Advance Praise for

SECRETS *of* SOFTWARE SUCCESS

"By recounting stories of individual companies' successes, *Secrets of Software Success* highlights valuable management insights for winning in the software industry."
> —Dr. Erwin Königs, CEO and President,
> Software AG, Darmstadt

"*Secrets of Software Success* is important reading for software professionals, entrepreneurs, CIOs, and CEOs. The authors lucidly present insights into what makes companies successful."
> —S. Ramadorai, CEO,
> Tata Consultancy Services, India

"A timely book for any leader interested in creating and sustaining success in these extraordinary times, *Secrets of Software Success* reveals how pioneering companies are transforming our world by delighting customers, managing growth, and building talented teams in a rapidly changing global environment."
> —Doug Burgum, Chairman and CEO, Great Plains

SECRETS
of
SOFTWARE
SUCCESS

SECRETS
of
SOFTWARE
SUCCESS

Management Insights from 100 Software Firms around the World

DETLEV J. HOCH
CYRIAC R. ROEDING
GERT PURKERT
SANDRO K. LINDNER
WITH RALPH MÜLLER

HARVARD BUSINESS SCHOOL PRESS
BOSTON, MASSACHUSETTS

Secrets of Software Success: Management Insights
from 100 Software Firms around the World
Detlev J. Hoch, Cyriac R. Roeding, Gert Purkert,
Sandro K. Lindner, Ralph Müller

WITH SPECIAL THANKS TO:
*Dirk Berensmann, Rainer Gawlick, Thomas Hoch,
Claudia Schopf, Rupert Stützle*

LIBRARY OF CONGRESS CATALOGING-IN-PUBLICATION DATA
Secrets of software success : management insights from 100 software
    firms around the world / Detlev J. Hoch . . . [et al.].
    p. cm.
    Includes index.
    ISBN 1-57851-105-4 (alk. paper)
    1. Computer software industry—Management—Case studies.
    2. Success in business—Case studies.   I. Hoch, Detlev J., 1954–

    HD9696.63.A2S43   1999   99-18402
    005.3' 068—dc21   CIP

The paper used in this publication meets the requirements of
the National Information and Standards Organization as stip-
ulated in *Permanence of Paper for Publications and Docu-
ments in Libraries and Archives Z39.48-1992.*

CONTENTS

FOREWORD

At the cusp of the twenty-first century, we have entered the fifth decade of the Information Age. It is now clear that information technology, like earlier technologies such as railroads, electricity, and telecommunications, is transforming society profoundly and changing fundamentally the nature of work, the types of products available, and service expectations. It was more than a century before the full impact of those earlier technologies was felt, and when the effect was complete, society and commerce were deeply changed. So it also will be with information technology.

After three decades of infrastructure building and transaction automation, IT use in organizations has moved from back-office support to the center of what a company has to do right if it is to survive and prosper. Software, of course, is at the core of this revolution. Ironically, as software has become more important for firms, less and less software is being developed by companies for their own use. Economies of scale and scope have driven the creation of an independent software industry. Microsoft, Novell, SAP, and Lotus are now household names. How to survive in this software industry is a genuine challenge, and extraordinary failures have occurred along with these successes.

This book represents the most effective analysis of the determinants of software success that the authors of this foreword have seen.

It is of equal value to software company managers, corporate MIS directors, and senior managers of information-intensive organizations. The book's authors have visited more than one hundred software companies around the globe (both large and small) and have interviewed more than five hundred individuals. In insightful interviews, they have teased out the differentiating characteristics of the successful versus the nonsuccessful firms in a way that is of great interest to managers. A rigorous research methodology was used, but the findings are presented in a highly readable and actionable form.

No industry is likely to become more important around the globe in the next twenty-five years, and thus it is interesting in its own right. This book identifies what can be done to dramatically improve the success rate of a software firm by clearly sifting out winning tactics from the losing ones. Many of the approaches suggested are not intuitively obvious to graduates of the Industrial Age. These recommendations, however, are right on target for the New World of the twenty-first century.

The structure of the book develops along the software industry's division into three segments: mass-market packaged software, enterprise solutions software, and professional software services. For each segment, the authors identify the entirely different management challenges that must be surmounted if the provider is to be successful. Those challenges are well articulated, and the appropriate and sometimes counterintuitive strategies for each are defined.

At the center of the book, however, is a very different approach demanded by this industry to human resource management. Rigid hierarchies of the Industrial Age, long career paths, and so on, don't work here. It is a genuinely different world.

This is one of those very rare books that is a "must read" for almost every manager. It is written in a highly readable fashion so that the messages are clearly and forcefully articulated. It is a distinguished contribution toward understanding the foremost industry of our time.

—Professor F. Warren McFarlan,
Albert H. Gordon Professor
of Business Administration
at Harvard Business School

—Professor Hermann Krallmann,
Technical University of Berlin

PREFACE

Witnessing the emergence of a new industry is a humbling experience.

In 1981, I was a member of a team that set out to contemplate a new, and sometimes bewildering, series of marketing issues for the European arm of Xerox. Xerox's famous Silicon Valley research lab Xerox PARC had recently invented several fascinating new technologies, such as an easy-to-use graphical user interface with screen icons. Xerox's senior management, however, wasn't sure how big the market would be for these and other inventions, or how they should be marketed. We were to define what the "office of the future" might look like and how Xerox PARC's inventions would fit in.

At a time when very few software packages were sold independently of hardware, we struggled with the answers to these unexplored questions. But two things became very clear to us. First, software was about to become a new industry in its own right, separate from the hardware business, and with tremendous potential. Second, and equally important, the uncertainty about the future, the speed of innovation, and the management challenges were all so great that it would take a tremendous amount of insight and capability for companies to thrive in such an environment.

As I watched this great software industry unfold over the ensuing years, these early thoughts became more than a reality; they became the roots of this book. The industry did indeed grow beyond most expectations, into a multibillion-dollar business, and many new companies arrived in the market with great products. Nevertheless, very few of them succeeded over time. In fact, most software companies failed—closed their doors and disappeared—before they even had a chance to really take off.

ADV Orga, for instance, a midsize enterprise solutions software company, once had revenues bigger even than SAP, today's world market leader. Yet it ended up being sold in 1989, following huge losses. Why? What had happened? Or WordPerfect, the Utah-based company: In 1990 it held 46 percent of the global word processing market. Six years later its share had fallen to 17 percent. It was then sold to another firm and never caught up with the earlier success again.

There were dozens and dozens of other examples. Why had these companies failed? And why had their competitors, such as SAP, Microsoft, and dozens of other prosperous firms, succeeded? Were there management strategy issues, personnel issues, or marketing issues that separated successful software firms from the failures?

IN 1996, *Microsoft Secrets* was published, a book that described one of the world's key software companies. The book was successful because it was the first to really analyze *how* Microsoft, in particular, became a rising star, producing multiple millionaires and *staying* at the top—while its many competitors often failed miserably. Although this gave me a lot of insight, I still wanted to know more, and so did many of my colleagues. Were these lessons applicable to the software industry overall, on a global scale? Were there some fundamental laws of software success yet to be revealed?

To answer those questions, we decided to survey a large sample of software companies worldwide, in the hopes of finding the secrets of software success. It was a journey that took a year and a half to complete, and by the end of the survey process, our team of three to five young McKinsey associates had traveled some 2 million miles—or 24 complete trips around the world. They rode Land Rovers through the desert, endured snowstorms in Canada, stepped around holy cows in India, and gazed across the endless prairie in North Dakota. It was an undertaking far beyond what we had expected and one that none of us will ever forget.

To find the secrets of software success, we also visited many other well-known companies—such as SAP, Oracle, IBM Global Services, Baan, Cambridge Technology Partners, CSC, EDS, Cap Gemini, and Siemens. In addition, we included many high-potential start-ups, such as BroadVision, pcOrder.com, Intershop, and BROKAT. We also purposefully included a number of "less successful" companies, so that their lessons would balance those of the successful firms.

Our survey itself asked many questions, touching on issues from market strategy to talent management to software development issues—both quantitatively and qualitatively. Fortunately, the software industry, by and large, responded enthusiastically to our plan to explore its successes and failures. This made our job much easier and very enjoyable. We had planned to interview only about 60 software companies, but in fact, additional companies *asked* to be included. So we kept adding companies and experts, and in the end the team had collectively interviewed about 450 top executives from over 100 software companies, usually including the CEO, CTO, CFO, and vice president of marketing and sales, as well as more than 50 industry experts.

Why the strong interest? Because there has never before been a fact-based survey on such a comprehensive and truly global scale in the software industry. Those we interviewed were as interested in learning the secrets of software success in this fast-moving and ever-changing business as we were.

Once we finished our survey, we decided that the results were much more than mere data. The interviews and the experiences contributed to a complete understanding and thus were important in fleshing out the data. For that reason we decided to undertake writing the book that you are now holding. The secrets of software success, we have come to find, are not only in the basic principles but also in the details of their application.

Before you turn to that, however, I would like to credit many of the individuals and institutions that made this book possible.

All credit for this book belongs primarily to the groups and individuals listed in the acknowledgments. Any criticism, however, belongs to the authors, especially for any bias in the choice of examples or simply for the fact that *success* as we defined it as a three-year profitability and growth measure, of course, can vanish quickly and has to be earned again every day. We are grateful for having had the opportunity to study the secrets of software success and hope every reader will be able to take away something of that spirit of magic and hard work.

One of our expert reviewers wrote, "As an old hand I found myself nodding in agreement as I read the book. . . . It is comprehensive and global . . . and its value is in collecting relevant experiences to provide context and understanding."

We leave to the reader to determine which of the secrets of software success of the late nineties can be applied in the future. There may be valuable insights even we have missed in the many anecdotes we report. Enjoy them!

—Detlev J. Hoch

ACKNOWLEDGMENTS

The *Secrets of Software Success* research and publication effort came together thanks to the valuable contributions of many individuals.

First, there would not be any basis for practical software management research without the 450 executives from 100 software enterprises around the globe who participated in the survey and who had their companies benchmarked against the others. (We offered from the outset of the survey to keep their specific names and company results confidential, unless we obtained their permission specifically for reference in this book. So we do not mention all in person here.) Without the great interest and patience of these 450 executives, taking time from their busy schedules, we would never have been able to experience this exciting time and publish this book. They all deserve very big thanks.

Some of those software leaders who *are* mentioned by name throughout the book often spent exceptional amounts of time with us for special interviews and questions, and they went beyond any expectations to support us. Among them were Kirk Arnold, Jerry Materella, Greg Baryza, Dan Bricklin, Pehong Chen, Susan Culler, Michael Markovic, Ernst Denert, Andrew Filipowski, Jerry Popek, Paul Humenansky, Peter Karmanos, John Keane, Sr., Elmer Kubie, Joe Liemandt, Paul McNabb, Tim Mead and Theo Schnittfink, Richard Roy, Stephan Schambach, Graham Sharman, Lal Singh, Pete Solvik, and Anne-Marie Westergaard. Several additional outside experts have provided guidance and counsel, in particular Professor Barry Boehm, Professor Brad Cox, Luanne (James) Johnson, Capers Jones, David Munn, Steve McConnell, Professor Paul Romer, and Julie Schwartz.

Within McKinsey, Ralf Felter and, later, Dirk Berensmann, Bernd Harder, Thomas Hoch, Ulf Kleinau, Stefan Schmitgen, and Stefan Spang formed the group of colleagues with whom the idea of undertaking this effort was first discussed shortly after *Microsoft Secrets* was published. Ralf Felter sketched the first research outline, which we used to form a dedicated practice development project program.

Many thanks for their great support and advice are due to the members of our steering committee: our academic advisors, Professor Hermann Krallmann from Technical University of Berlin and Professors Linda Applegate and Warren McFarlan from Harvard Business School, complemented by our colleagues Andre Andonian, Johannes Meier, Bruce Roberson, Stefan Schmitgen, and Lothar Stein, representing a blend of leaders of various McKinsey industry sectors and functional practices.

The operating committee of McKinsey GEO chaired by Herbert Henzler, with its members Andreas Biagosch, Axel Born, Klaus Droste, Michael Jung, Jürgen Kluge, Thomas von Mitschke, and Wilhelm Rall, has been a constant source of encouragement and guidance from the very first project idea discussion onward.

Timo Poser, Axel Roepnack, Claudia Schopf, and Rupert Stützle, complementing us as part of the full-time project team, were instrumental in conducting the numerous interviews, synthesizing the results, and preparing the publications. Arunima Aggarwal, Dirk Berensmann, Rainer Gawlick, Thomas Hoch, Ulf Kleinau, Jürgen Laartz, Peter Leukert, Hiltrud Ludwig, Dirk Markus, J.J. Richards, Detlev Ruland, and Jim Seaberg provided invaluable support and guidance as part-time team members throughout the whole project.

Beyond the project team and steering committee members and supporters, a number of colleagues have been instrumental in contacting and engaging the survey participants or in making special contributions—namely, Jens Bernotat, Neeraj Bharadwaj, Neeraj Bharagava, Claudio Bombonato, Steven Bradley, Ralf Felter, John Fors, Hans-Georg Frischkorn, Bernd Harder, Jeff Hawn, Masao Hirano, Chris Ip, Vivek Kalra, Ulf Kleinau, Ralph Klin, Axel Köhne, Bernd Kraus, Hans Kraus, Venugopal Krishnamurthy, Krishnan Turlough Padmanabhai, Corrado Ruffini, Chris Ryan, Stefan Schmitgen, Stefan Spang, Dennis Sweeney, Kyosuke Tsuda, and Dilip Wagle.

Michael Klotz from UBIS, Gert Koehler from Technologieholding VC, and Eberhardt Schmidt from BNed also helped with their contacts.

Some great insights for our work came from interactions with additional members of the leadership teams of McKinsey's worldwide electronics, telecommunications, IT, and multimedia sectors as well as our Business Technology Office—namely, Scott Arnold, Gerhard Bette, Michael Busch, Dieter Düsedau, John Griffin, John Hagel III, Endre Holen, Greg Hughes, Johan Kestens, Eric Labaye, David Mark, Frank Mattern, Jürgen Meffert, Mike Nevens, Marc Owen, Bill Pade, Jürgen Schrader, Jonathan Spector, Dag Sundström, Johan Vinckier, Holger Wohlenberg, and others.

We were also fortunate to be able to build on a rich foundation of functional knowledge and frameworks provided by a variety of McKinsey's Functional Capability Groups and Special Initiatives. Particularly, our Strategy Theory Initiative's next generation strategy frameworks from Bill Barnett, David Benello, Hugh Courtney, Kevin Coyne, Simon Fidler, John Hagel, Jane Kirkland, Jayant Sinha, Somu Subramaniam, Dag Sundström, Patrick Viguerie, and Lo-Ping Yeh—first discussed in Amsterdam in November 1996—served as a great head start. Furthermore, the materials provided by our Growth Special Initiative from Mehrdad Baghai, Charles Conn, Stephen Coley, Jürgen Ringbeck, David White, and others very much helped to structure our own approach.

The concepts developed by our Global Opportunities Special Initiative from Lowell Bryan, Jane Fraser, Jeremy Oppenheim, Wilhelm

Rall, Jim Rosenthal, Dominique Turcq, and many others offered extremely helpful intellectual leverage.

McKinsey's "Corporation of the Future" research effort by Byron Auguste, Patrick Butler, Jonathan Day, Ted Hall, Alistair Hanna, James Manyika, David Meen, Lenny Mendonca, Michael Patsalos-Fox, and Anupam Sahay is still the benchmark thinking on the implications of declining interaction costs to industry/corporate structures and served as an excellent basis for future trends analyses.

Another great source of intellectual exchange has been numerous discussions with and support from team members of various other client projects—namely, Stefan Albrecht, Oliver Bäte, Petra Becker, Klaus Behrenbeck, Sabine Bendiek, Jens Bernotat, Heike Berthold, Thomas Billeter, Chip Chandler, Dirk Daniel, Rupert Deger, Claudia Funke, Wolfgang Gödel, Stefan Hack, Marcus Hacke, Ralf Hauser, Uwe Heckert, Johannes Helbig, Dieter Henne, Christian Hofmann, Kathleen Hogan, Andreas Hölscher, Bill Hyuett, Viola Kaltefleiter, Bernd Kraus, Ines Krebs, Josef Leiter, Alexander Lewald, Mathias Lingnau, Ueli Looser, Andreas Reinhold, Helga Meier-Reinhold, Christian Reitberger, Felicitas Piegsda-Rohowski, Roger Roberts, Joachim Seifert, Martin Selchert, Matthew Stepka, André Stoffels, Detlef Struck, Armin Timmermann, Henri Vanni, Wolf-Dieter Voss, Gilbert Wenzel, Simone Wiegand, Bettina Wiesmann, Sandra Wu, Georg Zachhuber, and many others.

This book would be unreadable without the great assistance and support of Erik Calonius, our freelance editor, who was referred to us by our manager of client communications Margaret Loeb in the New York office. Erik was absolutely instrumental in making this book happen, and he deserves special thanks for his great journalistic skills, commitment, and team spirit and for his readiness to make "impossible" schedules happen. Similar deep thanks go to Hollis Heimbouch, senior editor from the Harvard Business School Press, who always asked us the right tough questions, gave us very valuable feedback, and supported the team excellently; and to Bill Matassoni, McKinsey's director of communications, who saw a potential in us when it was truly hard to see any yet and who always supported us with great enthusiasm. In addition, communication experts Torsten Oltmanns and Lang Davison helped us steer our thinking especially in the early stages of writing, while Saul J. Rosenberg, McKinsey's manager of sector and center communications, helped tremendously in the final stage.

Cornelia Boller, our executive assistant, 1996 through 1998, deserves special credit for always forming the communication bridgehead between a rather far-flung team and providing special motivation with her inexhaustible positive spirit and great sense of humor.

Sandra Oelert, our executive assistant since early 1999, must be given special praise for her meticulous quality support throughout the approval process and her great persistence and stamina in keeping us on track. Literally dozens of other helping hands within McKinsey's support staff also deserve special credit

Finally, the tolerance and understanding of our spouses and significant others, Eva Yvonne, Sandra, Angelika, Gesine, and Kathrin, and of our kids, Sabrina Nadine, Tatjana Marlene, and Mark Philipp, have been absolutely material to the success of this undertaking. It has been a great blessing to share this experience with them.

> —*Detlev J. Hoch, Sandro K. Lindner,*
> *Ralph Müller, Gert Purkert,*
> *and Cyriac R. Roeding*

1

"IT'S LIKE RIDING A BULL"

It is springtime in Scotland, in the year 1765.

A 29-year-old clock maker is working away day and night in his laboratory (Figure 1-1). He connects pipes and metal cylinders, heats water, measures movement, and takes the equipment apart again—over and over. For more than four years, he connects and disconnects pipes and metal cylinders.[1]

On January 5, 1769, the clock maker secures the first patent. The first working model of the invention is completed five years later. In the interim, the young inventor faces bankruptcy several times—and when he finally completes his first working model, most people ignore it.[2]

Source: From Robert H. Thurston, *A History of the Growth of the Steam-Engine* (Port Washington, NY: Kennikat Press, 1972).

Figure 1-1. The laboratory of the young engineer in 1766

It takes another 20 years for the world to realize the potential of the steam engine. About 75 percent more efficient than earlier attempts by other inventors, James Watt's invention has suddenly made steam power economically viable.[3] In retrospect, Watt's steam engine is seen as the start of the Industrial Revolution. Productivity increases dramatically by more than 100-fold. For the first time, human beings are released from some of the hardest aspects of labor.

TWO HUNDRED YEARS LATER

It is springtime in Boston, in 1978.

A 26-year-old Harvard MBA student is working on case studies late into the night. While other students calculate their financial data on paper, this student, who has an undergraduate degree in computer science from MIT, has requested time on a DEC minicomputer. Still, the work advances slowly. Whenever he needs to make a slight change in

Source: Photo courtesy of Bob Frankston/Dan Bricklin. Used by permission.

Figure 1-2. Dan Bricklin and Bob Frankston's "laboratory" in December 1978

the calculations, he must rewrite the entire program and request more time on the DEC machine.[4] The MBA student decides there must be a better way. Together with a good friend from MIT, he spends months working on a solution in their "laboratory" (Figure 1-2).

The two young innovators are Dan Bricklin and Bob Frankston, and their "solution" is the electronic spreadsheet. Numbers can be typed on a computer screen in a matrix of rows and columns. Every time one number is changed, all other related numbers are automatically recalculated. Bricklin and Frankston name their product *VisiCalc*.

VisiCalc is not a big mass-market hit when it is introduced for the Apple II computer in October 1979. Subsequently, Bricklin and Frankston sell only about 1,000 copies a month. As business customers begin looking at the software, though, they start to realize its potential. "When we first showed it to a computer store in Boston, the salesman found it somewhat interesting. But the store's *accountant*, who saw it, became so excited he started shaking," Bricklin told us. Budgeting that took 20 hours of manual work is reduced to 15 minutes. Errors that are commonplace in manual calculations are eliminated. Furthermore, the total cost for an Apple II computer, a Diablo printer, and the *VisiCalc* program is not more than $5,000. Many companies spend that on mainframe time every month.[5]

> **"The accountant got so excited when he saw the new software he started shaking."**

Bricklin's software becomes a bestseller. More than 700,000 copies are sold in six years. But *VisiCalc* is more than just a sales success. It is the piece of software that makes personal computers take off. It becomes the "killer application" for the Apple II computer.[6] Many customers purchase the $2,000 Apple computer *because* of the $100 *VisiCalc* software.

In 1996, the IEEE Computer Society honors Bricklin as "the catalyst for the rise of the personal computing marketplace we know today."[7] Bricklin is the first leader from the software industry to receive the IEEE Computer Entrepreneur Award, after hardware entrepreneurs Bill Hewlett, Dave Packard, and Gordon Moore. (Andy Grove, Bill Gates, and Steve Jobs eventually receive the award but not until *after* Bricklin.) And in 1997, *Business Week* describes *VisiCalc* as "the spreadsheet program that lofted the PC to stardom."[8]

JUST AS THE steam engine took over monotonous, mind-numbing physical labor, *VisiCalc* freed people from onerous mental labor. And just like the steam engine, it was the beginning of a technological revolution.

A WORLD ADDICTED TO SOFTWARE

Twenty years after Bricklin released his first software package in 1979, life without software is hard to imagine. Without software, paper letters would be the fastest form of written correspondence. No fax, no e-mail, and no business voice mail.

But that's just the beginning of the impact of software. Across industries, software now enables and fuels economic growth:

Software with wings. The Boeing 777 aircraft, introduced in 1995, was a $4 billion, highly complex design, involving "three million parts flying in close formation," as Boeing Computer Services president John Warner put it at a recent software conference in Boston.[9] Engineering the aircraft required thousands of experts—plus a lot of *artificial intelligence*. Before it was completed, 1,700 workstations in the United States and Japan had run special computer-aided design (CAD) software.[10] Once the plane is airborne, 4 million lines of basically error free code run it. "The Boeing 777 could be regarded as a bunch of software with wings," Edward Yourdon, a software expert, commented in his 1997 book on software projects, *Death March*.

Code on the road. Software is also driving cars. Consider BMW, for example. The luxury-car maker launched an international advertising campaign in 1998 that showed an *Apollo 11* rocket blasting into the sky. The text underneath read, "When you start up a BMW 7 Series, you activate 20 MB's of computing power. . . . That's more than on Apollo 11's mission to the moon."[11]

Health(y) software. In the early 1990s, Craig Venter, a scientist from the National Institutes of Health, set out to crack the human genetic code—through computerized, software- and hardware-powered analysis rather than through traditional research. William Haseltine, a biophysics Ph.D., picked up the idea and founded Human Genome Sciences (HGS) with the intention of completing the massive task in less than 20 years. Most scientists have doubted that it is possible to map the entire human genetic code, with all 100,000 human genes and their multiple subsequences, in any time close to that schedule. With the help of software technology, however, HGS is likely to outperform its target. According to company information, by 1997, more than 90 percent of the 100,000 human genes had already been decoded, including more than 1 million partial gene sequences. Gene-based medicine, enabled through this software project, "will have a profound impact on the future of medicine," Haseltine predicted in 1997.[12]

Software tasks today range from controlling nuclear power plants, recognizing customer purchasing patterns, enabling stock trading, and running banking systems all the way to running cell phone systems and exploring for oil.

Software—nothing but pure knowledge in codified form—largely drives and enables today's economy. Paul Romer, an economist at Stanford University who specializes in growth theory and who was named one of America's 25 most influential people by *Time* magazine in 1997, told us: "The software industry is the best place to understand the changes that we have to make both in our business models and in our understanding of the economy. We must stop thinking of physical objects as the only inputs and outputs that we work with."

Software is nothing but pure knowledge in codified form.

Even Pope John Paul II—arguably not among the first to declare fundamental changes—confirmed in *Centesimus Annus* (in Latin), "Whereas at one time the decisive factor of production was the land, and later capital, . . . today the decisive factor is . . . knowledge."

THE GLOBAL WEALTH AND JOB MACHINE

Knowledge businesses create a large part of today's wealth and jobs. The software industry has certainly created both to a large extent.

Soft ware makes *hard* cash

"My jet is bigger than your jet," *Business Week* headlined a recent article about wealth in the software industry. The article quoted

Daniel Case, chairman of Hambrecht & Quist, Inc., the San Francisco investment bank, who said that in Silicon Valley the question is no longer "Do your kids go to private school," but rather "Do they have a private jet?"[13]

In fact, the industry has produced about 22 people whose net worth is more than $300 million, as listed in *Forbes Magazine's* 1996 "Richest 400 People in America." That was more than in the pharmaceutical and the chemical industries combined (a total of 15), and more than in the food sector, which is traditionally well represented in the list by the Campbell and Mars families. Among the *very* big winners, software has also been overrepresented. Of the world's 40 richest people in June 1998, six came from the software firms Microsoft, SAP, and Oracle.[14]

At Oracle, the Silicon Valley database company, CEO Larry Ellison earned more than $6.5 million in stock between April 1997 and April 1998—not in the entire year, but *every day*.

"Regular" software employees do quite well too. Microsoft alone is estimated to have created between 5,000 and 10,000 millionaires. In Silicon Valley's San Jose, the number of millionaires grew by 44 percent in 1996, totaling 55,000.[15] The average growth rate of millionaires in the entire United States, in comparison, was "only" 7.5 percent. In San Jose, many new millionaires were programmers, and some were even assistants and receptionists at software companies.

> **Software companies make millionaires out of programmers, assistants, and receptionists.**

Company wealth

In Morgan Stanley's 1997 *Technology IPO Yearbook*, the software industry was rated the "top investment theme" in 12 of the previous 17 years, surpassing the PC business, semiconductors, networking equipment, and others. Of the top 50 initial public offerings (IPOs) that created the highest market value in the same time period, 11 were again software and software service companies. The closest runners-up were telecommunications, with 7 companies, and semi-conductors, with 6.

Database software giant Oracle was such a top IPO. It multiplied its market value more than 130 times, from when it went public in 1986, from $188 million to $25 billion in 1998. So did SAP in the 10 years after its 1988 IPO in Germany. When SAP went public *again* on August 3, 1998, this time on Wall Street, it was called "the largest listing in the 206-year history of the New York Stock Exchange."[16] SAP and Oracle were examples, not exceptions. In 1997 alone, 40 percent of the Software 500 increased their total software revenues[17] by *at least* half.

Market-to-book valuations soared due to such outstanding growth, high future growth potential, and low book assets. With a 1997 market-to-book ratio of 16:1 for its top 10 players, growing at 31 percent in each of the previous four years, the software industry held one of the highest ratios of all industries.[18] Only the pharmaceutical business came close. Ratios in other industries also kept growing, but their figures were still much lower, with 7:1 in telecommunications, 5:1 in retail, 4:1 in biotech, and about 3:1 in banking, petroleum, automobiles, and semiconductors.[19]

The wealth was not created only by mature software players like SAP or Oracle, which were started in the 1970s. Intershop, an electronic commerce software start-up founded in 1992, grew from 65 employees in 1997 to 265 within 1998 alone. When the company went public in Germany in mid-July 1998, the stock price jumped to 2.5 times the initial price on the first day of trading, despite start-up losses in 1997 and only $6 million in revenues. The software market is still a wealth machine for *new* start-ups as well, through which it has spawned jobs at all organizational levels and created wealth throughout the global economy.

The job machine and the search for more brains

"U.S. Brains Alone Can't Power Silicon Valley," the *International Herald Tribune* proclaimed in April 1998, describing the ever-increasing need for foreign software workers. Indeed, Aldy Duffield, human resource manager at Oracle, told us, "We need foreign programmers here. We simply cannot fill the all the positions with U.S. software engineers that we create," Duffield said. "There is a tremendous scarcity out there."

The software industry has indeed been a large job creator. By 1996, more than 2 million software programmers worked in the United States alone.[20] And more than 95,000 *new* jobs with IT-related skills have been created *annually* in recent years. Between 1987 and 1994, job growth in the software business was 9.6 percent, while in the United States in general it was only 1.6 percent.[21] The U.S. Bureau of Labor Statistics estimated in 1998 that computer scientists, computer engineers, and systems analysts would be *the* fastest growing of all occupations all the way through the year 2006.[22]

All these new jobs will not be filled, however. Only 25,000 students received a bachelor's degree in computer science in 1995, as the baby-boomers moved on, decreasing from more than 42,000 in 1986.[23] A recent study estimated that in the United States alone, 346,000 IT-related jobs were left vacant.[24] "The shortage of people is indeed our biggest obstacle to growth," Aldy Duffield of

> **Software jobs are the fastest growing of all occupations.**

Oracle told us. "We need about 150 new people every week."

The search for employees in the software business has led to sometimes astounding efforts. Sybase, for example, the large database company, leased a biplane and flew a banner across Silicon Valley, pleading, "Sybase Wants You."

Global opportunities

Silicon Valley is not the only region to spawn software jobs.

The Dallas area, for example, was home to more than 800 software companies in 1997. And Route 128 in the Boston area had a similar number of software producers. Looking overseas, Europe had more than 1 million programmers in 1996.[25] Germany's SAP, for example, hired more than 4,000 people in 1998, thus growing by more than one third within a single year. Japan had almost 1 million programmers in total in 1996 as well.

Software code is also being produced increasingly outside Europe and the United States.

JUNGLES. Of the 930 million people in India, 52 percent are illiterate. The average gross domestic product per person was $1,250 in 1996— 1/22 of the U.S. average, even at purchasing power parity.[26]

Despite this economic state, India's software industry flourishes. The industry grew from $10 million in 1987 to $2.2 billion in 1997, and recently at rates higher than 52 percent per year.[27] In India's jungle area of Kerala in the southern part of the country, shops sell Microsoft software in the same areas where people still commute in dugout canoes. Government-funded "software universities" in the same area specialize in teaching young professionals how to implement enterprise solution systems like SAP and Baan for large multinational corporations.

In total, more than 55,000 new IT professionals have been educated in India every year in the past decade, enabling most of them to enjoy a standard of living well above the Indian average. Although the programmers work for one-tenth the salaries of those in the United States, their income is still about 20 *times* that of the Indian average. The software industry has indeed become a key lever to the growth of emerging countries.

DESERTS. From Israel's capital city of Jerusalem, it takes a 40-mile trip through plain, dry land to reach the outskirts of Tel Aviv, leaving behind a huge sand desert that spans a long stretch eastward of Jerusalem all the way to the Dead Sea. Right at the border of this dry land, all at once four futuristic, 10-floor, glass-front buildings rise to the sky: Nice Systems headquarters, the Israeli company producing voice recording systems. The 500 people who work here develop and market software and hardware to compete against companies on a global scale.

Nice is not an exception in Israel—more than 40,000 people of the 4.9 million population work in the software business, and the number is growing fast.[28]

THE FLIP SIDE OF THE COIN

"Anyone can *start* a software company. That's the easy part," Joe Liemandt, CEO of Trilogy, told us. "The big question is what happens thereafter." Indeed, many more software entrepreneurs break it than make it. One of the reasons for this is that the software business operates at breakneck speed.

> **"Anyone can *start* a software company."**

Eighteen months to failure

Seventy percent of the computer industry's revenues (including the software business) were "from products that did not exist two years ago," wrote *The Economist* in 1996.[29]

That pace is too fast for many companies. WordPerfect, for example, the Utah-based word processing software company, lost its market leadership position in 1992 to Microsoft, mainly because it did not keep up. WordPerfect adopted the *Windows* graphical user interface 16 months later than Microsoft, it addressed the demand for integrated office software suites almost three years later than Microsoft, *and* it lost users in earlier releases because they came out more than half a year later than announced. WordPerfect was sold off to Corel in 1996. Their share in the word processing market decreased from 46 percent in 1990 to 17 percent in 1997.[30] WordPerfect has not been an exception.

Even those leaders who *are* successful in the business describe its pace as frantic and often scary. Success in one year does not mean success in the next at all, as Nathan Myhrvold, chief technology officer (CTO) at Microsoft, remarked: "No matter how good your product is—you are always exactly 18 months away from complete failure."[31] Dietmar Hopp, chairman of the supervisory board at the German enterprise solutions company SAP, echoed that sentiment: "We were always paranoiac, even in successful times, that someone would suddenly pass us on the Autobahn to market leadership."[32]

But the pace of change is only one part of the story.

Many can start a software company—very few can run it

While the potential for creating wealth and prosperity in the software business seems almost boundless, very few software companies remain or even become successful over time. Most software start-ups never make it to the IPO, and even many of those that do, fail later.

Only 6 out of 1,000 business plans for high-tech start-ups receive funding from venture capitalists.[33] And out of those 0.6 percent, only 10 percent go public (IPO). The majority—more than 60 percent—eventually go bankrupt or create very little value.[34]

These odds are troubling. But what is more distressing is that of the 10 percent of high-tech companies that reach the IPO stage, most do not grow to real success. As Morgan Stanley reported in its 1998 *Technology IPO Yearbook*, only *4 percent* of the analyzed 1,099 technology IPOs in the previous 17 years had created *67 percent* of the $744 billion shareholder value appreciation. In other words, 96 percent of all high-tech IPOs produce only one-third of the overall value beyond the time of the IPO. Oracle and SAP among others, are well-known, but rather rare, success cases. In fact, they are the exception, not the rule.

THE DIFFERENCE BETWEEN MAKE OR BREAK

The fact that a few spectacular success stories are countered by so many extreme failures was one of the key reasons that we wanted to examine the software industry in more depth: to understand the key drivers of success—and failure.

A better understanding of these drivers could also be highly useful to other industries:

► From an operational perspective, as mentioned before, software is increasingly becoming one of the key enablers of other industries.

► From a strategic management perspective, other industries are becoming increasingly knowledge driven and thus more similar in their management problems to the software industry.

What makes the difference between success and failure in the software industry? What causes one software company to shoot through the roof while another hits bottom? What determines whether a company remains a lasting, even growing, success, like Microsoft, SAP, and Oracle, or whether it enjoys only a short-term success like *VisiCalc* (which was replaced only three years after it was launched, by the competitor spreadsheet *Lotus 1-2-3*), or *Word-Perfect*, the previous market leader in word processing software (which lost segment leadership in 1992)?

What makes the difference between success and failure?

The answer is simple, but important: Although the product must be "good," it is the company's management that makes the *key* difference, both in terms of the people the company retains as well as in the actions the management takes. And although many entrepreneurs claim to know this, few even come close to doing it right.

Many software companies have good ideas, and they are able to secure financing, but few can turn the ideas into reality and sustain their success. "The right product at the right time is important," Joe Liemandt told us, looking back at his start-up experience. "But the management's ability to learn from mistakes and make the right decisions is what decides between making it and breaking it."

HOW THE WORLDWIDE SURVEY WAS SET UP

The key goal of the survey was to learn what factors make the difference between success and failure in the software industry. Accordingly, we decided the survey would have to reflect as much of the *entire* industry as possible: from industry segments to company size, from different business functions to geographic coverage. For example, the software industry is a global business, with successful firms located everywhere from the U.S. West Coast to India and Japan—so our survey also had to be truly global. Thus, while the Silicon Valley became an important location for us, it was by far not the only place we met software leaders.

EXPLORING THE INDUSTRY ON A WIDE SCALE

In total, more than 100 software firms contributed to the worldwide survey, covering 16 countries across North America, Europe, and Asia (for more details, see Appendix I). Precisely 94 software firms participated in the full survey, during which personal interviews, each about two hours long, took place with 450 of the companies' senior executives, usually including the CEO, CTO, CFO, and vice presidents of marketing and human resources. A small number (10) of additional important software firms (including Microsoft, as it has already been well-covered in *Microsoft Secrets*), several consulting firms, and selected experts from academia contributed on specific topics via expert interviews. Six of the world's 10 largest software firms participated in the full survey. In total, 15 companies interviewed had revenues larger than $1 billion, and another large group was in the $100 to $999 million range. It is not only the CSCs and SAPs that are included throughout the book, however, but also much smaller and younger companies with high future potential such as Intershop, pcOrder.com, and BroadVision. Mid- and small-sized companies with less than $50 million or $10 million, respectively, in revenues in fact made up for almost half of the survey.

To make sure we would gather an outside perspective on the industry, we also talked to about 50 senior executives and experts from other industry sectors—including the automobile industry, banking and insurance, consumer goods, entertainment, petroleum, pharmaceuticals and biotech, telecom, and basic materials. From those interviews, we discovered knowledge that could definitely be transferred from the software industry to many other industries.

Massive data

The interviews generated a large volume of information, both in quantitative and in qualitative terms. More than 2,000 data points were gathered in 80-page questionnaires for each of the companies, and the 200,000 total entries were compared and cross-analyzed in a custom-made database.

Equally important, however, were the qualitative insights we gained from each of the interviews. Many of the individual company stories throughout this book stem from these conversations with the top leaders of the world's most successful software firms. Often, the detailed stories give the real insights about what it takes to lead in an industry that attracts some of the world's smartest people.

The entire interview period lasted more than one and a half years, until midsummer 1998.

Clusters of performance: top third versus bottom third

To determine what differentiated successful and failed software businesses, we clustered the surveyed companies into a top-third group (successful companies), a middle-third group (average companies), and a bottom-third group (less successful companies), according to their market performance. To establish a clear basis for comparison, we purposely included companies in the survey that had characteristics of what is generally believed to be top-third and bottom-third market performance. This performance, as shown in Figure 1-3, was measured by the companies' return on sales (ROS) and their *compound annual (sales) growth rate* (CAGR). The success of start-up companies, which often have extremely high growth but very low profitability, was sometimes evaluated more qualitatively based on future potential rather than current performance, to make sure the clustering would be adequate. More detailed information about the clustering approach is included in Appendix I.

Once we clustered the companies into market success groups, we started comparing the top-third with the bottom-third to understand which management principles truly differentiated them. Consciously, we excluded the average companies in our analyses, so that the differentiation between successful and less successful strategies would be much sharper and less diffused by borderline cases.

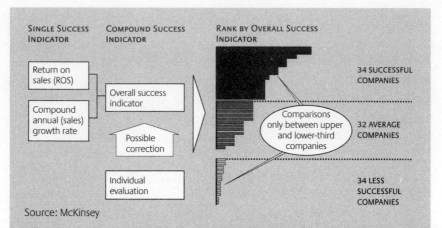

Source: McKinsey

Figure 1-3. Success of top-third versus bottom-third software companies

TESTING POTENTIAL PRINCIPLES AGAINST THE FACTS

More than 200 potential differences in management aspirations, actions, and style were tested against hard facts. For example, an important question was whether or not success factors varied for software companies in different regions, economic environments, and cultures. The answer we found was that whether the company was in the Silicon Valley in the United States, or Bombay, India, or Tel Aviv, Israel, or Munich, Germany, the key factors of success were basically the same around the globe. To show how successful software companies from around the world tackle similar success challenges in their environment, the book contains example companies from various regions covered in more depth such as Oracle from the United States, TCS from India, Nice Systems from Israel, Navision Software from Denmark, and sd&m from Germany.

DIFFERENCES IN THREE INDUSTRY SEGMENTS

While success factors did not differ much across regions, they did differ quite substantially across three industry segments: professional services, enterprise solutions, and mass-market products. Thus, we have drawn in-depth examples from these segments to show how their leaders succeed. Some of the examples are from SAP, one of the world market leaders in the enterprise solutions business, Microsoft in the mass-market product business, and Keane and Cambridge Technology Partners in the professional services business.

PROCESSING AND INTERNET FIRMS EXCLUDED ON PURPOSE

Intentionally, we did not cover processing service firms (like ADP and Shared Medical Systems) and typical "Internet companies" (like Yahoo! and Amazon.com) in the survey because neither one of the groups has its main emphasis on actually *producing* software code; rather, companies like these mainly *apply* software to do their business. The search-engine software for Yahoo!, for example, is not Yahoo!'s proprietary software development—the external developer Inktomi delivers it. This different business focus of Internet firms leads to a largely different business model: Most revenues do not stem from software licensing or from project fees. Instead, they come from advertising, as in the case of Yahoo!, or from sales of merchandise over the Web, as in the case of Amazon.com. Of course, the various business models of Internet firms also require a range of management techniques different from more typical software firms.

(*Note:* In contrast, Netscape, for example, *is* at least partially a software company by our definition because it does sell software licenses as a key source of revenues. So we kept the typical software activities of such "hybrid players" inside our arena of attention—whether it be a mixture of a software and Internet business, as in the case of Netscape, or a mixture of software and processing services, as in the case of CSC or IBM.)

EMBEDDED SOFTWARE LOOKED AT AS A TREND

Standardized embedded software (standard software built into, for instance, cars and telephones) is a recent development which we did not cover in detail in the survey, but we do discuss it in Chapter 9 in the context of important future trends that have the potential to significantly impact the future software industry landscape.

TACKLING THE MANAGEMENT CHALLENGES

The management of software firms is a balancing act. Success depends on simultaneously striking the balance *within* and *between* key management areas, from internal areas such as leadership, people management, and product development to more external areas like marketing and partnering.

Balance within key management areas. In partnering activities, for example, software leaders must give away market share to partners to stimulate overall market growth while they simultaneously retain a healthy share for themselves to maintain short-term profitability. In software development, the challenge is to build high-quality products while keeping the time to market as short as possible.

> **Even the most successful firms usually don't strike a perfect balance.**

Balance between key management areas. Success also depends on maintaining the balance *between* key areas, such as marketing versus development and leadership versus "followership."

Failure often stems from a lack of balance. But even the most successful firms don't usually strike a perfect balance in all dimensions. Improvement is possible for almost any firm, regardless of its current performance.

IT'S THE "COMMONLY EXCEPTIONAL" LEADERS AND SCARCE FOLLOWERS THAT MAKE IT HAPPEN. In the software industry, exceptional leaders are almost the rule. Dropping out of a university, maxing out on credit cards, or moving to the Silicon Valley from overseas and quickly improving their English—these are not uncommon characteristics to find among software CEOs. Facing strong potential competitors and technology that can change every three to six months, leaders need conviction almost to the degree of blindness to aspire to world leadership from the first day of operations.

Alone or in "teams at the top," the leaders go to great lengths to create a corporate culture that is sufficiently challenging and enjoy-

able to attract and bring out the best from scarce software programmer talent. Facing 346,000 unfilled positions in the United States
alone, as well as average U.S. turnover
rates of 21 percent, software leaders **Only the "coolest**
learn to attract and retain employees
with everything from family-style work- **places to work" attract**
places to sailing events with company **the top talent.**
boats, and perhaps tickets to Hawaii.

As long as leaders manage to retain their very best people, high
turnover, contrary to conventional thinking, does have some positive
aspects. New ideas and high energy, plus new customer and recruiting networks, are invaluable resources that come with new employees
from outside the company.

**IT'S THE DEVELOPMENT PROCESSES THAT CAN EITHER CRASH A COM-
PANY OR BOOST ITS PRODUCTIVITY.** A printout of the *Windows98*
source code would fill hundreds of books this size—and a single typo
in it would have the potential to crash the entire system. The size and
the vulnerability of such systems makes failure easy in development
projects. And this happens all the time. In fact, 84 percent of all software development projects do not finish as planned, and more than
30 percent are canceled altogether before completion.

Despite this situation, many software companies tackle the problems with surprisingly poor processes. Among developers, clear
development processes and methods are often unpopular. They are
assumed to "reduce personal freedom" and make work less interesting. In fact, the opposite is true. Software companies that have excellent processes, such as very clear team structures, extensive
stakeholder involvement, "daily builds," and software reuse, largely
ease frustration for programmers. The processes make work *more*
enjoyable. Boring rework and bug detection are reduced. At the same
time, product quality increases, and time to market shrinks. Some
development teams have even managed the "impossible": They
spread out over dozens of locations, thousands of miles away from

each other, work together from their private homes in Hawaii and on the outskirts of New York, and still produce award-winning software.

IT'S THE MARKETING GODS WHO MAKE SOFTWARE KINGS. A handful of software product companies are becoming the marketing experts of the digital age. They are usually the leaders in their product categories too: The fundamentals of the software product business allow only one or two companies in each category to become true winners. To *reach and sustain* a global market leadership position and also to *break* the leadership position of large established players, outstanding product marketing is *the* critical requirement.

But while a number of software firms spend more of their budget on marketing than fast-food giant McDonald's, only a few of them spend their money effectively. The firms that succeed insist on communicating a clear *value proposition* to customers, and that makes all the difference. Rather than advertising product features, successful firms advertise company brands. They cannibalize their current products by introducing new products up to twice a year, before the current version ever reaches the cash cow phase. They apply creative software *entry-pricing techniques* to build their customer base. They also take innovative approaches to PR, often letting their partners pick up the check for extravagant promotions. And they establish and communicate completely new platforms, build marketing alliances, and preinstall software—to reach, sustain, or take over the pole position and to become the "category killers."

IT'S "MARKETING TRUST" THAT DRIVES AND DIFFERENTIATES THE PROFESSIONAL SERVICES. Professional software services firms are experts at making customers feel at home. They invite small groups of top CIOs to "discussion circles," where they can address and exchange their concerns and ideas. They share implementation risk with their customers, to demonstrate their commitment to complete the project successfully. They publish articles and books to prove their expertise.

Professional services marketing is key, but it works very differently from software product marketing. The project is sold before any result is delivered, and therefore trust is key.

Professional software services firms are experts at making their customers feel at home.

While typically more conservative in their business practices, some service firms are getting louder and more like product firms in their promotional techniques. Aggressive advertising and sports sponsorship are some of these techniques. Indeed, the trust builders are expanding their trust base.

IT'S GROWING THEIR PARTNERS THAT MAKES SOFTWARE COMPANIES GROW THEMSELVES. Partnering activities are the area in which some software companies truly excel. Sustaining and managing growth is the key challenge for software companies in the future—and there is no growth without partnering activities in the software industry, whether it be between product or service firms. Alliances are not a convenience; in most cases they are a matter of survival.

Partnering has thus taken on a completely new dimension in the software industry compared to other industries—in the number, equality, and importance of partnerships. Some of the world's most successful software companies give away up to 80 percent of the total revenues they create with their partners. Sometimes they connect with dozens of new partners a day for R&D, marketing, distribution, or complementary products. Composed of very equal allies, these partnerships differ strongly from traditional supplier-manufacturer relationships in that they independently sign up customers, who have many choices of software partners available to them.

But despite the emphasis on partnerships, these relationships are often so informal that few written contracts confirm them. Partners move relatively freely in and out of huge partner networks called *partner webs* that are built on common technology platforms, with often hundreds, sometimes thousands, of partners. Fruitful, but very tough, competition within and between those webs spurs overall web performance.

THE OUTLOOK FOR THE FUTURE. The future of the software industry shows enormous growth—and strong management challenges at the same time. New Internet and embedded software applications will take standardized software into future cars, telephones, home heating systems, and many other devices. Software companies will need to once again reposition themselves to address this new generation of computing. *Componentware*, which will allow reuse of modular software to an unprecedented degree, plus the development of software in countries all over the world, will produce radical gains in software development, distribution, productivity, and quality. And a new form of "coopetition" among product and project players could alter today's business relationships significantly and offer new opportunities and challenges.

> Explosive growth creates tough new challenges for management.

RIDING THE BULL

The software industry was born about a half century ago. Since then, the software industry structure, as it emerged over five eras, spun out the professional services segment, the enterprise solutions segment, and the mass software product segment. While these are different industry segments, all of them relate and often depend on each other for complete solutions. It has been vital for software firms not only to recognize the high growth potential of each segment but also to understand the different key factors of success in them.

Standing back at a distance, observers can see the larger factors that have determined success. But just as important are the details, including company facts and stories, and these require a closer look to understand. For example, it is obvious that a company should properly train its partners. But the way that, for example, SAP set up its Partner Academy in multiple locations around the globe—an "institute of higher education" for training its partners in dozens of weeks-long courses, the first of its kind—is the detail that illustrates how far successful companies can go in outperforming the average.

Companies that recognize and address these success factors have been able to enjoy not only wealth and job creation but also the excitement of leading the pack. As Richard Roy, general manager at Microsoft Germany, told us: "It's simply a sexy business."

John F. Keane, founder of the $1 billion professional software service firm in Boston that carries his name, also expressed his excitement about the industry to us. But, after playing in the business for more than 30 years, he has offered a qualifying statement: "It's also like riding a bull. You really have to be aware of the bull's movements. Because every time you think you succeeded, you are thrown off the bull."

History has shown that time and time again.

2

A NEW BUSINESS CALLED "SOFTWARE"

It may seem as if the software industry began just recently, when Bill Gates and Company were emerging from Seattle's Lakeside High School in 1973. But the industry actually runs back much further, approximately 50 years, to names and faces that have been half-forgotten.

The story begins, in fact, with a man named Elmer Kubie and a phone call he received at home in February 1955. The call came from John Sheldon, Kubie's former boss at IBM's Technical Computing Bureau in New York City, who said he wanted to speak about a "matter of importance" to both of them.[1] When they met later that day,

Sheldon explained that he was about to try something completely new. At a time when software was written by either the hardware manufacturers or their customers themselves, he planned to start an independent company that would write software for others.

When we found Kubie living in retirement in upstate New York, he recalled that meeting. "John couldn't find anyone to do scientific calculations for him on various computers. And he thought, there is a big demand for such services, why not found a company that could offer programming services?"

One month later, on March 28, CUC was founded. It was the world's first independent software company. At the beginning, the firm consisted of Sheldon's New York City apartment, one secretary, four programmers, and $40,000 in capital. As Kubie took over the management, he became the first to ride the "software bull." He grew CUC within 13 years into a highly profitable $13 million business with 700 people. He also set the ground for a completely new industry: software.

AT THE FOREFRONT OF A GLOBAL GIANT

In the nearly 50 years since Elmer Kubie and John Sheldon founded CUC, the software industry has grown into a global, $233 billion giant, posting a 17 percent annual growth rate since 1993.[2] Along the way, the industry has passed numerous milestones: from the first megaprojects (that employed up to 60 percent of all available U.S. programmers at the time) to the first million-dollar software product, to the "$50,000 deal of the century" that laid the foundation for Microsoft's rise, and on to the takeoff of other multibillion-dollar giants like SAP and Oracle.

In addition, three different industry segments have emerged over the last 50 years: professional services, enterprise solutions, and packaged mass-market software (see Figure 2-1).

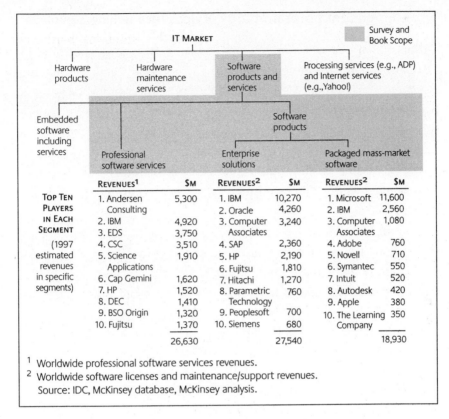

Figure 2-1. The segmentation of the IT market today

All this was far and beyond what Kubie and Sheldon had set out to do. It turned out, though, that CUC was the forerunner of all the major events and ideas to come.

THE EVOLUTION OF THREE INDUSTRY SEGMENTS

CUC's start-up in 1955 had set an example. Following CUC, software programming services that were offered independently from hardware vendors gained ground quickly.

Independent programming services (era 1)

Other software services companies entering the scene shortly after CUC included Computer Sciences Corporation (CSC), Planning Research Corporation, California Analysis Centers, and Management Science America. By 1965, only 10 years after CUC's founding, more than 40 major software services firms had set up shop in the United States, some of them employing more than 100 programmers.[3]

They offered custom-made solutions for one customer at a time. This could include IT consulting, software programming, and software maintenance.

But in addition to the big firms, the software industry was already teeming with small entrepreneurs, eager to get in. Within 12 years of CUC's start, more than 2,800 software service firms existed in the United States. The period from 1955 to 1969, in fact, was marked by the takeoff of large independent professional software services firms. (Appendix II at the end of the book explains this in more detail.)

In the beginning, several large software projects provided work and learning opportunities for independent software services firms. The *SABRE* airline reservation system, for example, contracted by American Airlines, cost a total of $30 million (American Airlines could have purchased four Boeing 707 planes for that amount of money).[4] *SABRE* was the largest civilian software project up to that time.

It was the U.S. government, however, that gave the early U.S. software industry the decisive push. The *SAGE* air defense system, begun in 1949 to protect the United States against bomber attacks, hired about 700 of the 1,200 programmers in the United States at the time. It lasted 13 years, involved several external software project firms after 1956, and cost some $8 billion.[5] *SAGE* laid the foundation for the supremacy of the U.S. software industry.[6]

The U.S. government gave the early software industry the decisive push.

Europe was behind the United States partly because its governments could not offer similar support following World War II and also

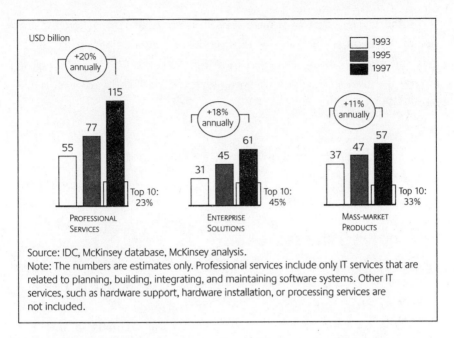

Figure 2-2. Worldwide revenues and growth rates in the three software industry segments

because computers were not as widespread in Europe. Still, firms like Sema, Computer Analysts and Programmers (CAP), and Logica were eventually started. Europe never truly managed to catch up with the United States again, however.

Professional services companies were the first independent software companies. While they have been joined in ensuing years by enterprise solutions companies and packaged mass-market software makers, professional services companies remain a vital part of today's software industry. With a 1997 global market of more than $115 billion, software services nearly equal the volume of the software product businesses, and in the past 6 years they have grown even faster than product revenues, at 20.2 percent annually (see Figure 2-2). Besides CSC, players include Andersen Consulting, Cambridge Technology Partners, Paris-based Cap Gemini, and Tata Consultancy Services from India, to name a few.

Although the software industry's first years were marked by the rise of the professional service companies, a new business idea and a new industry segment emerged in 1964, with the coming of Martin Goetz and a new Princeton, New Jersey–based software company named ADR.

Software products (era 2)

At the time, Goetz who was project manager at ADR, was working on flowchart software that he hoped to sell to RCA. Up to that point

Why not sell the same code a thousand times?

RCA, like all other computer makers, gave software away for free when it sold its hardware. Goetz's *Autoflow* program was to become one of those free programs on an RCA platform.

At the time, no one thought it was possible to make money by selling software products independently of hardware. But when RCA turned down *Autoflow,* ADR was left with $10,000 in development costs.[7] This forced Goetz into a bold move: He decided to approach RCA's hardware customers directly and *license* the software (while keeping the copyright) to them for $2,400 each. Unfortunately, only two of RCA's 100 customers responded and licensed *Autoflow.*

Goetz could have given up. Instead, realizing that IBM had a much greater customer base with its 1401 computers, he not only had the program rewritten again but went out and marketed it to IBM users. He managed to license the software product more than 2,000 times—despite fierce competition from IBM, who gave away a slightly less sophisticated program for free.

With this success, ADR started the *second software era*—becoming the first software company organized around the development and marketing of a software product. It was a company that did not sell an individual project but a predeveloped piece of software over and over again. The software product business was born.

Other companies followed this model. One of the biggest success stories of the time was a "file management" product dubbed *Mark IV*—a predecessor of today's database management systems.[8] It was produced by Informatics and created by an engineer named John Postley. Postley had helped develop the earlier *Mark III* system, but now he had much higher aspirations for the program. Since his managers declined to fund him, Postley was forced to raise $500,000 capital from customers who would license the new product named *Mark IV*. When the product came out in 1968, it was immediately successful, even in the face of competition from free software from IBM.

A breakthrough for *Mark IV* and many other software products, however, came after June 23, 1969. After much pressure from the U.S. Justice Department, pending antitrust lawsuits from several companies, and rising internal software development costs, IBM made a crucial announcement: It would stop giving away software for free along with its computers and would begin pricing hardware and software separately in the future.

Now customers across industries were forced to recognize that software actually cost money. Later, historians would call this date "The birth of the software industry."[9] While it was *not* the actual birth of the software industry (we believe CUC was the beginning), it was the launching point for many software product firms.

The IBM /360 computer, the first true standard platform, greatly facilitated that takeoff. In the early 1970s, software product firms for the first time could write software that could be used on more than 80 percent of the world's mainframes. In the United States alone, that meant over 50,000 potential users.

Meanwhile, Informatics was among *the* software winners in this new era. After IBM's unbundling decision, sales of its *Mark IV* file management system exploded: In late 1968, there had been about 80 installations; in early 1969, there were 170, and by 1970, there were 300. *Mark IV* became one of the most successful software products ever and the first software product with more than $100 million in total revenues.

In the product business, two very different segments came to be. The first was enterprise solutions based on mainframes and midsized computers, and the second, mass-market packaged software, would emerge much later with the PC.

Enterprise solutions (era 3)

IBM's unbundling decision cleared the way for another event, far away from IBM's U.S. headquarters. Soon, one of the world's largest software product players set up shop in a living room of a small house in Walldorf, about 60 miles south of Frankfurt, Germany.

Dietmar Hopp, a former system consultant at IBM's German subsidiary, sat over some beer with friends and told them the time had arrived for him to become an entrepreneur. His goal was simple and mirrored that of other product firms in the United States: He wanted "to develop software faster for clients, by developing standard software that will be used in as many companies as possible in the future."[10]

Hopp's venture became SAP (Systems, Applications and Products), a company with revenues of $3.3 billion in 1997. Other software firms also set up shop in the period from 1969 to 1981, the *third software era*, an era marked by the emergence of enterprise solutions providers. Examples are Baan, which started in 1978 in the Netherlands and reached $680 million in revenues in 1997, and Oracle in the United States, which was founded by Larry Ellison in 1977 as a database system provider and later successfully entered the enterprise solutions market. Later, smaller companies in this segment also set up shop, such companies as Navision in Denmark and Great Plains Software in the United States.

SAP's *R/3* is a good example of an important enterprise solution product. It "mirrors" business processes logically via large electronically linked databases and optimization software. That software controls business processes from human resource planning to plant management, from logistics to inventory management. Enterprise solutions software literally runs many of the world's leading companies.

SAP, alone, counts such big names among its clients as Mars, Johnson & Johnson, Anheuser-Busch, Lockheed Martin, Reebok, Adidas, Procter & Gamble, Rolls Royce, Honda, Mercedes, Bombardier, AlliedSignal, Deutsche Bank, IBM, and Hewlett-Packard.[11]

ERP software runs the world's leading companies.

ERP software, developed by companies like SAP, Oracle, Peoplesoft, or Baan, is the most important type of product in the $45 billion (1997) enterprise solution segment, which has kept growing at about 18 percent per year (see Figure 2-2). But other products besides ERP software are also part of complete enterprise solutions and thus belong in this industry segment. Examples are software *tools* for ERP installations, supply-chain management software, decision support software, call center software, and relationship management software, to name a few.

But at the time, these products were sold only to companies. The public had not yet recognized software as an independent business.

Packaged software for the masses (era 4)

Software products for the masses began to be available in 1979, when Dan Bricklin's spreadsheet program, *VisiCalc*, for the new Apple II personal computer was introduced. Eventually more than 700,000 copies of *VisiCalc* were sold in six years.[12]

Then in 1981, IBM asked a 25-year-old entrepreneur to develop an operating system for its new computer, the IBM PC, which it would allow him to market separately from the IBM hardware. In what has been called "the deal of the century," the entrepreneur bought the first version of the system from a small firm called Seattle Computer Products for a mere $50,000, without telling them it was for IBM.[13]

The entrepreneur, of course, was Bill Gates.

The development of the IBM PC, launched in August 1981, initiated a *fourth software era*, when an additional, yet most significant, software product segment quickly emerged: PC-based mass-market

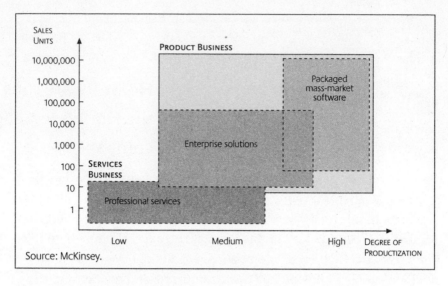

Figure 2-3. Degree of productization and unit volume in the three market segments

software. For the first time, the public could purchase software in shops and use it immediately. Because packaged mass-market software products are basically a complete customer solution in and of themselves, few additional services are required for installation (Figure 2-3).

These packaged mass-market software companies have become global giants. Microsoft reached revenues of $11.6 billion in 1997, making it the world's largest mass-market software product company and one of its best-known brand names. Other names, like Corel, Intuit, Autodesk, Lotus, or Ashton Tate, have also sold millions of programs around the world.

Today, packaged software products come in a wide variety of applications: from programming languages like C++ to operating systems like *Windows98*; from flight simulators like *Flight Unlimited* to personal accounting software such as Intuit's *Quicken*; and from *Norton Anti-Virus* to Netscape's Internet browser. There are virtually thousands of products in the market that are part of this software segment.

The $57 billion mass-market software product business (1997) has grown continuously in recent years by at least 10 percent per year (see Figure 2-2). Only drastic price declines make this growth figure look comparatively low, while in terms of volume it has had by far the highest growth of all three software segments. Interestingly, however, all of the world's top 10 mass-market product companies are still based in North America—despite worldwide efforts to catch up.

The face of the software industry today (era 5)

The *fifth software era*, the Internet and value-added services period, started in 1994 with Netscape's browser software for the Internet. Many new software firms like BroadVision and Intershop also sprung up, which started to sell software that used the Internet for data exchange. In addition, typical "Internet companies" like Yahoo!, Excite, and Amazon.com emerged, which did not make their key revenues from selling software anymore but rather applied software that often came from external software firms (for example, they set up Web services that delivered advertising revenues or merchandise sales). These firms are not software firms in the traditional sense (and thus they belong to a separate category in Figure 2-1).

HIGH COMPLEXITY DUE TO MULTIPLE PLATFORMS. Today, there are many competing platforms and standards in place. Hardware platforms range from mainframes to mini-computers and PCs. Software operating systems include *MVS, IBM OS/390, Unix, NT, Windows 95/ 98*, and *Windows CE* (for embedded software). Standard communications software applications include products from IBM/Lotus, Microsoft, Netscape, and Novell.

Furthermore, old systems must coexist with new ones. Banks, for instance, often rely on mainframe systems, while PC hardware and software is added on. This complexity demands that companies make their systems compatible with multiple standards or offer tools that help manage these linked systems.

THE DIFFERENCES BETWEEN ENTERPRISE SOLUTIONS AND MASS-MARKET SOFTWARE. The evolution of the software industry is also seen in the industry segmentation, as Figure 2-1 shows. The two main business types are software (professional) services and software products, with products divided in the two segments, enterprise solutions and mass-market packaged software.

Enterprise solution products always need customization. What differentiates enterprise solution products from packaged software is that it takes substantial time and effort to get enterprise solution software up and running. Pieces must be customized. A recent study showed that companies that install ERP software usually spend only 30 percent of the total software costs for the *software product license*. The remaining 70 percent are for *professional services* to implement the product.[14] Some software companies (like Oracle) offer these services themselves; others like Baan and SAP rely mainly on partners (i.e., professional software services firms like Deloitte & Touche or Andersen Consulting).

> Enterprise solution software installations take substantial time and effort.

Installations take months or years, not hours. While PC users nowadays are used to buying a software product and starting to work with it on the same day, installing enterprise solutions is a radically different matter. Take, for instance, the SAP *R/3* installation at Hewlett-Packard.[15] In 1993 the world's second-largest computer manufacturer decided to replace several custom-made solutions at its European Computer Manufacturing Operations unit with SAP's integrated standard software. It was, indeed, a major task to get the software running. A stunning 8,000 HP products, such as workstations, servers, software, and other equipment, had to be included in the project. This might explain why Heinz Henning, who is responsible for international SAP implementations at Hewlett-Packard, is quite proud of the time it took them—only 18 months, which is comparatively fast, given the complexity mastered.

Not for millions, but rather for thousands. Another difference is that enterprise solution products generally sell far fewer copies than mass-market products like Microsoft *Windows95*, as Figure 2-3 shows. In 1997 alone, Microsoft sold more than 60 million copies of that operating system.[16] SAP, as the world's largest ERP provider, on the other hand, installed its *R/3* software at about 16,500 sites worldwide—over a period of five years.[17] Other enterprise solution providers, like $60 million Simultan, an enterprise solutions firm in Switzerland, develop industry-specific solutions for 50 customers, and fewer, a year.[18]

In order to understand the software industry, it is important to understand which basic dynamics these segments have in common and which they do not.

THE DYNAMICS OF THE GAME

Two days before Christmas, in 1985, the unique journey of the first software services firm, CUC, ended. George Strohl, president of Computer Usage Company (CUC), was notified by a San Francisco court that his case had been converted to Chapter 7—bankruptcy. What had happened?

Managing software products and services simultaneously is a big challenge.

After Elmer Kubie left the company in 1968, CUC changed direction. The company started offering software products in addition to individual programming services, and it even entered the hardware market. One year later, CUC reported its first loss, of $430,000. The company changed leaders but kept the same mix of products and services. By 1985, CUC posted $2.4 million in losses on $1.5 million of revenues. That year, CUC's new president took the company into bankruptcy proceedings.

CUC failed partly because it got into software services and software products (and hardware) simultaneously,[19] without addressing the differences between managing software services and managing software products. It was a significant mistake.

While software products and software services businesses share some common ground, many aspects are different—including such "basic strategic forces" as cost structure, demand volume, competition intensity, geographic presence, and relationship management. These differences affect the management of software product and software service companies. Enterprise solutions firms, in particular, must continuously address these differences, as both products and services are linked to product installation.

Business dynamics in the product business

LOW ENTRY BARRIERS. Approximately 35,000 software firms exist worldwide that have more than five employees.[20] From Australia's Amicus Software Pty. Ltd., to Zimbabwe's Q Data DynamiQue Ltd., companies all around the world are players. They are all drawn in by low entry barriers to a field in which knowledge is more important than cash and equipment. "This business is 95 percent intangible capital," explained Joe Liemandt, founder of Trilogy Software.

> **"This business is 95 percent intangible capital."**

Low capital investments. Liemandt is a good example. In 1989, he dropped out of Stanford University to start Trilogy, a company based in Austin, Texas, and specializing in front office sales and marketing software. "I needed less than $100,000 in the beginning," he told us. "In fact, you want as little money as possible—that forces you to be efficient."

Venture capitalists, of course, like to invest in software companies for exactly that reason. "Software is very capital efficient," said Ann Winblad, of Hummer Winblad Venture Partners, a $200 million venture fund that was the first, in 1989, to invest exclusively in software firms. Winblad notes that her average software company requires only $3 million to start up.[21]

Our global survey showed that successful companies use on average seven times *more* start-up capital than the less successful ones. But compared to other industries, their capital needs are still very low—at about $5.1 million worldwide, and $8.4 million in the United States. "For a paper mill, on the contrary, you need $1 billion, before you even start, and then you write losses for years," Richard Roy, general manager of Microsoft Germany told us. "In software, all you need is a bunch of bright heads, a few desks in a garage, and an Internet connection." Besides those low capital requirements, high innovation rates often lower the entry barriers even further.

Low financial entry barriers boost innovation, and high innovation rates, in turn, lower the technical entry barriers. Low financial requirements lead to faster innovation and technological breakthroughs, as many start-up players join the market, compete, and strive for innovation.

The technological breakthroughs they create, like the arrival of the Web in 1994, often lower the entry barriers *again* for new players. A 1997 study showed that with the exception of Microsoft and IBM, 13 out of 15 leading companies in the Internet-based electronic-commerce software market were only three years old or younger. Among them were companies like BroadVision, iCat, Intershop, and Internet veteran Netscape (founded in 1994).[22] The reason: Young companies are often equally suited to tackle radically new opportunities as established players—and sometimes even more so. Said Joe Liemandt of Trilogy: "Many people graduating from college today have been using the Internet since they were 15—they're 25 now, and they're 10-year Internet *experts*. Technology is changing so fast, there is nobody who has better 'expertise' in the area." The smallest companies are often the fastest to respond to technological changes, as they are the most flexible and carry the least "legacy" along with them.

LOW MARGINAL COSTS LET COMPANIES REACH OUT FOR WORLDWIDE MARKETS. The development costs for the first copy of the Microsoft *Windows*95 PC operating system on CD were well above $1 billion, estimates software expert Capers Jones.[23] Producing the second CD, however, was vastly cheaper. It cost about $3. Traditional "production" costs hardly exist in software. That point was well proven at PLATINUM *technology* in Chicago, a $1 billion software company, where one of the main "production facilities" is a small $5,000 Kodak CD writer sitting on a desk on the fourth floor. The lonesome machine could produce several hundred CD-ROMs per day at $3 a piece.

In software product companies, virtually all the cost of software is in the design and coding of it (in addition to marketing and sales, of course). But while variable costs for product copies are low, the large up-front fixed costs for development mean that a great many copies must be sold. Only by selling to millions of people can Microsoft market its billion-dollar operating system for $209 per copy to its customers (as of April 20, 1998).[24]

Sometimes domestic markets—even the size of the United States—are too small to reach such high sales volumes. The German software start-up Intershop, for example, moved its entire headquarters to the United States just two years after its founding, to reach its largest market directly. Intershop is not alone. Many software product firms know only one target: the world. But only a tiny fraction of them succeed in that market.

THE RACE FOR MARKET LEADERSHIP. Immediately after the IBM PC arrived in 1981, hundreds of word processing packages were being created for it, including Samna *Word*, *Perfect Writer*, *WordStar*, and Microsoft *Word*. No one word processor clearly led the market.

Today the picture is much different. Microsoft *Word* leads with 62 percent of the word processor market in 1997, with only one major competitor, Corel, at 34 percent.[25]

This extremely high concentration in word processing is a classic example of the "law of increasing returns" that rules the software product business and that was first

The "law of increasing returns" rules the software product business.

described by Stanford economist Brian Arthur. The law states that a product that advances in market share tends to get even further ahead and sell even more copies, while one that falls behind tends to fall even further behind. Advantages or disadvantages tend to magnify rapidly. This law leads to a very high market concentration after a short time, leaving few winners and many losers. A number of reasons, described in detail in Chapter 6, account for the effect:

▶ The ability of programs to operate together and exchange information is critical; thus people buy the same software as the people they usually communicate with. Users enjoy "increasing returns" from their software as other users also begin to use it.

▶ Once users are trained on certain software products, they are less likely to switch to others because they would have to be retrained.

▶ Since software products are often difficult to evaluate objectively, decision makers often buy whatever is most popular.

In order to kick off the increasing-returns dynamic, high-tech marketing expert Geoffrey Moore said it is crucial to reach more than 40 percent market share within a certain niche within 12 to 18 months. "At that level of success—assuming your closest competitor is well behind you—word of mouth in the marketplace starts spreading the message that you are the market leader," says Moore.[26] Once that happens, Moore argues, market share can be expected to increase to well beyond 50 percent of the following 12 months' sales.

The law of increasing returns, indeed, shapes large parts of the software industry. In the enterprise solution business, for example,

SAP had a market share of 33 percent in the ERP market in 1997, according to Advanced Manufacturing Research.[27] It truly led the market and still does today.

How the race evolves. The winners of the race for market leadership usually emerge and secure their position in a shakeout among multiple players in the early stage, when a completely new product field is created. The players compete for the leading position in the new product field segment, trying to "set a standard." In enterprise decision support software, for example, at least 45 players competed in 1998. Only Oracle and IBM got close to a market share of 10 percent in this $1.5 billion game.[28] But once a few players achieve such an advantage in market share, marketing visibility, or in product performance, the effect of increasing returns begins to be seen.

Customers tend to flock to the market leader. After a while that drives most competitors out of the market. *MS Excel* is such as winner in the PC spreadsheet market. It controlled 60 percent of the market in 1998, leaving only 38 percent to the other competitor, *Lotus 1-2-3.*[29]

No security at the top. A leading position, however strong, may not last long. A technology shift or an aggressive move on the part of a fast player into a product field can change the game radically. From 1983 to 1987, for example, *Lotus 1-2-3* was the clear market leader in the spreadsheet market for DOS. But Microsoft realized new opportunities from technological innovation very quickly and became the new market leader.

Business dynamics in the professional services business

Leading *product* players reach their market leadership by selling ever more of the same thing—the same code—while their "production" costs remain at a constant $3 or so per copy. For professional services firms such cost structures and targets are completely out of range, however. Nearly constant variable costs and lower fixed costs make volume sales and market share much less important. For this reason, increasing returns do not exist in the service business.

To be sure, there are some important similarities between product and service firms as well, including low entry barriers, a constant threat of new entrants, and the same high pace of innovation.

But overall, the service firm business model is radically different.

ALMOST CONSTANT AND SIGNIFICANT MARGINAL COSTS. A 1996 McKinsey analysis of 22 companies showed that the cost of revenue is more than four times as high at software services firms than at product companies.[30] "We are not in the product business but in the people selling business," said Professor Robert Polillo, CEO of Etnoteam, an Italian services firm. Those people are expensive, repeatedly in every project. Even if Andersen Consulting builds a custom-made software solution for a customer today and a similar solution for another customer tomorrow, the cost of both of them is not radically different. Increasing the skill and experience levels in similar projects can usually not save more than 30 percent per project, a professional software services study noted.[31] That is quite different from the radical cost for the second CD-ROM copy in the product business.

NO INCREASING RETURNS, THUS MUCH HIGHER MARKET FRAGMENTATION. The difference in marginal costs clearly influences the market structure in the services segment. There is no race for market leadership, as in the product business. As marginal costs are basically constant in services, volume sales are not imperative. Furthermore, every solution is custom-made. The customer's desire to remain with the market leader, and thus to a "standard," is not as strong as with software products. There is no effect of increasing returns in this segment of the software business.

For these reasons, smaller local professional services providers can be very successful. While only a few companies usually win big in the product business, in the professional services segment there are literally thousands of companies offering comparable services. On average, more than 10,000 professional software services set up shop every year in the United States alone.[32] The market concentration with 23 percent of the total for the top 10 is low compared to the software product segments (see Figure 2-2). Even top-ranked Andersen Consulting, with revenues of $6.6 billion in 1997, reached a market share below 6 percent in the global software services market.[33] And despite huge mergers in this industry, such as by Coopers & Lybrand and PriceWaterhouse, professional services firms are unlikely to ever achieve global market leadership, as some software product companies do in their segments.

In fact, many software services companies remain geographically focused. In Europe, for instance, even some of the largest providers stay comparatively close to their home base. Companies such as Cap Gemini, Debis Systemhaus, or Siemens Business Services have all gone international and today generate a significant part of their revenues outside their home country (for instance, in the case of Cap Gemini, 75 percent of its revenues). However, so far they seem to have retained a focus on Europe. Offices overseas are still the exception, not the rule, and a global presence alone does not guarantee success. In fact, even small players offering the majority of their services in only one country can be very successful. Etnoteam, sd&m, and Sapient are good examples of that.

In professional services, a global presence is still the exception, not the rule.

Only a few service firms have aspired and managed to become truly global players with significant revenues in North America, Europe, and Asia. Among them are Andersen Consulting, IBM Global Services, EDS, CSC, Ernst & Young, KPMG, Pricewaterhouse-Coopers, Deloitte & Touche, and Cambridge Technology Partners. Recently, however, some regional service firms have started to follow the big global players. "We will be a global company within three to five years," John F. Keane, founder and chairman of Boston-based Keane, Inc., told us. "We are looking for acquisitions right now. The world is a world driven by technology, and technology is global. There are no doors barring it."

The challenge of managing the two business types simultaneously

Software product and service firms clearly depend on each other, especially in enterprise solutions installation. They also share common business dynamics, such as low entry barriers, fast innovation, and the threat from new entrants.

But a structured analysis of the importance of key success factors in our global survey also shows that the differences between software product and professional services business are quite substantial, as Table 2-1 summarizes.

While product companies must monitor their market share in terms of copies sold, for instance, professional services firms must concentrate on their capacity utilization rate.[34] Indeed, our survey results reveal that successful professional services firms achieve much higher capacity levels than their less successful counterparts.

Interestingly, the approaches differ not only *within* key management areas, like marketing, but even in the *relative importance* of the key management areas. While strategic and marketing issues are most critical to the overall success of product companies, superior human resource management and software engineering are most important in professional services.

The enterprise solution companies, in particular, cannot address this issue simply by coping with only one business type, as mentioned. Organizational separation and different marketing approaches for each business within the company must help solve the problem.

ADV Orga, the leading enterprise solution company in Germany in the early 1980s, with more than 500 employees, failed to do that. In addition to its other problems, there was no clear organizational

	PROFESSIONAL SERVICES	PRODUCT BUSINESS
Marginal costs	Almost constant	Almost zero
Market structure	Highly fragmented	Drive towards high concentration
Regional appearance	Mainly regional, with increasing tendency to globalization	Highly globalized
Customer relationship	One to one	One to few, one to many
Most important number to watch	Capacity utilization rate	Market share (installed base)
Relevance of management areas*	1. Human resources 2. Software development 3. Marketing and Sales 4. Strategy	1. Stategy 2. Marketing and Sales 3. Human resources 4. Software development

*According to significance analysis of key success factors in each management area.
  Source: Global McKinsey software survey.

Table 2-1. Dynamics of software product versus professional services business

separation between their product and service businesses. Whenever there were many service projects, developers were pulled off the product business to support those projects. As a result, product development was often put on hold and market launches were delayed. Furthermore, marketing was handled similarly for both products and services. In 1989, ADV Orga was sold with heavy losses. Meanwhile, ADV Orga's main competitor at the time, SAP, addressed those differences mainly via partnering in professional services and rose to global market leadership.

Despite the substantial differences between product and services businesses, they share some similarities. Their leaders, for instance, are similar in that they not only have to accept uncertainty, they have to thrive on it. In fact, leadership is one of the most important ingredients in software success.

3

EXCEPTIONAL SOFTWARE LEADERS ARE THE RULE

In 1989, the Berlin wall fell. At the time, Stephan Schambach was a 19-year-old student in Jena, a small university town in East Germany. Instead of continuing his studies in physics quantum theory and thermodynamics, he decided to take advantage of the opportunities brought on by the new political freedom. He realized there would be a large demand for computer services in East Germany. This was the beginning of an exceptional journey, one that many software leaders have taken. Like other leaders, Schambach tackled extraordinary challenges, convinced funders and followers of his entrepreneurial vision, and took his company overseas at the first opportunity.[1]

STEPHAN SCHAMBACH'S STORY

With about $1,000 in his pocket, the college dropout founded Netconsult, a computer consulting and system integration company. Success came swiftly. After two years, Schambach and his two employees made more than $1 million in revenues. In search of more capital and technology know-how, Schambach met Wilfried Beeck, the first German distributor of NeXT computer systems, a spin-off from Apple. Together, they turned Netconsult into a small successful computer business.

Aspiring to the virtually impossible

For Schambach, however, Netconsult's success was not truly satisfying. He was already looking for the next challenge and so turned his attention to a new medium, the Internet. At the time the Internet was in its infancy. Graphic Web browsers did not exist. Internet applications for business were unheard of. That was exactly where Schambach saw an opportunity, though. After a few market tests, he decided to provide standard software and electronic commerce solutions that would make the Internet "fit for business."

When Schambach shared this vision with his partners in 1995, they didn't buy in. Their current software service business was growing nicely. The Internet's future seemed enormously uncertain, and the costs for creating new software *products* for it seemed to be out of any scope. None of the partners could imagine how they would find enough capital. At the time, "angel investors" and venture capital were almost nonexistent in Germany.

Recruiting the top programmers

The first challenge was to find programmers who could create the new product in just a few months. When Schambach found Frank

Gessner and Ronald Fassauer, two 25-year-old computer science graduates from the University of Leipzig, he was so enthusiastic about his ideas that they simply could not turn him down. Instead of taking one of several attractive offers from major computer companies, Gessner and Fassauer signed up for the massive task at Intershop. In the following months, they *lived* in the office, working night and day.[2] They brought in mattresses and became "platinum card customers" of the local pizza shop.

Finding the funding

Schambach's partners were right about the banks. The best loan Schambach was offered was for less than $300,000—not exactly what he was looking for. His next idea was to run an ad in the *Frankfurter Allgemeine Zeitung*, one of the most prestigious German newspapers, seeking capital for an innovative new company.

This was not the usual way to start a business in Germany at the time—but it worked. Gert Koehler, managing partner and founder of Technologieholding VC, one of the first venture capital firms in Germany, read the ad excitedly. He met with Schambach and carefully asked him about his vision, his plans, and his personal background. "I lost my last doubts in that conversation," Koehler told us. Almost instantly, he offered to finance Schambach's young company with an initial investment of $1 million—making "Intershop" the first e-commerce software company ever financed by venture capital in Germany.[3]

"Now the challenge *really* started," Schambach recalled. Although Microsoft and others had not yet announced plans to enter the field, Schambach and Koehler sensed that the window of opportunity was small. They decided to introduce their first product by March 1996 at the CeBIT exhibition, the world's largest computer and software fair. That left them with exactly one month to prepare for the important event.

Meeting the press

Schambach in the meantime, found additional managers and started Intershop's first PR campaign. The challenges were substantial. At the very first press conference, only one journalist showed up. Schambach told the journalist that all other journalists had already come and gone, but he offered him an "extra" interview. The journalist was grateful and wrote a favorable story for a major newspaper. "It was great to get that article," Schambach told us. "It gave us exactly the publicity we needed at the time." Later, at the CeBIT exhibition of 1996, Schambach's and Gessner's product was showered with positive media reviews.

Internationalizing almost overnight

The CeBIT success was the kickoff for Intershop's next development. In the following months, Schambach moved to Silicon Valley. He had realized that he needed to be at the center of the world's rising electronic-commerce marketplace. Within a few months, Schambach started a Silicon Valley subsidiary and made it Intershop's headquarters.

In 1998, Intershop went public on the German stock exchange Neuer Markt with an IPO valued at about $300 million.

THE ESSENTIAL CHARACTERISTICS OF SOFTWARE LEADERS

While every industry boasts strong leaders, software leaders like Schambach have several strong characteristics in common. These characteristics are shaped by management challenges that are generally more extreme, in many cases, than those found in other industries.

First, software leaders must deal with very high levels of uncertainty.

They are technology visionaries
thriving on uncertainty

Software leaders must live on the cutting edge. In Schambach's case, it was not only starting a high-tech company in a remote region of East Germany that was surprising, it was also anticipating—almost through a flash of insight—the entire Internet revolution.

The number of visionaries in the software industry is impressive.

In 1987, driving from Frankfurt to Walldorf on the way home from an IBM presentation, SAP founders Hasso Plattner, Dietmar Hopp, and Klaus Tschira decided to create a new version of their best-selling SAP *R/2* enterprise solution software. The new *R/3* would utilize a much more flexible design.[4]

The number of visionaries in the software industry is impressive.

But on what system should the new product run? At the time, many universities had just begun using *Unix*, a new operating system that allowed networking between computers of different vendors, thus enabling a new system architecture, the client-server model. Despite these advantages, it was rather unstable and didn't meet the performance levels required for an enterprise solution application. And so, while it offered many experts advantages over mainframes, many practitioners thought it would never replace the leading mainframes of the time.

But Hasso Plattner disagreed. Advocating *Unix* for the new *R/3* system, he proposed a direction that seemed highly speculative and risky at the time.

He promptly ran into resistance within his own company. But he was convinced of his vision—and so used his influence as a major shareholder to get approval from the board. Four years later, in 1991, SAP introduced *R/3* to the world, installed on a tiny HP *Unix* workstation. People were stunned. "It was almost ridiculous," recalls Plattner. "They were saying, 'This little machine, with some memory drives attached—this is the great SAP?'" The little machine, however, set the ground for SAP's dominating position in the ERP market. *R/3* on *Unix* opened SAP to multitudes of *Windows* PC users and "blew away the green screen competition" with a "beautiful front-end," as Bruce Richardson, a consultant at Advanced Manufacturing Research in Boston, described it. On top of that, the performance of *R/3* on *Unix* was higher than that of *R/2* on mainframes.

R/3 became a killer product in the global ERP market. From 1992 to 1998, SAP's revenues in the United States alone grew from $45 million to $2 billion.[5]

It was Hasso Plattner's deep insight into technology, and his anticipation of future developments that made this success possible. Both Plattner and Schambach illustrate that software leaders must live on the cutting edge.

The software industry has produced many other well-known visionaries, who have transformed business worldwide—from Elmer Kubie, who believed way back that software could be sold separately from hardware, and John F. Keane, who started his software services company above a doughnut shop in 1965, all the way to Bill Gates and Larry Ellison, and others.

They are extreme risk takers— and hope for immense returns

On the way to making their visions happen, software leaders must be able to manage enormous amounts of risk. Our survey showed that leaders of successful software product companies take, on average, 25 percent less time to make important strategic decisions. The reasons for this are not so much that they have better information or market research but rather their willingness to take risks.

Successful companies make important decisions quicker.

Consider Joe Liemandt, who dropped out of school and founded Austin, Texas–based Trilogy Software, Inc., in 1989, a company that specialized in front office sales and marketing software. For Liemandt, risk taking came naturally. "If you are not ready to drop out of school, then you don't really believe in your idea," he told us. "I thought I had to drop out to capture the market opportunity."

No venture capitalist wanted to fund him, so Liemandt lived off credit. "Once I had 22 maxed-out credit cards," he told us. Two years after founding Trilogy, however, Liemandt reaped the returns of his willingness to take risks. He finally made his first sale, to Hewlett Packard—a contract worth $3.5 million. Other big-name customers like Boeing and Lucent followed. By 1996, Joe Liemandt hit the Forbes Richest 400 List and became its youngest self-made member, with an estimated $500 million net worth. In 1998, he had 850 employees and sales beyond $100 million.[6]

Liemandt and his company are not a singular case. Marc Andreessen was 22 years old when he cofounded Netscape and developed the Internet browser software. Bill Gates, Steve Ballmer, or SAP's Hasso Plattner are all risk takers as well. And all of them became multibillionaires by taking risks.

Gates, the Harvard University dropout, was worth $51 billion in July 1998. His software code, you could say, sells better than oil: According to *Forbes* magazine, the oil-soaked Sultan of Brunei ranked *third* in the list of the world's richest people in 1998, at $36 billion, *behind* Bill Gates and the Walton family of Wal-Mart. Until 1998, the Sultan had always been richer than Gates.[7]

SAP's cochairman and CEO, Hasso Plattner was rewarded with the thirty-fourth position on the world list, at $7 billion, for his insights on client-server systems, only topped within his own company by SAP's cofounder and chairman of the supervisory board, Dietmar Hopp—twenty-seventh on the list, at $8 billion.

Taking risks is part of the folklore of the software industry. In fact, Joe Liemandt likes to play the odds in Las Vegas with his associates. "It's good for morale," he says. "Nothing brings a group of people together like risk." One time, Liemandt bet one of his programmers that the programmer would not make a certain deadline. To make the bet more risky, Liemandt bet his Lexus

Taking risks is good for morale.

and agreed to drive the programmer's Ford Aspire if he lost. Lie-mandt lost and drove the Aspire for the rest of the year.[8]

But while successful software leaders love challenge, they are not crazy. They do not bet everything on one opportunity; instead, they take multiple risks that yield multiple options for success.

They bet on multiple options to prepare for all uncertainties

Microsoft, for example, didn't bet solely on the success of its *Windows* PC operating system but codeveloped the competing operating system *OS/2* together with IBM. SAP is another example. Instead of "shaping" the industry, SAP prefers to adapt to leading standards, investing in several simultaneously. As SAP's cochairman and CEO Henning Kagermann noted, SAP can watch the play unfold from the second row.[9]

Leaders of professional software services firms also manage uncertainty via options. Jim Sims, CEO of Cambridge Technology Partners, the Boston-based $600 million software service firm, ensures that Cambridge continuously invests in *several* new players that may develop a new technology standard. "We stay in touch with the newest technologies," Sims said. "We hope that one of those companies in the fund will win one day."[10]

On their way to winning, though, software leaders must accept occasional failure. In fact, failure is not the exception, but the rule—even among successful software leaders.

They'd rather "fail quickly" than avoid mistakes

"It's better to make six right and four wrong decisions, than to wait too long," SAP's Dietmar Hopp noted.[11] Jerry Popek, CTO of PLATI-NUM *technology* agrees. "It's important to move fast," he says. "That will often lead to mistakes. But mistakes can be corrected."

Consider how Pehong Chen reacted shortly after he started BroadVision. While the entrepreneur was right in betting on electronic-commerce solutions, he erred when he chose interactive TV—which *seemed* to be the "wave of the future"—as a platform for his products. In fact, Chen had his TV product near completion when he got his first look at the worldwide Web.[12]

"It became crystal clear to me that we were wrong and that we would lose everything if we didn't change tracks quickly," Chen recalled. Instead of having long discussions, Chen transformed the company into an Internet firm almost overnight—against the resistance of his managers. "I basically had to fire the whole top management team because they didn't believe in the change," he says. His swift actions made the difference, and by the end of 1998, BroadVision had a market cap of more than $700 million.

> **Chen transformed BroadVision into an Internet company almost overnight.**

Liemandt told us, "The key thing in this business is to make mistakes quickly, and correct them even faster."

They aim high

Software leaders also set extremely high expectations. When Flip Filipowski founded PLATINUM *technology* in 1987, he decided to build a *billion-dollar revenue company* within 10 years.[13] Filipowski felt he had to move fast because he saw the software industry moving quickly toward maturity. He also knew that in the software product business, only the leading players truly win. "For me, getting big fast was a question of survival," he explained.

Filipowski didn't quite make it. "It took us 11 years instead of 10," he admits—with a slight look of embarrassment. His embarrassment should be bearable, however: It took Bill Gates 15 years to get Microsoft to a billion dollars; Intel, Oracle, and SAP all took longer than 10 years to make it. Only John Morgridge and John Chambers of Cisco beat Filipowski. They made it in 10 years.[14]

In our global survey, we found an extremely strong correlation between high aspiration level and company success. Of the successful companies, 93 percent had a clear and ambitious vision, whereas only 25 percent of the less successful companies had that same aspiration level.

They are builders of highly dynamic organizations

On December 7, 1995, Bill Gates announced an abrupt change in course at Microsoft. Reaching back into history, Gates quoted from a remark made by Japanese Admiral Yamamoto on the day the Japanese attacked the United States: "I fear we have awakened a sleeping giant." The giant in this case was Gates's company, and the attackers were Netscape and the Internet age.[15]

Gates clearly saw the attackers coming. In the 20 months of its existence, Netscape had lifted its *Navigator* World Wide Web browser to worldwide leadership. The company had also staged one of the most successful initial public offerings ever. Meanwhile at Microsoft, "We had really somewhat missed the Internet boat," concedes Richard Roy, general manager of Microsoft Germany.[16]

That was about to change. Standing before hundreds of analysts and reporters, Gates announced that he would refocus every project and every product to meet the Internet challenge. Indeed, managers throughout Microsoft abruptly stopped several multi-million-dollar projects—and started Internet projects within hours. One of the managers, John Ludwig, walked into a room filled with programmers and ordered, "Clear that source code off your machines, and start

Microsoft rose to the Internet challenge.

working on Java today." The number of programmers working on an Internet browser rose quickly from 8 to 800.[17]

Nine months later, on August 13, 1996, Microsoft *Internet Explorer 3.0*, the new competitive browser, was introduced. It matched Netscape's *Navigator* in every feature. In the first week, more than 1 million users downloaded the free software. While the battle between the two companies was still being waged in 1998, one point was clearly made: Microsoft had managed to turn around a massive 20,000-person organization within little more than six months. It took an extreme conviction and a clearly communicated message of massive change from the top leaders to do so. Keeping the organization ready for such drastic changes is an ongoing effort. Said Intel's Andy Grove about managing in high-tech firms: "You need to plan the way a fire department plans: It cannot anticipate where the next fire will be, so it has to shape an energetic and efficient team that is capable of responding to the unanticipated as well as to any ordinary event."[18]

They build extremely flat, team-based organizations

SAP, with 20,000 employees and $5 billion in revenues in 1998, runs a three-tiered, flat organization. At company headquarters in Walldorf, Germany, part of a speech by Chairman Dietmar Hopp is pinned to the wall by the coffee machine. "To all those new to the company," it reads, "we are nonbureaucratic and encourage self-initiative here at SAP." It adds, "This entails that everyone is also somewhat responsible for things that are usually not within the regular job task."

In professional software services, building team-based organizations is also a key leadership task. "In professional services, it's the team that wins," John F. Keane explains. "But because of that, leaders are also key in professional services. In the product business, the product is the cohesive around the company, with leaders inventing and representing it. In services, the leader has to orchestrate and build an empowered team."[19]

Microsoft's chief operating officer, Bob Herbold, formerly head of marketing at consumer goods giant Procter & Gamble, says in an interview with the *Financial Times* that the software industry's team structure and flat hierarchies are what impresses him most about the industry. "At Procter & Gamble, most of the communication is written. It goes up and down a level, and it's relatively slow compared to this industry. So it might take four rounds of communication for you to find out that I am really upset about something. At Microsoft, we pride ourselves on getting to the point."[20] Managers in other industries agree. "Software companies like Oracle and Sun are so team based; we'd love to emulate them," says Texaco's oil exploration visualization center manager Michael Zeitlin. "Middle managers have the power to decide. They can simply act. That culture impresses me."[21]

They create a culture that attracts and retains talent

When we visited PLATINUM *technology* outside of Chicago, we asked various managers what impressed them most about their company. From Bill Veber, manager of the corporate data center, Michael Matthews, executive vice president of marketing, and developer Ron DeMott came the same answer: "Flip." The distinctive style of CEO Andrew "Flip" Filipowski, they said, made a big difference.[22]

Even Flip's office is distinctive, with hundreds of Indian dolls lining the walls and a big TV hanging from the ceiling with an Internet news service continuously running on it. In another corner, a supply of soft drinks rises six feet high. "First-time visitors are always surprised. Flip is really a very special person," said an executive assistant, flashing a smile as she showed us Filipowski's office. She's not alone: Nearly everyone we spoke with mentioned PLATINUM's leader and the culture he's created when they explain why they joined the company and why they enjoy working there.

Creating a culture that attracts talent is vital for software leaders, and, in fact, is one of their most important challenges.

TEAMS AT THE TOP

Many of today's start-up companies—and even the software giants—are not led by a single leader. Very few leaders, in fact, can claim to have all the skills required for success. Rather, many companies are led by leadership teams: The challenges for software leaders arising from the extreme pace and uncertainty in the industry are so diverse that it often takes more than one leader to tackle all the tasks. It takes a "balance between real team and single-leader capabilities," a deep understanding of which situations would be managed better by teams than by individuals, as expert Jon Katzenbach notes.[23]

The larger a company, the wider the range of skills and situations a leader must master. Leaders must either grow into these capabilities or bring in others who can handle them. Otherwise, they may just steer their company into disaster.

"We call them the twins," Theo Schnittfink, senior vice president of European operations of Cambridge Technology Partners, told us. He was referring to Jim Sims, founder and CEO, and to Art Toscanini, CFO.[24]

Prior to starting Cambridge, the two had already formed a team at Concurrent Computer Corporation, where Sims had become chairman and CEO and Toscanini was vice president and controller. **Vision, values, and vigor.** Together, they grew Concurrent into a $340 million business, with 3,500 employees, before selling the company to Mascomp in 1990. The two leaders have truly complementary skills.[25]

Jim Sims is the company visionary. Standing at a flip board, he genuinely enjoys talking about the company's values. "I am world class in core values," Sims explained half-jokingly. Sims also strives to motivate the company wherever he can. "Jim gets really nervous if something stays the same for a while. He forces us to reinvent ourselves every day," said Schnittfink.

Toscanini, in contrast, is much quieter. He tends to think first and talk later. He covers the analytical side, with very realistic views, and a firm grasp of the financial figures. He makes the business profitable. During our conversation, Toscanini sat calmly in his chair, pausing before answering questions and making his points very clearly. Sims, on the other hand, jumped frequently from his chair, pacing the room while speaking. The two complementary personalities have turned Cambridge Technology Partners into a $600 million company in little over seven years.

Twins populate the software business

A number of "twins at the top" lead the most successful software companies covered in our global survey.

CONTROLLING EXPERT AND TECHNOLOGY CAPTAIN AT SAP. At SAP, Dietmar Hopp, the cofounder, former CEO, and now chairman of the supervisory board, applies a down-to-earth, fact-driven leadership style, with an emphasis on planning and control. He ensures that SAP has enough capital and that the operations run well. Hasso Plattner, cofounder and now cochairman and CEO, takes the "technology visionary" role. Often referred to as "Mr. *R/3*" himself, Plattner was the driver behind SAP's technology. He enjoys yacht racing, where he frequently competes with Larry Ellison, who is a yachtsman himself. Plattner wrote the computer program that analyzes wind and water conditions himself, and he had great success at the famous Hobart-Sydney-Regatta in December 1996, when Plattner's yacht won in record time.[26] Plattner's fresh personality and his preference for showmanship contribute significantly to the popular image of SAP in the United States as an aggressive and innovative overseas attacker.

MR. FUTURE AND MR. PROCESS AT ORACLE. In 1991 Oracle was in serious trouble. Customer satisfaction was declining rapidly. Ellison's hyperaggressive salespeople had been selling large quantities of software at huge discounts, and they were even selling software that couldn't be delivered. As a result, Oracle was forced to restate its 1990 earnings and lost $12 million in 1991, the first loss after years of fast and profitable growth. Ellison admitted later, "I have never been really good at running a sales force or a large service organization." He was much better at creating new products and articulating Oracle's vision. With more than a billion dollars in revenues, however, Oracle's organization needed effective processes.[27]

With the aid of a headhunter, Ellison found Ray Lane in 1992, who had been running the Dallas office of consulting firm Booz, Allen & Hamilton. Lane, often referred to as "Mr. Process," quickly took on the organizational challenges as chief operating officer, reorganizing the sales force, building Oracle's service operations, and establishing rigorous management processes inside the company. By 1997 Lane had helped grow the company to $5.7 billion in revenues and net earnings of $821 million. The stock price rose from $2.76 to $38.50. Ellison himself said that he owes much of Oracle's success to Lane, "past, present and future." The two have a yin-yang partnership: Ellison functions as Oracle's public face and conveyor of its vision, and Lane ensures that Oracle delivers. Bill Marshal, an Oracle consulting manager, observed, "As a combination, they're much stronger than they are as individuals."

Grow or go—the life cycle of leaders

Unlike many entrepreneurs, Larry Ellison had the strength to recognize he needed help. By acknowledging his skill gap and willingly sharing control in a new leadership team, Ellison saved his company.

Many entrepreneurs fail to do that. A study of high-tech leadership found that companies that did not back the CEO with a complementary leadership team tended to be less successful. Of the most successful companies, only one third had the same, single leader that they began with.[28]

Two European software services companies clearly demonstrated what happens to companies when leadership teams don't grow along with the company. Both firms were in the $70 million range and wrote losses. Both had grown quite fast under their original leadership, which made it impossible for the initial executive team to be in charge of all ongoing operations. The right thing to do would have been to establish a clearly structured organization with several strategic business units managed by strong second-tier managers.

In both companies, leadership's reactions to the challenge were wrong. In the first company, the leaders refused to give away control. Middle managers became frustrated with their lack of decision-making authority. Many of them left the company, depriving the firm of its best management talent. Meanwhile the managers were unable to oversee all operations and, by trying to manage everything, lost their grip. Eventually the company was sold for 30 percent of its revenues.

Leadership teams must grow with the company.

The second company suffered the opposite fate. Its leaders gave up control completely, and soon the regional managers were managing their units as if they were local emperors, paying little attention to overall company interests. Top management was flying blind. As a result, some of the company's projects reached an ROI of minus 180 percent. This company finally exchanged its leadership, putting in place an experienced leadership team. Four years later, it was sold for 150 percent of its annual revenue. It was, at least, an acceptable price for a professional services company at that time.

THE MINDSET TO WIN THE RACE

When dealing with extreme challenges, successful software leaders need one asset more than any other. They need an attitude—one that may best be described by leaders outside the software business. "We say 'Why?' and our friends in software say 'Why not?'" Roger Davis, managing director of Citicorp Securities' $1 billion global insurance banking business, told us. "We are trying to adapt this 'Why not'-style step by step, from the top down and vice versa. It simply takes an important shift in thinking."[29]

This "Why not" attitude is especially crucial when software leaders tackle one of their most difficult challenges: shaping the corporate culture—a culture that must attract one of the scarcest commodities in the software business: great employees.

After all, the software industry's greatest competition is not only for the customers' business but also for the best talent. Indeed, the race has become so competitive that recruiting efforts can feel like a war.

4

WINNING THE WAR FOR SOFTWARE TALENT

In 1995, Saurabh Srivastava sat in his office in New Delhi, India, and pondered a significant challenge.

IIS Infotech, a $40 million, 400-employee firm of which he was president, had been enjoying double-digit growth for many years. Future demand looked good for products ranging from Year 2000 software fixes to enterprise solutions installations. Nevertheless, Srivastava was troubled. He had tried to recruit just 50 of India's annual 5,000 top-notch computer science graduates. But despite a lot of effort and very attractive salaries, he had managed to sign up only 10 of them. "We got a lot of okay people, but the really great ones were almost impossible to get," Srivastava told us. "I knew this situation was going to be a real threat to our future. Without more and more of India's best computer scientists, we just couldn't sustain our growth."[1]

Srivastava decided to tackle the problem. When computer science professor R. K. Arora from the renowned Indian Institute of Technology (IIT)—the "Indian MIT"—complained about a funding shortage at their New Delhi facilities, Srivastava immediately offered to help. "I said, you need money, we need people, so let's throw it together," he recalled. In an advertisement to top students, IIS and IIT offered a nine-month intensive program that included theoretical training at IIT and practical project work at IIS. ITT got involved through an organization called FITT (Foundation for Innovation and Technology Transfer), a body set up by ITT for such purposes. It concluded with an advanced degree in computer science—and most importantly a guaranteed job at IIS Infotech.

In 1997, the program brought Srivastava 40 top programmers, and in 1998, 80 programmers. "For that success, though, we basically had to backward-integrate and build our own talent factory," said Srivastava.

GLOBALLY SCARCE BRAINS

The scarcity of software professionals is the major barrier to growth in the software industry and one of the key challenges of software leaders.

According to a recent study by the Information Technology Association of America (ITAA) and Virginia Tech University, 346,000, or approximately 10 percent, of IT positions in the United States were vacant in 1998. In Silicon Valley alone, there was a shortage of 200,000 computer industry workers.[2] In Silicon Valley, workers can simply walk across the street to competitors and receive pay raises of $10,000 to $40,000 for a very similar job task.

In other markets, the lack of qualified personnel is as troubling as it is in the United States. India faces severe constraints to its software growth due to the shortage of talent. One reason is the enormous growth of the $3 billion Indian software industry, which multiplied its size 50 times in the past 10 years and is still expanding at 50 percent annually. The other reason is the number of Indian developers lured away to Silicon Valley—more than 15,000 every year.[3]

In Germany, the situation is not much different. While other German industries have suffered from the highest unemployment rates in years, many German software companies struggle to find qualified people. The smaller and less well known companies are especially desperate. The human resources manager of a small software provider in Munich told us that while he used to receive hundreds of resumes after posting a newspaper ad, today he gets only about 15 from the same ad. Well-known companies face similar problems. In 1998, Andersen Consulting planned to hire an additional 700 people for its German offices, about a 40 percent increase. To reach such a number of *top* people, Andersen had to look outside Germany—including Switzerland and Austria—because there weren't enough to be found in Germany alone.[4]

A NEW DIMENSION FOR RECRUITING

The scarcity of top software workers requires previously unheard of efforts.

Attracting top students from top universities

In the summer of 1997, Andersen Consulting flew a group of 100 German university students to Nice, France. The group, selected from 2,000 IT students, was treated to three days of luncheon buffets, evening parties, and daytime seminars. In the end, 40 percent of them were impressed enough with Andersen to sign up with the company as full-time employees. Andersen's success triggered five similar events in the following year. [5]

SAP has begun to sponsor classes at the University of Heidelberg, and it is present at all important job fairs, to lure top students to the company. Smaller companies, like IDS, a partner of SAP, are sometimes even more active. August Wilhelm Scheer, CEO of IDS, a consulting and software tool firm, leverages his position as a professor at Saarbruecken University to scout new talent. Scheer introduced a new major in the fall of 1998 called "consulting." The classes focus on SAP (and Baan) software implementation techniques—which is also the key focus of IDS.[6] A number of Scheer's new hires have come from his university classes. The same technique for finding new talent exists at Etnoteam, a professional services company in Milan, Italy. Three professors from the local university founded the company— and every year, the top 10 percent of their students usually receive a job offer at Etnoteam. As many as 80 percent of them have accepted the job.[7]

Creating personal ties with candidates through current employees

Cisco tries to build relationships with prospective employees even before formal interviews. Advertisements encourage potential employees to call and "make a friend" at Cisco. By chatting with a Cisco employee very informally—with someone who has a similar background and interests—candidates form their first informal communications with Cisco. By advertising in local movie theaters across Silicon Valley, Cisco received 100 to 150 responses every week from applicants who were looking for "new friends." Within Cisco, more than 1,000 Cisco employees volunteered to help with the program. The potential rewards were attractive: Each prospect they "befriended" and who was ultimately hired was worth a lottery ticket for a free trip to Hawaii.[8]

"Make a friend" at Cisco.

Many companies in the global survey offered large bonuses to employees for finding job candidates that are subsequently hired. At

PLATINUM *technology*, as much as $5,000 is paid for every new hire. Internal referrals are significantly more cost-effective than referrals obtained from outside services. "The quality of referred people is usually very high, for two reasons," Marc Ugol, senior vice president of human resources, told us. "First, the referring person generally has a very good knowledge of the recruit's capabilities and attitude, and second, they wouldn't put their reputation at risk with a low-quality referral."[9] Other companies do the same, but with different twists. To emphasize the quality of the hire, for instance, CSC pays a bonus one year after the hiring—but only if the new employee is still with CSC. At Compuware, employees publish their own job advertisements in newspapers in order to get more referrals. "They basically turn it into their own business," said Ron Watson, director of human resources.[10]

Involving venture capitalists in recruiting efforts

Venture capitalists provide a more indirect, but often as powerful, access to employee networks and qualified personnel. They are especially helpful to start-ups, which generally lack large numbers of direct contacts and a widely known brand name. "When I finally decided to take some outside capital, it wasn't because I was interested in the money. It was because I was interested in gaining the help of John Doerr and his venture firm, Kleiner Perkins," says Jim Clark, cofounder of Netscape.[11] In an interview with the *Red Herring* magazine, John Doerr recalls: "We helped Jim to assemble a really first class team in under 90 days: Two VPs of engineering, VPs of sales and marketing, and a world-class CEO, Jim Barksdale."[12] Likewise, when BroadVision started up in 1993, it also didn't need outside capital. (CEO Pehong Chen had sold his previous start-up company, Gain, for more than $100 million.) Nevertheless, Chen requested a small amount of venture capital from Sutter Hill Ventures and Mayfield Fund. "A renowned venture capitalist is like a quality stamp. And moreover, they have excellent people networks," Chen explained.[13]

Recruiting over the World Wide Web

Nearly all the software companies in our survey used the Web for recruiting purposes. But the differences between "using" and "truly applying" the Web are great. Some companies excel at recruiting on the Web both in terms of how *many* candidates they screen and how *aggressively* they search for them. At Cisco, the human resources department receives more than 100,000 applications and resumes in electronic form via the Web per year. More than 40 percent of the 5,000 annual new hires are recruited electronically. The Internet is also used to identify target candidates. For example, most prospects visit Cisco's Web site from their jobs—even if they work for direct competitors. Those are especially interesting candidates for Cisco. Recently, a message would pop up when these candidates surfed Cisco's home page, saying, "Welcome to Cisco. Would you like a job?"[14]

> **Cisco's HR department receives more than 100,000 electronic job applications yearly.**

Tapping global sourcing opportunities

The shortage of engineers in Silicon Valley has led to an ever-increasing demand for foreign workers. More than 40 percent of all U.S. software companies hire skilled immigrants to help overcome the local labor shortage, according to the Information Technology Association of America (ITAA).[15] Since many companies develop parts of their software at offshore subsidiaries located in places like India, they also try to adapt those local programmers to their corporate culture and to transfer them back to the United States to fill the vacant positions at headquarters.

The sourcing of talent from India has become so commonplace that applications for U.S. H1-B high-tech immigration visas have swamped the government agencies. In 1998, the annual 65,000 cap on H-1B visas for high-tech and other specialty jobs had been reached by May. U.S. companies, dependent on the imported skills, lobbied Congress to raise the cap from the current 65,000 to 115,000 until 2001.[16] That bill has caused great controversy in the U.S. Congress.

Stepping into completely new territory

But despite the lobbying in Congress, immigration laws remain a problem for U.S. firms that want to hire talented programmers from overseas. That was exactly the problem that Doug Mellinger, founder of U.S. custom-software design company PRT Group, faced in 1994. To attract new talent, he made great efforts to build an offshore development center in India. But that could not solve the problem either: Many large customers simply refused to take the time to travel to far-off India for crucial review meetings.

These constraints led Mellinger to step into completely new territory to solve the problem. In 1996, he opened up a new subsidiary, only a four-hour flight from New York, but far enough away to avoid immigration restrictions.[17] The location was the island of Barbados in the Caribbean. And the perks to attract talent—and customers, too— ranged from plenty of sunshine to free refills of the fridge. "In the mornings, we play tennis," says one recruit from Bangalore, India. "Then we create software."

Programmers flocked to Barbados, solving Mellinger's problem. Within two years, 300 arrived from Bombay, Malaysia, Manitoba. Customers like J.P. Morgan and Chase became so excited about the highly qualified talent pool close to the United States, that they invested more than $12 million in equity and contributions to help finance future expansion. PRT's sales on the new high-tech island soared from zero to $19 million within two years.

The need for software people has created many innovative approaches to recruiting. But which factors motivate software employees to take a job—and stick with it?

WHAT MOTIVATES SOFTWARE WORKERS

Allowing individual work styles

Software companies must accommodate an enormous range of work styles and personalities if they want to attract enough talent. A glimpse at the recruiting home page of pcOrder.com, an aggressive start-up in Austin, Texas, tells the story:

> We are as varied as we are talented. Some people can only concentrate in a dark room with The Chemical Brothers blasting, other people prefer Classical and believe that lack of light really is bad for your eyes. Some people "look professional" as an excuse to shop for nice clothes; other people wear a clean T-shirt and shoes when they want to dress up. Some work from 5 A.M. to 5 P.M; others don't believe in the cruel and unusual abuse of alarm clocks and never show their faces before lunch time.

Software companies must accommodate an enormous range of work styles.

This range of personalities, work styles, and backgrounds was indeed what we found when we visited more than 100 software companies around the world.

Take Jacob Ramsgaard Nielsen, a programmer at the Danish software company Navision Software. When Nielsen was 20 and had just finished high school, he walked into the Navision company headquarters close to Copenhagen and asked for a job. Nielsen was willing to stack boxes if he needed to. But after a quick assessment of his skills, the need to carry boxes never arose. Nielsen could not only grasp complex technical issues quickly, he could also communicate them in a very simple, understandable way.[18]

Nielsen started as a technical writer in a team of young, innovative developers. Although he was without a university degree, he was accepted as an integral team member. Indeed, he came to learn that while degrees are an important entry ticket in other industries, in the software business it is often not even required, as long as the scarce technical talent and the skills are there.

Money is another incentive for software workers. Or rather: stocks.

Sharing profits—and reaching millionaire status

In 1993 Heather Beach, 25, took a $28,000-a-year job as a receptionist with Silicon Valley software start-up Siebel Systems. Since start-ups are always short on cash, Beach agreed to receive part of her salary in stock. Three years later, when Siebel went public and quadrupled in value within six months, the receptionist's fortunes soared. While Heather Beach may have been the first software receptionist to become a millionaire by the age of 30, she was hardly the only software employee in the seven-digit club. According to Payment Systems, a Florida-based research company, more than 60 people in the Silicon Valley alone reach millionaire status every single day of the year.[19]

Successful companies entice recruits with stock option plans and instant wealth.

Stock options programs are also very effective software worker motivation tools. These programs offer huge potential benefits for both employees and the company.

For employees, the benefit is simple: getting rich. According to the *Washington Post*, each of Microsoft's 21,000 employees gained—on average—more than $1 million in 1997 alone, on the

value of their annual stock options. Bill Gates and Steve Ballmer, incidentally, did not participate in the options. They own so much stock
that giving them options would be absurd; so they're among the few
"optionless."[20]

For software companies, the benefits of stock options are twofold.
First, options encourage employees to perform well because company
success equals personal gain. Second, stock options, which are usually
exercisable only after two to five years, are a powerful incentive for
employees to stay with the company. As Randall Bolton, CFO of
BroadVision, told us: "Our stock options program is our most important retainment factor. All of these people could walk out the door
and get better offers in terms of compensation—but they would lose
all their options." How important stock options are for retainment is
evident in an example from Cambridge Technology Partners, the professional services firm from Boston. After stock prices had fallen in
the stock market turmoil in later 1998, CEO Jim Sims announced to
employees worldwide via a video conference that he would lower the
price in retrospect by up to 50 percent for all options less than two
years old—to keep them from becoming worthless. At the same time,
though, he also said that the new price would be valid only for people
who stayed on for additional time as well.

Baan, the Dutch enterprise solutions provider, recently pursued a
similar strategy in its attempt to return to better times than in the second half of 1998. "In a bid to hold on to programmers, they are allowing employees to exercise their stock options at a price that would
have been laughably low a few months ago."[21]

For start-ups, stock options and equity share programs are especially important. They overcome smaller starting salaries and the ego
deflation of not belonging to a big player like IBM or Oracle. Instead,
start-ups can offer highly attractive compensation schemes. Employees are often eager to sacrifice parts of their cash payments in
exchange for equity (like Heather Beach)—as long as the millionaire
status follows when the company goes public.

In several European countries, tax and labor laws make stock options unattractive or even illegal. This places the European companies at a disadvantage in hiring software workers. The leading European firms are finally starting to attack the problem, however. SAP in Germany, for instance, has recently introduced a costly substitute for options—a

Europe and the Far East are just catching up on incentives.

"virtual" stock options program. Employees may buy "virtual shares," which give them benefits comparable to "real" stock options. SAP pays the "virtual stock gains" directly from its cash flow and takes these large costs as additional personnel costs.

Other German companies overcome the legal limitations by simply moving to the United States. Says Stephan Schambach, CEO of Intershop communications: "One benefit of moving the headquarters to the U.S. was to be able to offer stock options to the employees, even if they remained in Germany. This is a key advantage to the German recruiting market." His developers work for a slightly lower than market compensation, but since the Intershop IPO in July 1998, many of them are likely to have cashed out well.

In general, our survey showed that linking performance and financial rewards directly is a key to success for software companies. Almost all the surveyed successful companies use variable performance-based bonuses, apart from stock options. These bonuses, on average, were twice as high at successful companies than at less successful ones. Moreover, the bonuses were linked more rigorously to employees performance. At sd&m, for example, a midsized German professional services company, first-level managers could earn up to 150 percent of their base salary in bonuses. European software companies indeed seem to be a trendsetter toward more performance-based salaries for employees.

But while becoming somewhat rich via stock options was clearly on the wish list of many software workers we talked to especially in the Silicon Valley, it was definitely not the most important factor for most software employees in the worldwide survey. After all, the volatility of the stock market can shatter many of those dreams quickly, as the latter half of 1998 showed.

MONEY IS NOT ENOUGH

Getting rich was not the main reason that software workers joined particular companies. A "softer" factor counted more than hard cash. "The key reason for people to join our company is our culture. In fact it has become famous all over the country and really helps us to attract key talent," said Anne-Marie Westergaard, HR manager at Navision Software, a Danish company that sells enterprise solution software for midsized companies. Many employees at Navision Software agreed. In general, company culture is one of the most important factors for software workers when choosing their "workplace."

Company culture is a powerful recruiting inducement.

The advantages of a strong corporate culture

While company cultures differed in many ways among software companies around the globe, they all shared some common goals.

ATTRACTING AND RECRUITING THE BEST EMPLOYEES. A software company doesn't have to copy the culture of another. In fact, a distinct culture sets it apart from competitors. Great Plains Software, for example, a company of almost 1,000 people that produces ERP software, attracts 3,000 applications annually, although it rarely advertises; and its location—Fargo, North Dakota—is hardly a high-tech hub. Still, like Denmark's Navision, Great Plains has a reputation as a "one local family, one goal" place to work. It made *Forbes Magazine*'s list of the "100 best places to work at in the U.S." in 1997 and 1998.

ONGOING MOTIVATION. The culture of software companies also has a significant impact on the performance of the employees. At Navision Software, where emphasis is placed on making people feel valued and at home, employees demonstrate a willingness to work long hours when needed. "There are weeks, especially before major releases, where people work 24 hours a day or stay in the company for a couple of subsequent days, bringing along sleeping bags," says HR manager Westergaard. "And there is no special incentive for that. People do it because they know it's important."

So what exactly does Navision Software mean by its "culture"?

What great software cultures look like

CLEAR MANAGEMENT COMMITMENT. All great company cultures share one common element. Culture is a key top management task—even if those tasks can sometimes be a bit demanding and slightly awkward.

At Navision Software, the top leaders are willing to do almost anything if it makes employees feel valued. Following a straining, but important and ultimately successful project, Lars Hammer, a software engineer at Navision Software, was invited to a company-wide meeting on the lawn in front of the building, along

Software leaders dance the hula.

with all other employees. During the meeting, Hammer was asked to step forward for "an experiment." He had to take off his shirt and imagine himself on vacation. Hawaiian music started to play, colleagues handed him a drink and put flowers around his neck. Two of the company's founders appeared, dressed in wigs and grass skirts, and started dancing the hula. After the performance, they handed the stunned employee a check, which would help him make the vacation illusion come real.

To be sure, not all software leaders go that far. But Navision Software succeeds in what the software industry seems to have a particular interest in—creating an environment that is fun. Other motivating factors at Navision Software are aerobics classes and a company rock band. The company's headquarters is located 500 yards from a beach near Copenhagen, in a green area of grass and trees, with a small pond in the middle, stocked with ducks. Inside, interiors are in Scandinavian wood style, and an art gallery brings in frequently changing exhibitions. Meanwhile, the kitchen prepares free breakfasts, and the company's private cook prepares lunch. Refrigerators carry soft drinks and even beer. For Navision Software employee Lars Hammer and other employees, these perks indicate how valuable people are to Navision Software's management.

And that's not all. To drive home the point that Navision Software's leaders truly care about culture, they even hired a "corporate culture manager." While Navision Software may be an extreme example, it is not alone in having leaders who take on the active key role in shaping a clearly differentiated culture.

At SAP, a "one-family approach" is maintained throughout the German offices. This "family" even has a "father." Cofounder and chairman Dietmar Hopp is called "Vadder Hopp" ("Vadder" is German slang for "father") by the developers. SAP's "family" commitment is deeper than just nicknames, though. When **Fathering a** a mandatory managed-care act was introduced in Germany, SAP announced it would **software firm.** take over the full amount for all employees, although only half was legally required. (When it was determined that this gesture interfered with German tax rules, SAP instead gave employees an additional vacation day.)

When programmers at PLATINUM *technology* told us that the greatest thing about their company was "Flip," they were not referring solely to the fact that Andrew "Flip" Filipowski wears a pony tail and avoids suits and even ties. His way of interacting with employees is also highly personal and unique. He answers and sends voice mails to and from anybody in the 4,000-person company, and gives personal updates to all about the "corporate front"—even if the news is not pleasant. When PLATINUM laid off 400 peo- ple after a phase of rapid growth through **Daily voice mails** acquisitions, Filipowski announced the layoff **from the billion-** via voice mail, explained the reasoning in detail, and gave a personal statement about **dollar CEO.** how difficult it was for him. The message had its effect. Some of the workers who were laid off sent e-mails to Filip- owski and expressed their gratitude for his personal remarks.

Filipowski has shaped a culture at PLATINUM where team spirit, individual performance, and a passion for technology are encouraged. "Key for me is to create an environment where the best people can blossom to their full potential," he told us.

CULTURAL CONGRUENCE: CONVEYING A CLEAR MESSAGE. As enjoyable as many software cultures appear to be, most employees realize that the "fun" is there to motivate them to work better and harder toward the company's specific goals. Indeed, it is important that a company's culture stimulates overall and individual performance and that the cul- ture clearly reflects the work values that are most important in reaching *specific* goals.

Celebrating a passion for technology. "We're not just keeping up with information technology trends, we're setting them," says Jerry Popek, PLATINUM's CTO and a renowned computer scientist. "We are a technology company," Michael Matthews, EVP of marketing, added. "Our primary goal is to provide our customers with cutting- edge solutions which help them to master business challenges."

PLATINUM CEO Filipowski, meanwhile, actively builds a cul- ture that attracts exactly the talent he needs to create these cutting- edge solutions. At PLATINUM, the company's best engineers are treated twice a year to a conference at an attractive location, where technology gurus (like Sun's head of Java technology development or even Microsoft's CTO Nathan Myhrvold) are invited to give presentations. The excitement these events create among PLATINUM's top people was obvious during one of the conferences at the Chicago Renaissance Hotel recently. Developers were enthusiastically discussing what they had learned in previous meetings, sharing it with top management. In sum, PLATINUM's high-tech culture attracts large numbers of developers who love to work on the leading edge of technology. This starts a cycle, one that attracts even more good programmers afterward.[22]

Living for customer value. At Compuware, the Detroit-based enterprise solution company, technology does not play nearly the role it does at PLATINUM. "We are a low-tech company," said Jim Prowse, executive vice president of corporate marketing and communications. "And I mean this in a very positive way. We are not striving for cutting-edge technology, since we believe this is often the bleeding edge. Instead, we provide our customers with mature technology solutions which really work. Our main goal is adding business value."

These objectives, again, are reflected in Compuware's culture. Peter Karmanos, Jr., who cofounded the company 26 years ago, created a set of company values every employee measures business decisions by. The values emphasize solid, customer-oriented work and the creation of business value. Compuware does not believe that intelligence is the only criterion on which hiring decisions should be made. "The most important criterion for new employees is their fit into our culture. First and foremost, they must be mature personalities who adhere to professional working styles and habits," says Ron Watson, director of human resources.

Lifting personal achievement above it all. At pcOrder.com, performance and motivation go hand in hand. Here the culture comes close to what has been called the "Get to work on Sunday culture" or "mercenary culture."[23] "We play hard and reward big," says 27-year-old

Christina Jones, president and founder. Indeed, pcOrder.com claims to offer the highest combined compensation packages in the industry. Extra perks for the best performers include use of the company boat, waiting on the lake in front of the building, new company cars, and vacations in the Caribbean or Las Vegas. Top performers and their work habits are introduced on pcOrder's Web sites as "stars." But while the perk package is high, so are the expectations. While we were meeting with pcOrder.com's CTO, Phil London, for example, we couldn't help notice that London was scheduling business meetings for Sunday, the last one starting at 8 P.M. London commented that that was not unusual at pcOrder. "The market is here—now—and we have to penetrate it quickly to set an industry standard," he explained.

Essential to such a culture are people who enjoy a total commitment to their job and who tolerate a rather limited private life apart from the company. Naturally pcOrder.com recruits fresh college graduates almost exclusively. The average age of its employees is about 27, very low, even within the industry. Andy Palmer, VP of marketing, pointed out two other characteristics of the "performance culture": strict accountability of the employees for the bottom-line performance, combined with a high amount of variable compensation.[24]

Company culture can promote success.

Employees are even accountable for the recruiting they do at pcOrder. They must take a mentorship role for new hires—and even responsibility for the new employee's performance. In fact, the mentors' bonuses partially depend on the success of their hires.

Despite all the emphasis on company cultures that attract *and* retain software workers, the turnover rates, especially in the United States, are traditionally very high. And they are not likely to decrease soon. Regardless of how hard employers try to motivate their employees, opportunities elsewhere draw workers away. Successful companies must learn how to manage this.

TAKING ADVANTAGE OF
HIGH TURNOVER

On average, every fifth person in the software companies we interviewed in the United States moved to another position by the end of the year. Annual turnover rates of about 21 percent are the rule, and more than two thirds of these are "walk-aways"–people who leave the company not because they are asked to leave but because they get a better offer somewhere else.

Software industry turnover is about 21 percent.

A 1997 study showed that across 19 different industries, ranging from aerospace to utilities, the software product and services industry was in fact the industry with the highest total turnover in the United States closely followed only by consumer goods and banking.[25] The software industry numbers are comparable in other parts of the world, with the exception of Europe, where turnover is at about 7 percent. But even in Europe, new start-ups with attractive stock option programs, and a decline in IT graduations in the last few years, are likely to increase the turnover rate significantly in the years ahead.

Many software companies, however, have learned to live with high turnover, as our survey has shown, and in fact even draw some benefits from high turnover rates.

Meanwhile, software employees *also* showed a new understanding for building their "human assets."[26] The trend among knowledge workers toward *managing* their own careers has received a significant boost in recent years. Now, software workers prefer working more like entrepreneurs: working under the corporate roof, to be sure, but acting in their own self-interest—well aware they can exchange one corporate roof for another, if better opportunities come along.

Take Bob Hagman, for example. After more than six years at CSC and SAIC as developer, Hagman quit to get his Ph.D. in computer science at Berkeley. Afterward he worked for eight years on high-end software at the Xerox PARC research lab. This job, he told us, was highly challenging and rewarding. But it was theoretical work, work that Hagman says left him feeling unrewarded. A position with Sun Microsystems promised practical applications of his talents—and so Hagman decided to jump into the commercial world again.[27]

At Sun, Hagman was coarchitect of the now-famous CORBA architecture, a standard that enables software components to work together. When he left Sun two years later for a job at Oracle, it was because Oracle people convinced him that he could pursue his ideas even better with them. But a year later, after feeling that he did not get enough "buy-in" from Oracle's management, he left for a small Silicon Valley start-up, Vitria Technology in Mountain View, California. Hagman says he's very satisfied with this position now. But can he imagine another change? "Of course," he said.

To be sure, changing jobs was not always easy for Hagman. But overall, Hagman was happy to try different things. He thought it was great *not* to have a secure job, but multiple opportunities instead.

Bob Hagman is not alone—thousands of managers and developers do the same every year in the software business, especially in the United States.

A new definition of *stability*

Common belief assumes turnover rates of more than 10 to 15 percent represent a threat to the corporate culture and employee motivation. Knowledge is assumed lost with departing employees, while the integration of new employees takes time and significantly lowers productivity. Overall, the corporate culture becomes difficult to sustain.

Our survey, however, found that the software industry—forced to deal with turnover rates of 20 percent or more—has learned to live with it.[28] In fact, most of those interviewed at companies that had such turnover rates said it was perfectly acceptable. At Oracle, "a 20 percent turnover rate is not regarded as being too critical," Kerry Lamson, former vice president of marketing, told us, adding, "On the contrary, it helps us to constantly bring in new thinking and new ideas." Indeed, we found that many companies find their high turn-over not a problem, but rather an opportunity. [29]

Turnover-driven innovation

Turnover as a facilitator of innovation and performance? While this may seem like a nice way to justify management failure to retain the right people from the start, our worldwide interviews indicated that turnover may in fact increase the quality of **New hires bring** the final software product. "High turnover is **fresh perspectives.** not such a bad thing," agreed Aldy Duffield, human resources manager at the Oracle headquarters. "It allows us to renew ourselves and our products." After all, the software business thrives on new ideas, and turnover can support exactly that.[30]

Who has fresher ideas? A person who has stayed with the same company for 15 years or someone who has worked in different companies, market segments, or countries in those same 15 years? A fresh pair of eyes usually contributes significantly to the team, many software companies seem to feel. Anne-Marie Westergaard, HR manager at Navision in Denmark, says that Navision purposefully hires new people who have "done something completely different." "These are the people that bring in the best ideas," she says.[31]

Furthermore, new employees usually want to prove themselves and so often join teams with high aspirations and performance drive. This attitude can be contagious. Says John Wookey, vice president of financial applications at Oracle, "Bringing in new, highly motivated employees helps us to sustain our aggressive, high-energy work pace. The attitude and drive of these new employees is highly contagious and keeps aspirations high."[32]

It is difficult to "cannibalize" one's own young. For that reason, successful software companies know that external people—those without a stake in old products—may be more likely to change or toss away old products and ideas. Successful companies in our survey, in fact, hired external managers to work with new products twice as often as less successful ones. The renewal rate of the product portfolio was also much larger at companies that hired managers from the outside.

External employees, after all, don't have their hearts attached to old products. They are ready to "eat the young"—because it is not their *own* young.

At Oracle, the principle is widely applied. Unlike earlier days, Oracle's managers today are often external hires, says Elizabeth Wiseman, Oracle's director of human resources development. "Many people at Oracle see this change as one of the key success factors in the turnaround after 1990," said Wiseman.

Turnover-driven recruitment

New hires also bring contacts with them for further hires. At Netscape, for instance, posters around the offices ask, "Who is the smartest person you ever worked with? Could we hire her, or him?"

Turnover is clearly advantageous. But if 20 percent of the workforce is continuously exchanged, where does stability come from? How can companies develop steadily if every fifth person leaves the company every year?

PREVENTING THE DOWNSIDES OF HIGH TURNOVER

One of the biggest problems occurs when the best and brightest leave.

The CEO of a small software company, which had suffered from several walk-aways of experienced project managers, told us somewhat desperately, "This was a real catastrophe. I could basically go out of business if that happens one more time." He added, "They took with them not only core knowledge but very good customer relationships as well."

It is a balancing act to maintain turnover while ensuring that *key people* stay.

Identifying and retaining key people

The key people are the ones that drive the business—the best programmers, the salespeople with the best customer contacts, and the most creative marketing people. They deserve and require special attention, for two important reasons.

THEY DELIVER THE HIGHEST VALUE TO THE COMPANY AND ARE RARELY REPLACEABLE. The core knowledge of new products often resides with the core employees. When Christoph Filles left UBIS development in Berlin with two other core developers, for instance, he had just developed version 1.0 of *Bonaparte*, an innovative software product for business process modeling. After the developers' departure, UBIS experienced severe problems. Version 2.0 of the product could not be completed without their help, and it was nearly cancelled. Finally, Filles accepted an offer to return—this time as *head* of development. A new company was formed exclusively focusing on the *Bonaparte* product. The company revived thereafter.[33]

How do companies retain the best and the brightest?

THEY RECEIVE THE BEST COUNTEROFFERS FROM OTHER COMPANIES. Hiring people away from other companies is one of the key recruiting methods in the software business, especially on the West Coast. One of the largest software firms in the Bay Area, for instance, told us that they have seven internal headhunters calling possible recruits and hiring them away from competitors and other players. Oracle has exclusive contracts with about 10 headhunter firms as well, creating so much revenue for them that Oracle receives significant "volume" discounts. Companies are willing to spend in order to lure key personnel.

One software company recently courted a high-potential recruit, and when he accepted, they paid for the relocation of his 27 dogs, each in its own cage. "Can you imagine talking to the airlines about transporting 27 dogs in a single plane—when each one of them is the size of a pony?" said the company's recruiting director. "If you can, then you can imagine how crazy this job market is."

One Silicon Valley–based company has devised a system that regularly calculates the "walk-away value" of its best employees in order to make sure that managers work hardest on retaining the ones *most likely to leave*. A dollar figure expresses how much value from stock options an employee would lose if he or she left the company early, before their stock options had matured. Managers then decide whether to give their top performers more stock options to raise the barriers to leaving. Thus, the walk-away value is an information system for managers that helps prevent the best from leaving prematurely.

Testing the cultural fit when recruiting people

A key issue in avoiding the downsides of high turnover is to ruthlessly test cultural attitudes during recruitment, to avoid a deterioration of the company culture by the many people going through the organization.

Some software companies consider how well a potential employee "fits" as the most important qualification. Peter Karmanos, CEO of Compuware, the $1 billion systems management company near Detroit, introduced a special recruiting program when he realized that his company's culture would be diluted by fast growth. In a meeting with his management team, he defined the Compuware culture with them. From then on, new employees were to be tested to determine whether they would fit into Compuware's culture. "Take integrity," Karmanos said. "If somebody shows up with the employee directory from his former employer, that's a sure ticket out of the game," he told us.[34]

At Navision Software, testing an applicant's work attitude is just as important. Prospective employees are taken into the breakfast room. "Look, this is our breakfast room. Have a look into the fridge," the applicant is told. "You see, there is a lot of stuff in it, so we can feed you if you have to work for a couple of days in a row." Candidates accustomed to regular, 40-hour weeks will probably bow out.

Bringing new hires up to speed and reducing "time to productivity"

High turnover compels companies to integrate, train, and utilize new employees as fast as possible.

When Beau Parnell, Cisco's director of HR development, realized the difficulty of getting its 5,000 new hires a year up to speed, he approached CEO Chambers and got clearance to establish "Fast-Start," a collection of employee-oriented initiatives. Now when new employees begin at Cisco, they are supported in several ways. "Facilities teams," for instance, are automatically alerted by the software that tracks the recruiting processes, so that every new employee starts with a personal phone number, a computer system with internal Web access, and an e-mail address, as well as training on all of it. "Buddies" are assigned to new hires to answer their questions and help them with their new job. The managers of new hires receive e-mails reminding them to review the employees' personal goals and departmental initiatives. Parnell considers it his personal mission, he says, to help Cisco "achieve the fastest time to productivity for new hires in the industry."

"Oracle University"— a real-life, virtual-reality school.

Similarly, Oracle emphasizes intensive training to prepare the ground for new employees, said HR manager Aldy Duffield. In earlier days, lack of training often led to stress, burnout, and high turnover, she added. At "Oracle University," a real-life and virtual-reality school, new employees get an opportunity to learn Oracle methodologies and core concepts.

All these measures—identifying and retaining key employees, testing cultural fit, and bringing new hires up to speed fast—enable successful software firms to exploit the benefits of turnover rather than to suffer from it.

GREAT TALENT MANAGEMENT IS NOT "NICE TALK"—IT'S TOP-LEVEL STRATEGY

Overall, the software industry has some of *the* best practice examples in the attraction, motivation, and retention of top knowledge workers.

The reason for this is that software companies have no choice but to become talent motivation experts: They face one of the highest levels of worker scarcity and turnover of all industries. Especially in core regions like Silicon Valley—with very high industry density, fierce competition for employees, and particularly high turnover—there is an imperative not only to apply but to truly master people management principles. As the number of such highly competitive regions increases globally, so does the importance of these principles.

After all, most of the assets of software firms "go down the elevator at 6:00 P.M.," as John Keane put it. Attracting and motivating these "assets" is vital, as they are the ones producing and marketing the valuable code. [35]

5

SOFTWARE DEVELOPMENT

COMPLETING A MISSION IMPOSSIBLE

On July 6, 1998, Chek Lap Kok, Hong Kong's new airport, officially opened for business. The $20 billion complex was one of the world's largest construction projects ever—literally rising from the bay. Dozens of contractors and construction phases were coordinated to accomplish thousands of different and complex activities occurring at the same time, which were often interrelated. At one point in the project, half the world's dredging fleet was involved. And yet it was completed more or less on time and within budget. But from the day it opened, Chek Lap Kok experienced embarrassing and expensive problems: Electronic signs showed faulty information, phone systems shut down, baggage disappeared. Passenger and cargo traffic ground to a standstill.

The airport lost $600 million before the problems were solved. Ironically, none of the problems had anything to do with the massive construction project itself. They were all due to computer hardware and software problems.[1]

Software has a reputation for going haywire and taking both company and client down with it. Such problems range from the Denver airport disaster, and the explosion of the first *Ariane 5* prototype in 1996, to the recent explosion of Boeing's *Delta III* rocket.[2]

The software firms are not always to blame, however. Sometimes they are pressured to perform under unrealistic deadlines. Other times, the clients continually ask for new features, just before the end of the project. The problems also stem from the enormous, underlying complexity of software per se; unclear customer requirements as to what functionalities the software should have in the first place; and uncertainties throughout the development project itself.

But software companies that install the right kind of procedures have made enormous progress in avoiding these failures. First of all, successful companies do not ignore uncertainty—they address it. They also establish quality control mechanisms that simultaneously speed up the whole process. And they reach for new paradigms such as building software from reusable components.

These companies, however, are by far not the rule; in fact, they are the exception.

ONE THING IN COMMON: FAILURE

An astonishing *84 percent* of all software projects do not finish on time, on budget, and with all features installed, according to a survey by the Standish Group, which studied about 8,000 software projects in the United States in 1995.[3] Furthermore, more than *30 percent* of all projects were cancelled before completion. The rest ran significantly over deadline and were 189 percent (on average) over budget. Based on the study, the number of cancelled development projects in the United States alone was estimated to be close to 80,000.

Another study found that more than 50 percent of highly complex projects are cancelled.[4] In other words, from the beginning of such a project, the chance for failure is *higher* than for success.

About 80,000 software projects initiated have never been completed.

That is true of projects at software product firms as well as at professional services firms. The study found only small differences in the rate of failure in the two industry segments. Total costs of cancelled projects were approximately $81 billion in the United States in 1995. Worse, estimations of lost opportunity costs are in the trillions of dollars.

Such problems have been recognized for years. Take, for example, the (in)famous case of the *MasterNet* system at the Bank of America.[5] Planning to become a major player in the trust business, Bank of America decided to build a leading-edge software and computer system in the fall of 1982. The system was designed to help manage complex investment and property portfolios on behalf of large corporations, government agencies, and individuals.

After 18 months of detailed research and analysis, a $20 million budget was approved. Premier Systems, a specialized software consulting firm, founded by industry pioneer Steven M. Katz, was hired. The planned completion date was nine months later, on December 31, 1984. But New Year's Eve 1984 came and passed. No system emerged. And what's more surprising—no one was unduly alarmed about it.

After all, there *was* steady progress. Yet another year of effort elapsed. Finally, in mid-1986, one and a half years behind the initial deadline, the bank held a much-applauded *preview* for its major corporate customers. Not everything ran perfectly, to be sure, but most of the bugs seemed easy to fix.

But more bugs popped up every day. Staff worked overtime constantly, often staying past midnight. Their efforts didn't help.

When the new system was finally put to real work in March 1987, 27 months late, it didn't perform as promised. The bank fell three months behind in delivering account statements. It began to lose credibility with customers, and its trust business deteriorated. Corporate customers withdrew accounts worth $4 billion. Finally, the Bank of America's management cancelled the project. They transferred the remaining trust accounts—worth $34 billion—to an affiliate in Seattle, one whose system worked.

The $20 million software project had become a nightmare, one that cost the Bank of America much more than the $60 million in cost overruns. Software development can seem like a never-ending problem, and it still does today in many cases.

SOFTWARE DEVELOPMENT—MISSION IMPOSSIBLE?

Brad Cox, the creator of software for the NeXT computer, said, "The way software is built today is still in the hunter-gatherer stage. It's like a pre-Sumerian civilization."[6] But why? Why is software development so prone to failure?

Extreme complexity involved

Most large software products consist of several million lines of source code. The *Windows95* operating system, for instance, has approximately 11 million lines.[7] Each line of code contains at least one execution command that affects other parts of the program and has to interact with many other lines. This book, for example, contains about 11,000 lines of text. Thus, a printout of the *Windows95* source code would fill approximately 1,000 books this size. Set on a bookshelf they would add up to almost 28 yards of books. And each little typo in one of these books would have the potential to crash the whole system.

There are other reasons for the complexity of software code, ranging from the high number of interactions between different modules of a software system to the fact that the famous "80:20 rule" cannot be applied. Indeed, close to 100 percent of a software program has to be accurate to work even somewhat correctly. No wonder that Capers Jones remarked, "Large software systems are among the most complex entities man ever built. They are much more complex than the construction of a large office building or a supertanker. Maybe the construction of the Egyptian pyramids was comparable given the relatively simplistic technical environment of its time."[8]

> Large software systems are among the most complex entities humans have ever built.

Extreme uncertainties from the outset

In traditional business operations, an upstream-downstream image is often employed to describe product development processes (Figure 5-1). At the project outset, during the "upstream phase," uncertainty is high, both in terms of the final outcome as well as in terms of schedule, cost, and other project parameters. As the project progresses, the uncertainty decreases and the project turns into the downstream phase. In that phase, the project is usually more stable, and uncertainty is lower and in fact, decreases almost to zero at shipping or project completion date. Maintenance and customer service at the tail end have relatively low uncertainty.

The software industry has even more uncertainty than many other industries. This stems from a number of issues:

UNCLEAR CUSTOMER REQUIREMENTS. In the software business, the needs of customers are very difficult to assess. Often, the architecture

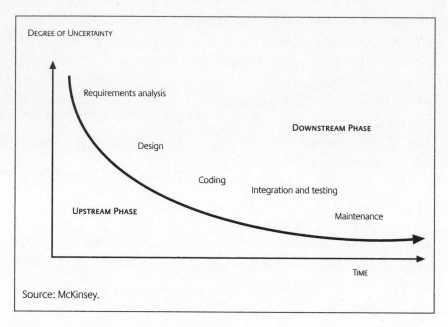

Figure 5-1. Upstream-downstream framework

must be left open to incorporate later changes; otherwise, expensive reworking could ensue. When Andersen Consulting designed an information system for a major transportation company, how the new system would be used was hard to predict. Reasons were a rapidly changing freight traffic market and the lack of any existing comparable system that could have been used to verify estimates. Paying attention to that uncertainty Andersen Consulting had to design the system architecture in an especially flexible way that allowed switching between different execution modes for transactions without any additional development effort. The execution modes had different resource consumptions, and thus switching between them could be used to balance system load.[9]

For software product makers, the challenges are even greater. For one thing, software requirements are usually more vague. For another, the product design must be more open, not only to address a broad range of needs but also to be extendable for later upgrades.

DESIGN NOT ENTIRELY PREDICTABLE. Sometimes, decisions on how to structure software are made that later prove to be wrong. Object Design, a Route 128-based object-oriented software technology firm, originally included a complex feature in the design of a software project. It was meant to save system resources by combining cache memory for multiple tasks. In the course of the project, though, the company discovered that the feature in fact harmed system performance rather than helping it, an effect that could not easily have been predicted before the coding.[10] Object Design ended up dropping the feature.

CHANGING REQUIREMENTS. Often requirements that are correctly defined at the beginning later change. Yahoo!, for instance, estimates that it had to rework substantially its MyYahoo! personalized Web site three times before launching it in 1997,[11] just to take into account new features that competitors were launching in the interim.

CHANGING TECHNOLOGY. Software systems, and especially software products, are highly dependent on the technological environment in which they work. Take Object Design and their so-called *ObjectStore PSE Pro for Java* product, a database development tool. This product draws heavily on Sun's *Java Virtual Machine* technology. In the course of Object Design's product development, however, Sun shipped several versions of its *Java Virtual Machine*. By the time they introduced version 2.0, Sun suddenly switched to a completely new method to define communication between Java modules and code in other languages. Object Design had to alter its product to keep up with the changes. "It took us six weeks just to cope with the changes," Object Design's former vice president of engineering, Greg Baryza, said. "But things like that

> **Software development is affected drastically by sudden changes in other companies' software.**

happen all the time. If you want to lead the market, you have to accept that and live with it."[12]

HOW SOFTWARE PROJECTS COMMONLY FAIL

Failure is common in the software business, and poor time estimates cause more problems than all others combined, says software expert Frederick P. Brooks.[13]

Estimates on the time it will take to complete a software project vary widely—on average—by a factor of 2.5, said software expert Barry Boehm.[14] "It is not only difficult to estimate a project accurately in the early stages, it is theoretically impossible," added Seattle-based software book author Steve McConnell. His statement reflects the fact that the final product design and features become clear only during the course of the project, not at the outset. The high uncertainty at the beginning of a project makes it impossible to impose a firm schedule and deadlines.[15]

Many organizations are not willing to take this into account, however. Managers demand an accurate schedule and cost plan right from the beginning. "In fact, far too many software project managers agree to come up with estimations based on no analysis or a poor up-front analysis," Steve McConnell told us. "That would never happen in a construction project, for example."

The reasons for such surprisingly nonanalytic approaches in a highly analytical business like software are manifold.

Overly optimistic developers. Many developers, especially the less experienced ones, tend to assume that everything will go well. This is not true for development projects, where Murphy's law applies—if something can go wrong, it will go wrong. Thus, even when developers are committed to their own schedules, they often cannot deliver.[16]

"Let's add more people." The next common mistake is the assumption that increasing staff for a project usually shortens schedules. This does not hold true for two reasons: For one, development work often cannot be partitioned among many workers. Interdependencies require certain tasks to be done sequentially. As Fred Brooks put it: "It takes nine months to bear a child, no matter how many women are assigned." Second, as more people are added, the time spent on communication increases substantially.[17]

Adding more people usually doesn't save time.

Underestimating the efforts required to make products out of projects. Professional services companies have often followed another failure pattern: After having developed a number of more or less similar systems for several clients, they have tried to develop a *standard product* with the same functionality for dozens, if not hundreds or thousands, of users. They were often wrong.

The reasons are simple: Mass-market and enterprise solution software products must be designed more broadly than custom-made code in the service business, as they must address many more possible applications and challenges. In addition, software products must comply with more technical environments than services software, as customers run different operating and hardware systems. Furthermore, products must be documented more thoroughly to allow anyone to use and perhaps extend them.[18]

Fred Brooks estimates that the effort required to create a successful product is about three times as high as for a comparable individual system. And if the product is a component of a larger system, this factor can easily increase to a factor of 9.

External pressure from marketing, customers, and management. Marketing departments at product companies, or individual customers at professional service firms, often try hard to shorten schedules. Understandably, they have a desire to shorten time to market or meet external deadlines.

Unrealistic expectations are also common on the management front. Wishful thinking is one pitfall, as is a tendency to use overly optimistic schedules to increase pressure on the development group. Development managers often neither have the experience nor the authority to negotiate successfully with the top leaders. "It is very difficult to make a vigorous, plausible, and job-risking defense of an estimate that is derived by no quantitative method, supported by little data, and certified chiefly by the hunches of managers," Brooks explained.

Impossibly tight scheduling is another factor. "Unrealistic schedules may be a motivation factor for some people," explained Greg Baryza, Object Design's former vice president of engineering. "But software developers are extremely analytic and smart people. If your schedule is unrealistic, you end up with nobody paying attention to it at all." In fact, Baryza says he gets worried when the number of *Dilbert* comics around the programmers' desks begins to rise—Dilbert, the fictional engineer who is afflicted with incompetent bosses and "stupid corporate policies."[19]

The fact of the matter is that stress is the cause of more than 40 percent of all software errors, author Robert Glass reports.[20] These mistakes can make enormous amounts of rework, which acts in combination with the original underestimates to spiral the stress level even higher.

Stress causes 40 percent of all software errors.

Software expert Barry Boehm gives an example from TRW, where he helped build a command and control application system, designed to run on a network of several computers. The requirement analysis contained a clause that the system had to be robust, in case one of the computers in the network failed; but in the design, the clause was overlooked. Design inspections had simply not been done very thoroughly, because of the enormous scheduling pressure. Later, when the system was coded and the defect was detected, the entire architecture had to be redesigned. Several major modules had to be changed, and a lot of code had to be rewritten. Furthermore, the documentation and test cases had to be rewritten. As Boehm recalled, the company ended up with a 20 percent budget overrun on the two-year project "just because of that single mistake."[21] By adding this class of defects to its high-risk checklist, TRW improved the chances of avoiding such defects in future projects.

Feature creep. Software firms also suffer from changes as the product is under development, a phenomenon called "feature creep." "Nobody would force a builder to rebuild the basement after having put on the roof, but in the software industry, that's common practice," says Jerry Popek, CTO of PLATINUM *technology.*

Popek says that when he was with Locus, Inc., the company developed an operating system for large computer networks. IBM saw the product, liked it, and asked for one basic change—to make it compatible with the gateways of IBM computers. It was a small request that took a lot of work and a year to fulfill. "We had to redesign the whole system and rewrite 50 percent of the code," Popek said.[22]

At professional services firms, important customers take on the role of the "requirement adders and changers." From all parts of the client organization, "small" changes or additions drop into the feature creep list. Or worse, the wishes do not show up in the list but are rather left with the individual developers or consultants. That often makes it completely impossible for the professional services firm to track the feature creep.

CHAOS RULES

The somewhat chaotic state of the software industry was studied by the Software Engineering Institute (SEI) at Carnegie Mellon University, Pittsburgh. The institute established a scale that measured software development organizations from a state of chaos (assigned a maturity level 1) to a state of constant improvement (assigned a maturity level 5).[23]

Only *four* organizations won a level 5: Lockheed Martin's shuttle group in Houston; a unit of Boeing in Kent, Washington; an India-based software group of Motorola; and a Japanese company. As for the rest of the software firms studied, *75 percent* were listed at level 1—chaos.[24] Why?

75 percent of all software firms rated as chaotic.

First, many software developers don't apply generally accepted development processes. This is rooted firmly in the software image of itself as a young, creative, upstart industry—without the need for a lot of discipline.

For another, managers have incentives *not* to focus on good processes. Diligent process management costs time and money. The average investment for moving up one maturity level on the SEI scale could cost several thousand dollars for each developer. "The payback from process improvement does usually not come in the project where it is started," explains Jerry Popek, PLATINUM's CTO. Popek says there's a constant tradeoff between spending money on the current project and "bringing the current project to an end somehow, and deal with process improvements later."[25]

HOW TO COMPLETE THE IMPOSSIBLE MISSION

"Software development is not about doing some things right—it is about doing *nothing* wrong," said software expert Steve McConnell. Indeed, succeeding is tough. Yet some companies do it again and again.[26]

Preparing for the uncertainty, rather than ignoring it

Successful companies do not ignore the extreme uncertainty of software development processes in terms of schedule and costs. Instead, they prepare for it.

ESTABLISH FLEXIBILITY. One way to succeed is by keeping the features of a product flexible, but not the deadlines. For example, a company will decide to issue a certain product at a certain time. But the features of that product will be prioritized according to a "must-do, should-do, and could-do" scale: *Must-do features* must be incorporated into the system by definition—to make the system run and to provide the basic features. *Should-do features* are implemented if time is left. *Could-do features* are normally delayed until the next release—unless a miracle occurs.[27]

When Object Design created the *Objectstore 6.0* project, design and marketing experts locked themselves into a room to review the required product functions. After several meetings, the functions were ordered as A, B, and C features. Marketing and development people *jointly* approved the classifications—and committed to the plan. "Such an approach takes some effort, but it is the key to make sure the right features make it into the product," Greg Baryza, Object Design's former vice president of engineering, explained.

ADAPT TO THE UPSTREAM-DOWNSTREAM. At Paris, France–based Ilog, a provider of software tools, development projects have two distinct phases. The upstream phase is structured to "make the creative juices" flow. Group sessions are scheduled to produce ideas. "We are sitting in a circle and hold hands," said Patrick Albert, Ilog's CTO, half-jokingly. Ilog recognizes that the creative process takes time. "People chat a lot in the hallways, coffee corners are crowded," said Albert. "The entire place doesn't look at all as if we actually did any work."[28]

The investment in creativity in phase 1 pays off later, says Albert, with more and better ideas, and a better architecture.

In the second phase, the downstream phase, the company then changes its face completely. Implementation of the first phase ideas become the focus—"no distractions permitted." People concentrate on their work and drink their coffee in their offices. Meetings are more focused and shorter. Timely shipping of the product becomes the key.

SPEND TIME TO SAVE TIME. In a study of projects undertaken for TRW, Barry Boehm notes that late fixes to software design costs an astonishing *50 to 200 times* the effort of an immediate fix.[29] That statistic underlines the importance of getting things right in the upstream part of the development process. "Upstream activities might seem as though they are delaying the 'real work' of the project,"

> **Late fixes in software design can cost up to 200 times an immediate fix.**

said Steve McConnell. "In reality, they are doing just the opposite. They are laying the groundwork for the project's success."[30] Furthermore, the product architecture chosen in the upstream process affects not only the actual project but often the product's success in the future. A superior product architecture bears many advantages in terms of expandability, scalability, and maintainability of the later product and can thus be a real competitive advantage.

Leaders of many successful software firms emphasized how important the early phases of a development project are. That is where problems should be resolved.

Strongly invest in people

"A talented software developer can be *10 times* as productive as an average one, even if they have the same amount of past experience," Steve McConnell told us.[31] Development managers we spoke with agreed. "A talented carpenter makes many decisions while he builds a good piece of work, and he can't really say what they are. He intuitively does the right things," said Greg Baryza. "It's the same for a developer. Many decisions about architecture and coding are rather intuitive, based on long experience and talent. It's difficult to codify them, but they make a huge difference."

Some of those "code artists" can be *extremely* skilled, says Jerry Popek, CTO of PLATINUM *technology*. Once, when he was still CEO of Locus, Inc., an important customer needed a new version of

the *Locus* product that could run on a new platform. The deadline
was three weeks. Popek knew that such a request, at best, would take
a five-person team at least six months. Popek was about to decline the
customer's inquiry when David Butterfield and Evelyn Walton, two of
his best developers, approached him with a proposal to complete the
massive task within the deadline. Popek doubted it was possible, but
he agreed because they had "nothing to lose."

Butterfield and Walton, with another developer, set up a "war
room" for the project. They worked day and night, slept at the office,
and—classically—lived on delivered pizza and Coke. Three weeks
later, the "impossible task" was done. The product ran smoothly on
the new platform. "I was stunned," Popek recalls. "It was not only
their effort and motivation. When reviewing their work later, I saw
that they had worked in an extremely efficient way, almost intuitively
making the right decisions and avoiding the usual traps and pitfalls."

The implication from such experiences is crucial. Software development projects should be staffed with the best people. "It's better to
wait for a productive programmer to become available than it is to wait
for the first available programmer to become productive," Steve
McConnell told us.

The same also applies to teams.

CREATING POWERFUL TEAM STRUCTURES. Not every programmer is a
star player. "As organizations grow, you will get mediocre developers—it's nearly unavoidable," said Andrew Filipowski, PLATINUM's
CEO. "There are simply just a handful of the top guys out there."[32]

But successful companies learn how to mix the star players with
those that aren't quite as proficient. An example of this is a team set-
up equivalent of a hospital surgical team with one or two top programmers assisted by others.

For example, an "administrator" in the top surgeon's team deals
with office space, supplies, and basic personnel issues. An "editor"
takes the surgeon's raw ideas and produces good documentation with
references and further information. A "tool smith" creates and

maintains special tools needed by the surgeon and his operating team, such as basic development or testing tools. Finally, a "tester" builds the scenarios to check the surgeon's individual work pieces and oversees the test of the complete product.[33]

HOLDING ONTO TOP TALENT. When one of PLATINUM's top programmers said he would have to leave the company a few years ago because his wife had a good job offer in California, COO Paul Humenansky simply refused to comply. Rather than lose the good employee, Humenansky arranged to have terminals hooked up in the developer's new house in California—and also in his cabin in the Sierra Mountains. From then on, the happy employee (obviously not a morning person) rose at noon, took a swim or a hike, and worked for PLATINUM from 3 P.M. until 3 A.M. "I'd be out of business today," said Humenansky, "if we hadn't established processes to overcome geographic boundaries in development."[34]

Since then, as PLATINUM made acquisitions across the country, remote employees made even more sense. "We had no choice. The question was, move them all to Chicago and thus, lose all the people, or let them stay at their location," Humenansky explained. The people stayed, and PLATINUM invested in telecommunication infrastructure and process integration.

Invest in process for higher performance and more freedom

As mentioned earlier, the Software Engineering Institute experts rated 75 percent of all software development organizations at a maturity level 1, in a state of "chaos." Cooperation between developers is often in an ad-hoc state—inconsistent, uncodified, and not tested for quality. Nevertheless, software developers and managers are still somewhat reluctant to establish rigid, elaborate development procedures and processes. They assume such efforts hamper creativity and morale in the teams.

But when taking a closer look, the facts disprove this common belief. In fact, the opposite is true. Investment in process improvement pays off. Costs are paid back by better quality and shorter development time, and morale rises as less time is spent on finding more and more bugs at the end of projects.

In fact, the successful companies we studied delivered software containing on average one third fewer defects than the others did, which was reflected in increased customer satisfaction. According to Barry Boehm, fixing mistakes accounts for about 50 percent of typical development time. "This is an enormous source of inefficiency and risk," said Boehm. "And the fixing effort soars the longer the defects remain undetected."

So in addition to avoiding dissatisfied customers, software companies can save time and effort by adopting quality-assurance processes. In a University of Southern California study, it was found that as the companies improved the maturity level of their development processes, they actually saved time overall.[35] On average, the total development costs decreased by 5 to 10 percent for every level they rose from 1 (chaotic) to 5 (constant improvement). At Lockheed,

Lockheed's quality-assurance program reduced design defects by 90 percent.

which attained a level 5 rating, the results of its mature process were striking: After five years of continued software process improvement, defects were reduced by 90 percent, time to market by 40 percent, and development costs by 75 percent.[36]

CREATIVITY AND MORALE GO UP, NOT DOWN. Most software developers are not advocates of processes—they assume processes make work "uncreative." A survey of more than 60 development organizations that had run software process improvement programs, however, showed the opposite. About 60 percent of the people in companies using elaborate processes rated their morale as excellent or good, as opposed to only 20 percent in the least process oriented companies.[37]

The result was consistent for developers as well as for managers. And more than 80 percent of the people actually *applying* processes disagreed strongly that processes hampered creativity or made the organization rigid and bureaucratic. Our survey interviews confirmed these findings again.

MANY "PROCESS IMPROVERS" AT HAND. A large number of process improvement methodologies exist. One is the *capability maturity model* approach created by the Software Engineering Institute, and another is the SPR methodology of Capers Jones and his firm, SPR, Inc. Most of the tools and methodologies focus on assuring quality right from the start. They also stress avoidance of rework and better documentation and testing. A number of smaller consulting firms specialize in applying and teaching these methodologies.

Two of these methodologies are particularly important: *stakeholder involvement* and the *daily build*. These techniques have been particularly useful to the successful companies in our global survey.

Involve project stakeholders extensively

In the Standish Group's survey of 8,000 U.S. software projects, user involvement turned out to be the single most important success factor in software development processes. Our global survey confirmed this point. And it also showed that the involvement of both traditional end users as well as of other stakeholders, such as the marketing department, was critical.

End-user involvement is critical to success.

CUSTOMERS SLEEP AT SOFTWARE COMPANIES. Successful companies in our survey rated the importance of customer involvement 20 percent higher, on average, than the less successful companies. The advantages are many. Early customer involvement clarifies their requirements, which can prevent extensive rework in the downstream phase. Meanwhile, explaining the costs of additional features to users early helps them prioritize all the features and prevents expensive, unnecessary "gold plating." Finally, allowing customers to preview the software helps programmers discover gaps and mistakes in the software product.

The world's leading software firms are pouring more and more resources into user involvement. Microsoft has its own *usability labs*—separate rooms equipped with one-way mirrors, cameras, and other equipment. All of them observe and record tests by end users.[38] Intuit became famous in the early 1980s for literally "following users" to their homes to identify their specific needs.[40]

Customers are usually very supportive and ready to contribute. Some of them even become overnight guests at software firms. When Netdynamics, Sun's Silicon Valley–based network application tools subsidiary, developed its version 2.0, one customer basically *lived* an entire week at the development site, to interact more closely with the developers.[41]

Professional services companies need an even stronger customer involvement than product firms. Lack of end-user buy-in can lead to total project failure. Furthermore, during the project, customers have to make many decisions that impact schedule, cost, or functionality. Customers who are closely involved better understand the implications of their decisions, and they usually make faster and better decisions: They have more realistic expectations and understand tradeoffs between additional features, costs, and time.

At Cap Gemini, Europe's largest professional software services company, all "extra requests" from the client are tracked, and the client is rigorously charged for them. But before *any* request is fulfilled, Cap Gemini's consultants challenge whether the client even needs the additional features—although the client would pay for them. For example, clients often change user interfaces or report formats. Those changes are rather cosmetic in nature and do not add real value but are costly to implement. "Sure, we could

Customers should pay for extra requests made during development.

charge for unnecessary features the client asks for and have a short-term advantage," CEO Paul Hermelin told us. "But in the long run, the client would realize it, and we would lose his trust."

In many cases, Cap Gemini's clients drop their requests back once they understand the implications. And afterward, they are often more satisfied with Gemini. A recent study proved that customer satisfaction usually increases significantly with closer involvement.[42]

Many of the points also apply internally, especially to the marketing department.

MARKETING EXPERTS MARRIED TO DEVELOPMENT MANAGERS. At Object Design, every feature added to product releases *after* the requirement definition has been set must be approved by a special "company change board." "Only the really important changes come through," said former vice president of engineering Greg Baryza. "And we drop other functionality in exchange, to keep feature creep at a minimum." Baryza named tracking and controlling changes during development projects as one of the most important success factors to keep deadlines. Marketing and development people have to make the tradeoff jointly between customer interest in additional features and the effort to implement them. If the opinions vary widely, Baryza does not step in, to make sure there is a joint decision mutually supported by developers and marketing experts: "I tell the marketing and the development guy: You two are married. And I am not going to be marriage counselor," he said half-jokingly.

> Marketing and development work closely together in successful firms.

It is not only feature changes, but also the general project success that should be tracked with the users.

FREQUENT PROJECT REVIEWS WITH ALL STAKEHOLDERS. At BROKAT, a provider of secure transaction processing software, all stakeholders are constantly informed of project progress. Customers and marketing people have access to an electronic project tracking system. "This gives them complete clarity and good sleep," said CEO Boris Anderer. "And it enables us to identify possible risks very early."[43]

BROKAT is not a singular case. Successful companies in our global survey rigorously tracked their projects' success—and shared the results with all stakeholders. The intervals between major project reviews were on average more than 40 percent shorter in successful product firms than in the less successful ones. For professional services firms, open reviews, together with clients, were crucial: They directly affect the client's perception of the project's performance. Project reviews took place more than twice as often in the successful service firms.

Project reviews take place more than twice as often in successful service firms.

Besides extensive stakeholder involvement, the *daily build* is a powerful tool in software development. Only a few companies in the survey had managed the challenging task of setting one up, but the companies who did, reported substantial benefits.

The daily build: eliminate defects first thing in the morning

Unlike car companies, which spend six to nine months to build a car prototype, software companies build a prototype every day. It's called the *daily build*.

When a car is designed, one group is responsible for designing the engine, another the brake system or the automatic transmission. The prototype is extensively tested, and necessary changes are identified. A key challenge stems from the interdependence of the parts. Changes in engine design, for example, affect other parts under the hood. A larger engine suddenly takes away space from the air conditioner; it has to be moved, and so must other parts next to the engine. Six to nine months are required for one car prototype to be completed.

Similarly, separate software teams are responsible for developing parts of the final software product. They build them, test the features, and correct the defects. Finally, a prototype is built to test how the system works as one. The difference is that with their digital medium, software companies can build a prototype frequently.

> **Of the successful companies, 94 percent use daily or at least weekly builds.**

In our global survey, we found that *94 percent of the successful companies completed daily or at least weekly builds*, whereas *the majority of less successful companies did them monthly or less often.* Many of those companies without daily builds said they wanted to have such processes in place—but they were finding that aspiration difficult to achieve.

So how does a daily build work? And why is it desirable, even if it is difficult to establish and increases project overhead?

HOW THE DAILY BUILD WORKS. Development teams work on their specific modules independently. At the end of the day, they test and debug this code by inserting it into a copy of the *previous* prototype to see it perform in the context of the whole system. Once it works with the previous prototype, they provide their code for a new daily prototype. All other teams do the same, and at the end of the day all new modules are available. At night, all the modules are linked automatically—and a new prototype is built. This prototype—the current daily build—automatically undergoes a series of tests, to check what happens when the modules interact. The next morning, every developer coming to the company receives a list of all the defects that occurred during the overnight test, plus a copy of the new prototype. The first task for the developers is to correct all those defects found during the last build. Then work continues on new features.

WHY DAILY BUILDS ARE SO POWERFUL. It is easy to imagine what happens in organizations that build prototypes once a month, or even less often. It can take weeks to detect certain errors that were seeded a long time before. Without interaction tests, developers can find only those defects *within* their own modules, but never those *between* interacting modules.

With daily builds, defects are fixed right after they are created, which reduces the time needed to find and correct them. Integration errors are reduced substantially.

So, while it is difficult to establish, the daily build has tremendous advantages. Overall, daily builds clearly improve productivity and the quality of the end product. They provide a far better status control for the whole project, and they improve morale. "The morale effects are startling. Enthusiasm jumps when there is a running system, even a simple one," said Fred Brooks. So once again, like other seemingly "tedious processes," this one improves both performance *and* morale.

> **The level of enthusiasm jumps when there is a running system, even a simple one.**

The two preceding examples—daily builds and stakeholder involvement—illustrate the power of good development processes. But despite increasing productivity and quality levels, the improvements are still incremental. A truly revolutionary performance improvement in software development is yet to come.

No silver bullet?

For decades, development managers have called for new "magic solution methodologies" that could bring a radical or truly revolutionary improvement in software development. The suggestions for magic solutions have never ceased—but the solutions have never materialized. In his 1986 article "No Silver Bullet," Fred Brooks argued that no single software development support tool would produce a true order-of-magnitude improvement in programming productivity in the decade that followed. His prediction proved true, and, in fact, there is no silver bullet yet.[43]

So will the progress be only evolutionary, and not revolutionary? Is there a way to leapfrog beyond current development productivity?

There is. *Componentware* is about to dramatically change the development game.

FROM HUNTERS AND GATHERERS TO MODERNISTS

Software expert Brad Cox has said that software development is in "the hunter-gatherer stage," reflecting the low process quality in the software industry. He also says that software production lacks something most other engineering disciplines have long adopted: The reuse of standardized components.

Reusing components: enormous potential benefits

Car makers don't make their own air-conditioners or ABS systems. Computer makers don't produce their own CPU chips or motherboards. These components come from providers that have specialized know-how. But unlike car or computer makers, software companies cannot make use of well-developed, high-quality components. They have to build everything from scratch. It is like a car maker casting its own nuts and bolts.

The lack of premanufactured components creates quality problems, and—at least to some extent—also extreme uncertainty. Most software experts agree that a shift to software components would help. Brad Cox has observed: "If software development could move from a 'build everything yourself' to a 'simply assemble prefabricated reusable components' model, that would mean a major productivity and quality boost for the entire industry."[44]

THE FUTURE HAS ALREADY BEGUN. Paul Humenansky, COO of PLATINUM *technology*, thinks componentware is about to change the entire software industry. At his company, the future has already begun. For *ProVision*, for example, a database backup product, PLATINUM already uses a component-based development approach. Instead of coding it from scratch, *ProVision* is completely "assembled" from predeveloped components. The product was completed in a stunning six months. "Normally, this would have taken at least 12 to 14 months," said Humenansky.

PLATINUM already uses component-based development— with stunning results.

Beyond time savings, a small sample component like an *Install* program shows the other practical benefits of reuse. *Install* programs are used to guide users through software installation processes. Two years ago, each team at PLATINUM used to create its own *Install* after finishing the product coding. That often took up to four full days. Humenansky decided to have a common *Install* developed. Now it is used by all teams. Of course, the teams save time—they just take the component, adapt it and use it. But what's more: Users have to deal with only *one Install* program and one user interface, which makes their "PLATINUM experience" much more consistent. Moreover, the quality of the new *Install* is vastly better because it has been developed and tested more thoroughly. After all, such extra efforts pay off because the component is used over and over again.

Major difficulties in using components

Paul Humenansky is convinced that component-based development will become "the new paradigm" in the software industry. "I firmly believe that companies that cannot do this won't survive," he said. "It is stunning, though, how few companies can really do it right now."

LARGE UP-FRONT INVESTMENTS REQUIRED. The reason that few companies take the lead in component-based development is simple: Implementing a reuse strategy is difficult. The up-front investment is rather large. Standard components take at least three times the development effort compared to software used only once.[45] In addition, developers have to be trained in object-oriented development. A technical infrastructure needs to be created for storing and "publishing" components.

ENTIRE MINDSET OF DEVELOPERS IN NEED OF CHANGE. "The whole culture has to be 'reuse'," said Humenansky; "otherwise you end up with reusable components which are used exactly once." At PLATINUM, Humenansky took his 100 best developers and set up a "componentware team" that reports directly to him. "It's an organizational issue; you need to push this down from the top," he explained. The team develops all the components for PLATINUM and also *markets* them to the other teams at PLATINUM. "You have to set this up like a marketplace," said Humenansky. "The team offers support for the others, it has a hotline for other teams, and they do training and documentation for their components."

AWARDS FOR STEALING CODE. Indeed, reuse is rewarded at PLATINUM. Every year at developer conferences, those teams that have been best at reusing software receive significant rewards and bonuses. One award goes to the "team that stole the most code." "Last time, we had a developer who claimed he could create applications without coding a single line, and he proved it to us," Humenansky told us excitedly.

Componentware on the horizon

Given the huge benefits, it is likely that component reuse will be adopted on a wide scale in the software business. Most large software companies have at least recognized the trend and are investing in it. While actual software reuse is still limited, research on software reusability "is active and energetic, even if not yet totally successful," reported Capers Jones.

Future common standards for components, such as standard functionality for customer invoicing, will further make component reuse take off. Meanwhile, software like SAP *R/3* has shown high potential for standardization. *R/3* and other standardized ERP solutions, like Baan's or Oracle's, are replacing most custom-made ERP software, and large productivity and quality improvements are being made.

The biggest push, of course, comes from software product firms: They have a tremendous interest in standardized components. It is a new growth market for them, a new market where leading players can win big.

Brad Cox, the strong critic of today's software development practices, is convinced that the component approach will provide the huge benefits promised. One of his recent articles about componentware is titled "There Is a Silver Bullet."

EXCELLENT DEVELOPMENT
SETS THE GROUND

Overall, software development is an extremely challenging task and a high-risk undertaking. Immense complexities and a large number of potential traps and pitfalls need to be managed. Only a few companies can handle that well. They focus on finding and leveraging the most talented developers and CTOs and then applying a whole range of elaborate tools and methods to reach success. From user involvement and team structures that resemble emergency rooms to daily builds of the entire software system, excellent software firms tackle the development challenges head-on and succeed in a seemingly impossible mission.

The vast majority of software companies can improve their processes. After all, better processes not only vastly improve productivity and product quality but—against common belief—also make the workplace more enjoyable and more creative.

6

MARKETING GODS MAKE SOFTWARE KINGS

Those that don't market themselves superbly are likely to face extinction.

In 1991, David Pensak, a computer scientist with advanced degrees from Princeton and Harvard, brought together several software developers from DuPont Corporation. They wanted to develop a "firewall" system, one that would protect companies linked to the Internet from outside hackers. By 1994, Pensak and his colleagues had finished the product, and it worked well.

But by then, the developers also faced insolvency. Sixteen copies of the program had been sold, at an average price of $40,000 each.

Revenues in 1994 totaled $256,000—versus $1.1 million spent in product development.

Fortunately, Shaun McConnon saw the product, realized its potential, and offered to turn the company around. McConnon had been Sun Microsystems' East Coast sales vice president and following that, managing director of Sun's Australian subsidiary.[1] After investing $150,000, he was named president of what was by then called Raptor Systems, Inc. His first acts were to hire more salespeople and to boost the annual marketing budget from $300,000 to $1.5 million.[2]

Two years later, the company broke even. The marketing effort, which included advertising across the media, "was critical in raising the profile of the company and making it a success," McConnon told us. But he wasn't finished. In 1996, he took Raptor public, raising $56 million. And two years later, he sold his "marketing company." The price Axent Technologies paid for Raptor Systems: $249.6 million.[3]

Those that do market their software effectively are likely to succeed.

MARKETING CHAMPIONS MAKE THE WORLD'S TOP SOFTWARE

While software is a technical business, the fate of software product companies—be it mass-market product or enterprise solution firms—largely depends on marketing. And so McConnon isn't the only software product maker who puts extraordinary emphasis on marketing for exactly that reason. Karl-Heinz Killeit, former CEO of KHK, a German enterprise solution software maker, explained his company's early rapid success with his one golden rule: For each new developer, he also added two new sales and marketing people.

Such stories are common. In fact, successful software product companies spend massive amounts on marketing and sales, on average more than *twice* their R&D costs. Microsoft, for example, spent almost $2.9 billion on marketing and selling in 1997—more than 25 percent of its revenues, versus about 16 percent for R&D.[4] Oracle spent 33 percent of its revenues on marketing and sales, versus 11 percent for R&D. And the Silicon Valley start-up company Broad-Vision spent more than 65 percent on marketing and sales, versus 30 percent on R&D.

Our survey reconfirmed this relationship: 41 percent of the employees of the successful product firms we interviewed were in sales and marketing. In the unsuccessful firms, only about 31 percent were involved in sales and marketing.

Why is marketing so crucial for success, and even for survival, especially in the software product business?

Software product companies know it's not enough to be *one* of the top players in a particular product segment—it is crucial to be *the* top player. Several reasons account for this race for market leadership.

Recovering massive R&D costs

In 1997, for example, Microsoft spent $1.9 billion on R&D.[5] For *Windows95* alone, Microsoft spent an estimated $500 million.[6] A simple calculation shows that at an average market price of $100, Microsoft had to sell more than 5 *million copies* of *Windows95* to amortize this investment, not even taking into account marketing, sales, and other significant expenses.

Even small companies have to create a mass market. Raptor Systems had to sell over 100 copies of its firewall system just to recover its multimillion-dollar investment in development. That may not have been many copies in comparison to Microsoft's needed sales. But it was steep considering that in the first three years exactly sixteen copies were sold.

The law of increasing returns

Making the masses buy is key to the recovery of large R&D expenses. But very few software product players *can* make the masses buy. Henning Kagermann, cochairman and CEO of SAP, told us: "Achieving market leadership draws in even more customers. It's a self-reinforcing growth cycle—the more customers you have, the more you will get." This self-reinforcing cycle, the *law of increasing returns,* is one of the key reasons for the crucial importance of marketing for software products. What is the reasoning behind this dynamic?

"The more customers you have, the more you will get."

First, interaction standards start the cycle. Whenever one person uses a particular kind of software, the chances are heightened that others working with that person will use the same software, too. Different file formats, different application software, and different operating systems can kill any "virtual cooperation." At Chrysler, for instance, employees began to raise concerns that the company was using too many incompatible programs. So in 1997, the company installed *MS Office* on 25,000 desktops worldwide—the same software for everybody.[7] From then on, *MS Office*, regardless of its technological superiority, was the leading PC software at Chrysler.

Second, personal switching costs increase over time. Once users learn how to use a certain product, they become less inclined to switch to a competitor's. They will even loyally purchase updates from the same company, rather than take a chance switching vendors.

Third, trust in market leaders facilitates buying decisions. Corporate IT decision makers tend to buy into prevailing front-runners when they make their purchasing decisions. "A bank that selects the standard transaction solution and then falls victim to a hacker is probably just one of many banks in the same situation," says Boris Anderer, CEO of BROKAT Information Systems, a secure transaction software provider. "But a bank that selects a less known solution and is the victim of a hacker may soon be looking for a new IT manager." It's an echo of the common refrain from the 1970s: "No one ever lost his or her job for buying IBM." Individual buyers also tend to go with the market leader. They take comfort in the attitude that "that many people can't be wrong."

Indeed, the successful players in our survey realized that only the first players in each mass market can win. Some 52 percent of the successful software product companies stated, "In our market seg-

> **It's not enough to be *one* of the top players.**

ment, we set the standard." Of the less successful ones, only 19 percent could say that.

The road to the top

The well-known winners of the industry have generally reached world market share leadership in at least one segment: Microsoft with the operating system *Windows* and with the application *MS Office* on the PC desktop; Oracle with its databases; and Lotus with *Lotus Notes*, the e-mail software.

Marketing is the clear path to such market leadership. Three key questions related to that are addressed throughout the chapter:

▶ How can software product companies *build* market leadership with marketing efforts, either as a start-up company or as an established player with a new kind of software product?

▶ Once software companies have achieved market leadership, how can they *sustain* it?

▶ Which marketing strategies can attackers use to successfully *break* the market leadership of an established player and make it their own?

Starting with the first issue: Start-ups always question how to use marketing to build market leadership. But few really find the answers, says John Doerr, general partner of the venture capital company Kleiner Perkins. "Most Silicon Valley start-ups get their technology to work but never squarely hit the marketing strike zone," he explains. "There is a tremendous marketing and management deficit in the valley."[8]

It's not just spending marketing dollars. Doerr says that even companies that market themselves prolifically still miss the point. The really big winners, he says, are not those that simply market a superior product. Rather, they are those companies that enter the market not only with a superior product but also with what he calls a *"value proposition."*[9]

Intuit, he says, is a good example of that.

BUILDING MARKET LEADERSHIP

One evening in 1983, Scott Cook overheard his wife commenting on the amount of time it took to manage their personal finances. Cook, who had spent four years in marketing at Procter & Gamble, sensed an opportunity. Together with Tom Proulx, an undergrad at Stanford who knew how to program, they created *Quicken*, an inexpensive personal finance software package. It was the forty-third personal finance software package in the market.[10] The company, Intuit, was launched with loans from friends and by tapping into Cook's credit card balance.

By 1997, Intuit's sales had reached $600 million. *Quicken* clearly led the U.S. market with more than 70 percent market share.[11] How did Cook do it? As Doerr mentioned, it was not solely by the technological sophistication of the program; it was by creating a compelling value proposition.

At a time when most competitors were still heavily focused on promoting technical software features, Intuit was focusing on solutions and a clear value proposition. "Scott had a fixation on what the benefit of the software product was, not what it did," said Eric Dunn, Intuit's chief technology officer.[12] Cook even wrote the advertisements. And while competitors appealed to logic ("Automate your banking"), Cook appealed to emotions: "End your financial hassles."[13] Intuit's product development teams became famous for following users home to observe them using the Intuit software and learn about their needs.

Even when Intuit was on the verge of bankruptcy, in 1985, Cook still *invested* in marketing. Intuit had just $95,000 left in the bank. Three of the seven remaining Intuit employees left when Cook couldn't pay their salaries anymore; the others worked without salary.[14] But when Cook withdrew their last reserves from the bank, he didn't pay the wages. Instead, he invested all of it in magazine and newspaper ads.[15] It was a new kind of marketing for Intuit, which had hitherto marketed its software through banks.

The new advertising, in newspapers and magazines, worked. Marketing remains Intuit's focus. Intuit, incidentally, has been called the "McDonald's of personal finance,"[16] but, in fact, while McDonald's spends about 18 percent of its revenues on marketing, sales, and administration, Intuit spends even *more*: some 24 percent on marketing and sales alone in 1997.[17]

Building the product portfolio

The key to a good value proposition is a *product marketing story*. Getting the story right—before jumping into the market—is a critical concern. Great product and marketing ideas do not always spring up easily during evenings at home, as in Intuit's case. In fact, many of today's leading companies followed other approaches to develop their product portfolio. The founding team of BroadVision, the Silicon Valley start-up, for instance, conducted nine months of intensive market research before ever starting to build BroadVision's first product, *One-To-One*, which is software that facilitates e-commerce. The product was apparently well thought out—revenues at BroadVision have doubled every year since the market launch in 1996.

> Great ideas often begin in the market research lab.

BREEDING NEW PRODUCTS INSIDE THE COMPANY. Another successful method of product portfolio development is through internal entrepreneurship. BMC, a Texas-based software company specializing in systems management, for instance, encourages R&D employees to produce new ideas. Anouar Jamoussi, a member of the R&D group, for example, was promoted to "product author." He had presented a new software product idea to the top management. The idea was approved, so he, as the author, became the "business manager" for the concept, shepherding it to market. As part of this program, authors receive a percentage of the revenues generated by their ideas in the first and second years, an amount that is scaled down in subsequent years. "Everybody in R&D wants to become a product author," Jamoussi explained. "It is not only financially rewarding but also prestigious." And, say BMC managers, the company has built much of its early growth on this system.[18]

BUYING BUSINESSES TO CREATE THE WINNING PRODUCT PORTFOLIO. Some companies prefer to find many of their ideas outside the corporate roof. Bill Nelson, CEO of GEAC, a Toronto-based software applications provider, buys into new ideas through frequent acquisitions. In 1996 and 1997, GEAC acquired 11 new companies. The software division of Dun & Bradstreet was such an acquisition, filling a gap in GEAC's portfolio with its integrated enterprise decision-support systems. Although D&B's revenues were twice GEAC's, the

> **Many companies buy into good ideas by acquiring other companies.**

acquisition was applauded by investors, which hiked GEAC's stock sixfold between May 1996 and May 1998.

Acquisitions have also been part of Intuit's strategy. In 1993, for example, Intuit doubled its size by purchasing ChipSoft for $306 million, an acquisition that added income-tax return software to Intuit's portfolio.

Being first does not always mean being the best

Once the value proposition and product portfolio are built and the marketing strategy is set, the right marketing tactics determine success. The right tactics start with the right timing.

While building new businesses fast is indeed a prerequisite to success, being *first* in the market doesn't mean a sustained victory. Often, the first players are those who have invented the new technologies. But history shows that the superior marketing players often eclipse them.

Superior marketing players often eclipse the earliest movers.

The first Internet browser, for example, was developed early in 1993 at the University of Illinois' National Center for Supercomputing Applications (NCSA). It was named *Mosaic*. Marc Andreessen, the lead programmer, had just obtained his bachelor of science degree in computer science at the university. Andreessen and his team tried to launch the product—with limited success. The market did not yet fully embrace the significance of the browser tool. In addition, serious quarrels with the university about the rights to the browser did not allow the team to market the tool as aggressively as needed.[19] To be sure, there were other reasons for *Mosaic*'s limited success as well, but the market readiness and marketing approach were among the key factors.

Subsequently, Andreessen left and cofounded Netscape together with marketing-savvy Jim Clark, cofounder of Silicon Graphics. Netscape evaluated the market and introduced the browser in April 1994—just before Internet usage started to explode. By June 1996, 26 months after the company's start, 38 million users had installed the Netscape browser.[20] "Our initial plan was just to make a browser that was more popular than *Mosaic* and to build a large installed base of customers as quickly as possible," Clark commented in a 1997 interview with the *Red Herring* magazine.[21]

Netscape enjoyed the first real market success for a browser—in contrast to *Mosaic*, which was the first to enter the browser market.[22] In August 1997, Netscape reached a market cap of $3.4 billion. In contrast, Spyglass, a small company affiliated with the University of Illinois that marketed *Mosaic*, had reached a market cap of $94 million by then—less than 3 percent of Netscape.

The history of the hardware and software market, in fact, is littered with companies that introduced new, revolutionary products that failed—not because they weren't first in the market but because they were unable to attain a mass market. Winning that mass market takes the right timing of the launch, and also the right customers.

Highly focused customer selection

In New York, we met with the CEO of a midsized software company that offered 14 product lines, with various subproducts, based on seven different operating platforms. The target customer group was not really defined, the CEO conceded. Any company with a request simply received the "best-fitting" product.

Compare that case to BroadVision. The Silicon Valley start-up clustered its potential customers in specifically designed matrices that listed the customer's needs and other criteria. A score determined the target customers that could be most profitable for BroadVision. Those customers immediately had a key account manager assigned to them. BROKAT, the young German software company in the secure Internet transaction systems segment, also applies such a highly structured customer selection process and has benefited from it. BROKAT grew quickly from its start in 1994 and had reached a size of already 250 employees by 1997.

Both BROKAT and BroadVision managed to address a basic marketing challenge: They targeted a customer group with sales potential large enough to recover their massive R&D costs—but kept the target group small enough to fully satisfy the needs of that group. Such a focused, well-served customer group is the starting point for market leadership, as it offers a "crystallization point" for further growth.

Boris Anderer from BROKAT told us that they pursue a *bowling alley market development* approach as described by Geoffrey Moore's *Inside the Tornado*. Just as Documentum used pharmaceuticals as its head bowling pin, BROKAT's head bowling pin is secure Internet banking, which will eventually "knock over" various other secure e-commerce application segments such as insurance, retail, or telco.[23]

To actually alert the target group to their presence, however, software companies go to great length to make themselves known.

The PR megaphone

Outstanding public relations and advertising skills are required in the software industry to reach market leadership fast—"outstanding" even when compared to many other marketing-intensive industries.

CREATING "SELF-FULFILLING" SUCCESSES. This was a marketing approach we found used at software companies around the world. PR events, for example, can communicate to the public that a new product is on its way to market leadership even *before* it has taken off. Before long, it *is* the market leader—a self-fulfilling success.

On March 5, 1997, a PR event took place at the luxurious Oberoi Tower Hotel in Bombay, South India. On the thirty-sixth floor, special guest Bill Gates was launching the product of *another* company, Ramco Systems, a young Indian software division. Ramco's product, *Marshal 3.0*, an enterprise solutions suite, was based exclusively on the Microsoft *NT* operating system, and because of that, Bill Gates was more than ready to provide support: "Ramco is a role model for the Indian software industry," he said. "It has grown on a firm partnership with Microsoft."[24]

Before the launch, Ramco was hardly known in the software world. After all, its parent company, the Ramco Group, specializes in cement and textiles. But with Gates's participation, perception changed. *Business Week* ran an article titled, "The Business Rajahs," and other publications similarly took note.[25] "Once we get the stature," Mr. Ramachandran, Ramco's CEO, told us, "the revenues fall into place." In 1998, Ramco was still searching for a viable role in the enterprise solution market, up against top players like SAP, Baan, and Peoplesoft. But at least the PR machine had drawn in some new clients, in Europe and in the United States.

PR AS A TOP MANAGEMENT TASK FOR LARGE PLAYERS ALSO. PR is equally critical for large players to build "category killers." For the launch of *Windows95*, Bill Gates personally chaperoned a PR extravaganza, with thousands of guests at the Microsoft headquarters in Redmond, Washington, and live statellite feeds to hundreds of U.S. computer stores.[26] Meanwhile, SAP's top managers frequently run "Sapphire user conferences" for thousands of visitors, featuring information about "the future of enterprise computing," *and* extravagant dinners.

The World Economic Forum in Davos, Switzerland, is another example. At the meeting, Bill Gates met with Ferdinand Piech, the CEO of Volkswagen. During a break, both climbed into the new VW Beetle, taking off for a ride through the Swiss town. The press followed, of course, and by the time the ride ended, the world had a new story: That Gates and Piech had decided to build Microsoft applications into the Beetle, among other new VW cars. The Microsoft product additions, in fact, would not only let the driver access his e-mail but allow technicians to service the Bug and other VWs via the Internet. *The Economist, Business Week* and even daily newspapers speculated about all the features.[27] It was an outstanding promotion and a well-prepared plan.

Our global software survey confirmed that outstanding software managers take PR and other public events as a personal, top-level responsibility: Top managers of the successful software companies spent up to 35 *percent* of their total time on general conferences, public appearances, media contacts, and interviews which involve no direct sales activities. These top managers clearly invest in awareness. Managers at less successful companies took a third less of their time on such events.

OBTAINING FAVORABLE PRODUCT REVIEWS. Smart PR doesn't stop with conferences and other large events. It also includes the "technology evangelists," experts sent out by software companies who "preach the word" to third-party developers, magazines that publish product reviews, and customers (at fairs like CeBIT). In 1997 Netscape even started to intensively train its technology evangelists in what director Marty Cagan calls "Netscape Charm School."[28] Four times a year, candidates for the missionary's job are educated on communication skills, customer responsiveness, managing relationships and effective presentation.

Technology evangelists travel the globe to convince opinion makers of their products' superiority.

The evangelists are sent out across the globe to convince key people of the special performance of their software products—reviewers who write crucial press articles that evaluate new software, corporate decision makers, IT department heads, and general journalists. When Miko Matsumura from Sun's JavaSoft division showed up at the Net-Info 97 exhibition in Thailand, for example, several IT publications carried Matsumura's picture on the cover.[29] His message about "the bright future" of Java was at least heard.

Aggressive advertising to support the PR

When SAP launched its *R/3* product in the United States a few years ago, one third of the $6 million product launch budget was set aside for advertising.[30] Similarly, when KHK, the Frankfurt, Germany–based enterprise solutions firm, went into business a few years ago, it also heavily stressed advertising. In fact, 10 percent of its budget went into ads.

Our global survey reflected the emphasis among successful firms on advertising. Successful companies spend, on average, 7 *percent* of their revenues on advertising, versus 3 percent for less successful players. That compares to a huge consumer goods and marketing company as McDonald's, which spent about 6.7 percent of its revenues on advertising in 1997.[31]

Start-up companies are particularly aggressive advertisers. Take

Pointcast, the Silicon Valley Internet business start-up: When it received its first $8 million in financing from its investors (such as Silicon Valley Venture Capitalist Mohr, Davidow Ventures), nearly all that money went for advertising. Intershop, the German start-up, meanwhile spent 20 percent of its revenues on advertising in 1997.

Large companies are increasingly innovative in their advertising. At the end of 1997, for instance, SAP advertised 10 free SAP installations for midsized German businesses in a "lottery." SAP's goal was to reach those customers as a new growth target. Some *1,600 businesses* applied and filled out lottery forms with detailed information about themselves. On top of this success, SAP benefited further by not picking up the $6 million costs for the free installations: They were shared by *twelve* partners, including IBM, Microsoft, Sun, and KPMG.[32]

Effective advertising can even become a "survival factor." Steve Jobs made advertising a key component of his 1997 and 1998 turnaround of Apple. "It's the beginning of a comeback," Jobs commented on the ad theme. "That is, to teach customers that people can change the world to the better if they are truly passionate."[33] This "intellectual-emotional appeal" was what Jobs requested for the Apple campaign. "Think different" became the worldwide slogan, one that was to set up Apple as a brand for "visionaries and unconventional thinkers."[34] Pictures of Gandhi, Einstein, and Picasso emphasized the spots' message.

"Think different."

Software firms are also increasingly using the Internet as a *core* advertising media. In April 1998, Microsoft signed a double-digit million-dollar online advertising contract with communication service giant Deutsche Telekom.[35] This was by far the largest advertising campaign on a German Web site to that point. For one year, a Microsoft advertising button was installed on the Web home page of T-Online. For Richard Roy, general manager of Microsoft Germany, the money was well spent: "The 2 million customers of T-Online make its home page one of the most frequently used pages in the German language Internet and secures first-class advertising contacts for us," he explained.

Advertising the brand, not the technology

Despite revenues that have grown rapidly to more than $1 billion and an advertising budget of 7 percent of revenues, Chicago-based PLAT-INUM *technology* used to have a relatively low profile in the market-place. That, said Michael Matthews, VP marketing, was probably because PLATINUM was not employing its advertising dollars *effectively*. "We were spending a lot for advertising, but the effort was quite unfocused," he told us. "I am refocusing this now," he added. "We will probably end up with a slightly lower budget—but now we will spend it on brand building."

Many software companies share this problem. Heavily technology driven, they tend to focus their communication on product features. We have found, however, that the greatest success from advertising is reached by marketing *company brand names*, not *product features*. The successful companies we surveyed spent 78 percent of their advertising budget on the company name, and just 22 percent on specific

> **Successful companies spend 78 percent of their advertising budget marketing the company name.**

product features. Less successful companies did it exactly the *other* way around.

THE ADVANTAGE OF COMPANY BRANDS. Brands serve to hold the value propositions in the minds of consumers even if the products themselves change or are discontinued. Value propositions are key to building market leadership, John Doerr has said. In addition, brands help a company recruit because they have the ability to convey positive images of the company and its culture.

For Intershop, the e-commerce start-up from East Germany, the company name was crucial for the company's successful start: "Inter-shop" was the name of an upscale East German retail chain carrying rare Western consumer goods, before the wall came down. Stephan Schambach, the founder of Intershop, used the name for his software start-up, which produced software for "virtual" shopping. Schambach advertised the name heavily. The media took notice, liked the story behind it, and featured Schambach's new company in the largest papers.

Meanwhile, larger companies must compete to build *global* brands. For Microsoft, this has become one of the key goals of its communication strategy. "We have a global market, we are a global player, and we need global branding," says Peter Hartmann, marketing communications director at Microsoft Germany. "We try to attach very clear positioning to the brand." Their goal: To make the name "Microsoft"—rather than specific product names or features—synonymous with *competent, user-friendly,* and *reliable*.[36]

So far, the efforts have paid off strikingly well. In a 1998 survey, *97 percent of all U.S. consumers recognized the brand* (topping even consumer goods giants like Nike and Campbell Soup).[37] Even in China, Microsoft was recognized by 43 percent of all consumers, according to Princeton, New Jersey–based research firm ORC International. "Companies like GE have been around for a hundred years, and it took them decades to build their global brand name," Jeff Brown, senior vice president of ORC's Corporate Reputation Division, told us. "I have never seen a company like Microsoft getting to the top that quickly."[38]

Oracle has also invested heavily in building a unified, worldwide brand: In 1997, Oracle replaced it regionalized ad strategy with a single $100 million global budget assigned to Think New Ideas, a U.S.-based ad agency. The budget made up more than 6 percent of Oracle's revenues, but Oracle CEO Larry Ellison was pleased. "Apple is the only life-style brand in the industry," he stated. "It's the only company people feel passionate about. My company, Oracle, is huge; IBM is huge; Microsoft is huge; but no one has incredible emotions about our companies."[39] That, he hoped, was what the new ad strategy would correct.

MARKETING BUSINESS VALUE PROPOSITIONS. While communicating technical product *features* is indeed not the most effective way to

spend marketing dollars, it does make sense, however, to market the
business value proposition of products *together* with the brand. This
becomes especially important for more complex products like enterprise solutions, where the product design leaves more room for differentiation in the market.

Some of the successful players have rigorously focused on combining the general value proposition of the company brand with the
business value proposition of their products. For example, on SAP's
Web site the brand value proposition "SAP—We don't just make better software. We make better compa-
nies" is directly linked to the product
architecture with its expandability and
the high integration level. As its motto
states, "SAP's strategic product architecture links all areas of an enterprise." The site then explains that the
"open interfaces" in SAP's software are the key to enabling communication between legacy systems, SAP systems, and external systems,
providing "enormous scalability and flexibility."

> **The more complex the product, the more important the business value proposition.**

A very similar approach is taken in Baan's advertisements: "[Baan]
creates flexible, easy-to-integrate products and services . . . This is
Baan—Simply Better Business."[40]

To be sure, SAP and Baan are certainly not the first companies that
have successfully used "total value proposition marketing." After all, the
Apple Macintosh became a rising star in the 1980s both for the Apple
brand *and* for the value proposition of an easy-to-use, fast user interface, one featuring icons rather than green screens and cryptic code.

Making customers try out the product

Millions of computer games have never made it off the retail shelves.
Doom, though, was a worldwide sensation in the early 1990s. By 1996,
Doom II, the follow-up version, had already sold 1.6 million copies.[41]
How was this success possible? From the very start, in 1993, *Doom*
was *partially* for free. The first few levels of the game could be down-

loaded over the Internet without cost. Once "locked in," a large fraction of the millions of downloaders became customers for the subsequent levels of the game.

A key step to building worldwide market leadership is enticing target customers to *try* the product at least once. This initial contact is vital in order to get the customers to *stick* with the software later. Attractive pricing strategies are key for that. Netscape, for instance, has followed the *Doom* approach by giving its basic browser away for free. But that strategy works only if there are other revenue streams. In the case of Netscape, the company could make money charging for its server software and for browser upgrades instead. But when no other revenues exist to subsidize free products, other pricing schemes are required.

FIXED COSTS CONVERTED TO VARIABLE COSTS. IBM's "San Francisco project" has been designed to reach small developers of enterprise solutions software. Instead of putting a price tag on its development tool, IBM tells the users, "Pay us when you make the first money with our product." IBM takes a share of the revenues only when developers have successfully marketed the software product. There are no fixed costs for the developer at the beginning, and IBM wins if the developers grow successfully (by using IBM's tools). Meanwhile, a small European software company is testing a "usage-based pricing model" in which user companies pay for the software based on the *time* they use it. "Software is a service," the CEO told us. And Pandesic, a 1997 joint venture of SAP and Intel, installs electronic commerce platforms against usage fees that are based on *volume*.

FIXED PRICE—GUARANTEED. Especially for smaller companies, the costs of implementing enterprise solutions are of considerable concern. SAP, for one, addresses this concern by offering fixed-price SAP implementations for small- to midsized businesses (businesses with less than about $130 million annual revenues). The package not only includes the software license but also the hardware, the installation, and a range of services.

PIRACY: ONE OF THE MOST COSTLY WAYS TO BUILD MARKET LEADER-SHIP. Software piracy steals $2.4 billion from the North American software industry every year.[42] In China, "copy plants" produce more than 54 million illegal software packages annually.[43] In the United States, it is estimated that one in three software packages is pirated. And some Far East markets have piracy rates of 99 percent, according to Business Software Alliance (BSA), an intellectual property rights organization sponsored by the world's top software makers. "These are one-disk countries," said Bob Kruger, vice president of enforcement at BSA.[44] "Once we make one sale, it's a closed market."

Software piracy is illegal, but it serves one indisputable purpose in the marketing of a new product: The first try by *private* users is "facilitated" by the zero price. And pirated copies, regardless of their origin, still help establish a software maker's market leadership—even if it is clearly one of the most expensive ways to reach it.

Many software companies seem to be only half-concerned about piracy. A "pirate hotline" in Europe, sponsored by well-known software firms, has been set up in recent years to give callers a chance to "blow the whistle" on illegal software use. About half of the 2,000 calls per year concern illegal business users, and half *private* users. The sponsoring software companies, however, specifically request that illegal *private* use *not* be tracked, the manager of the hotline service told us. Only professional offenders are tracked down. The other calls are put away in the files.

A concerted multichannel effort to reach target customers

Going global and launching products fast is important for software companies on their way to market leadership. But next comes the establishment of a powerful sales force to sell the products and to find the most effective sales *channels* and flood them. The goal is to start a concerted, fast-paced distribution firework that builds market leadership against competitors.

USING A VARIETY OF THIRD-PARTY SALES CHANNELS. *Preinstallations on hardware* have become one of the most effective sales channels in the mass-market software segment. Hardware vendors or value-added resellers (VARs) choose the software most attractive to consumers and preinstall it on new PCs. In April 1995, four months before the *Windows95* product launch, 45 PC manufacturers had already decided to have the software preinstalled on their equipment.[45] Among them were the biggest players: Compaq, Dell, Packard Bell, HP, and NEC. Even IBM, Microsoft's key competitor in PC-operating platforms at the time, decided to preinstall *Windows95* on its entry-level "PC 300."

Intuit frequently used preinstallations on its way to market leadership in the personal finance software field. In 1996 alone, 6.2 million *Quicken* units were preinstalled on PCs.[46] Of the 12 largest PC equipment manufacturers, 9 put *Quicken* on their machines, including Compaq, IBM, HP, Packard Bell, and Toshiba.[47]

The importance of *installing* software on PCs (not just *supplying* it) is illustrated in an example from Lotus. A few years ago, Lotus offered its office package *SmartSuite/Amipro* in PC packages for free. But it came as a CD-ROM—not installed. A natural barrier was raised. "I saw the *SmartSuite* CD," one potential user told us. "But quite honestly, I was already using *MS Office*, which came pre-installed from my local vendor, and I didn't want to spend the time installing *SmartSuite*." Lotus *SmartSuite* never became a serious threat to *Microsoft Office*.

> Microsoft rented an armada of 500 trucks to deliver millions of copies of *Windows95* within days of its release.

Flooding the retail stores. For the U.S. launch of *Windows95*, Microsoft increased its production capacities seven-fold and rented an armada of 500 trucks to transport the packages to the retail stores. Millions of copies were made available within days. More surprisingly, about a million copies were obtained by customers *during the first four days* of availability in North America.[48]

Looking Glass Technologies, a game software company in Cambridge, Massachusetts, is also a master at handling retail placement. The company makes sure that store retailers have cardboard display stands featuring the Looking Glass products. There are also posters and other in-store advertisements. Looking Glass spends 20 to 30 percent of its revenues on marketing, and the majority portion of this amount goes into in-store marketing. Looking Glass spends about $300,000 *every month for each game* promoted in the stores.

The Internet is also playing an essential part as a sales channel—not only for software but for other types of merchandise. Some of the younger software companies we interviewed had done more than just market their own software heavily over the Web. They had in fact based their entire product line on the assumption that Internet sales and transactions soon would boom dramatically: BroadVision provides one-to-one electronic commerce platform software; BROKAT specializes in software for secure transactions over various electronic distribution channels such as the Internet; and Intershop provides a whole product line of e-commerce software.

Involving systems integrators as multipliers. Many of the enterprise solutions companies we met are experts at marketing through partners: SAP, for example, receives a large share of its orders through systems integrators that implement the SAP systems. Other companies, like Intellicorp, a small Silicon Valley company, provide software tools for SAP installations, and thus cooperate with a number of larger professional services firms as well.

PROFITING FROM EAGER SALES FORCES. When Ross Perot left IBM in 1962 to start EDS with $1,000, one of his main incentives for leaving was to top the incentives he had found at IBM. After all, it was still January, and Perot, the aggressive IBM salesperson, had already reached his sales cap for the year. There was no reason left for him to excel.[49]

Overall, we found that highly aggressive sales forces are crucial to spur success—and incentives are the tool that drives the sales team. Kerry Lamson, vice president of applications product marketing at Oracle, knows that well. "There is no upper limit for a salesperson here. A high-performing salesperson can easily earn $1 million a year," he assured us.

Our global survey verified the importance of strong incentives for the sales force. Salespeople of successful software companies earned *on average* 38 percent of their total compensation through a variable share, with some top achievers reaching far above that. In less successful companies the figure was 20 percent or even less.

European companies on average offer less attractive incentive packages. One German software solutions provider offered *no* incentives at all. The result: The company's revenues reached just $18 million after 20 years in business, and the profit margin, about 4 percent.

Other Europeans, however, have learned the lesson. Soon after SAP had entered the U.S. market in the late 1980s, Klaus Besier, SAP's U.S. top executive then, scrapped the sales cap.[50] Any U.S. salesperson was then able to earn significantly more than the previous cap of $140,000. This no-sales-cap approach marked a significant departure from German practice. As *Business Week* wrote at the time, "Some SAP top managers still suffer from the thought that a salesman can now earn more than themselves." With this change, some salespeople could earn $2 million. Revenue increases justified the rewards, though. By 1993, revenues at SAP America tripled to more than $100 million.

The world aspiration

Companies striving for market leadership have to play the global game—just as SAP did when it entered the U.S. market in 1988—because in software, the market is truly the world. Big U.S. players have also realized that. On August 24, 1995, when *Windows95* was launched, PR activities in the United States included bands and jugglers, balloons and buffet meals under billowing tents.

But what was remarkable was that *Windows95* was launched in *12 other countries* and *12 different languages* in the same week, and with equal amounts of energy. Of 15 TV and movie advertising spots produced for Microsoft by the agency Wieden & Kennedy in 1998, in fact only 7 were produced for the United States; the other ones were *simultaneously* made for Japan, France, the United Kingdom, and Germany.[51] This is an international approach of a new quality.

Even some start-up companies go global *right away*. California-based BroadVision, for instance, had its *first* product launch in Japan—not in the United States—to demonstrate its world aspirations from the start. "The Web is global. It doesn't make sense to constrain ourselves to one country," Bob Runge, former VP of marketing, told us. Within the first *nine months* of its existence, BroadVision spread to 7 countries. "We had no choice," Pehong Chen, BroadVision's CEO, explained. "We had to reach the total potential market as fast as possible."

> **Silicon Valley–based BroadVision had its first product launch in Japan.**

Inso Corporation, a software product company we met in the Boston area, could reach its potential market only by going global: The company, after all, was in the business of making foreign language modules for mass-market software. Within four years, Inso was in 30 countries—and 30 languages.

U.S. SOFTWARE GOES GLOBAL FASTER. Contrary to common belief, U.S. companies "go global" faster than the Europeans. In our survey, we found that the U.S. companies go overseas within an average of 2.6 years after starting, while the European players wait 3.7 years, more than 40 percent longer.

Marketing on a global scale requires some risk-taking and a clear global focus, as the story of one German software company illustrates. This company first tried to expand into the United States in 1987, two years after its founding. This initial attempt failed, however, because of the "different business rules" in the United States, the founders told us. The second attempt, in 1989, was stopped when the company decided it would "rather wait" for the next program version.

Three years later the next move was canceled—until the entire product suite could be completed. Then, in 1995, the fourth attempt was canceled—a large partner was not yet ready. Finally, in 1996, the company took its first international steps, opening a few small sales subsidiaries. It was a small operation rather than a truly global one, and, as a result, international sales were a disappointing $3 million (after more than a year of operations in almost 10 countries)—or less than 5 percent of the company's total revenues.

Europe does have some potential role models. But there are some outstanding European players in the globalization race as well—not only SAP, but many of them start-ups—which could serve as role models for other European firms. Intershop is one. Stephan Schambach, Intershop's young CEO, flew to Silicon Valley a few months after he started the company. Within half a year, he moved the entire company, *headquarters and himself*, to the valley: The U.S. market was much larger, he reasoned, and both competitors and potential partners were on the West Coast. (The company kept several software developers and a marketing unit for Europe in Germany.) Schambach realized the internationalization was going to cost his start-up $10 million, more than its annual revenues at that time. But he knew it was worth the cost.

Companies launch incomplete products. In the rush to get products out into the world, software companies often make compromises. Selling somewhat incomplete products is common practice, and so is the acceptance of "bugs" in the products. This is especially true for companies that are still on the way to market leadership. The idea is to stay ahead of the competition by offering new products faster— even at the risk of offending some consumers.

At CeBIT 1996, the software and computer fair, one start-up

company presented its first electronic commerce software package. The following year, the company's CTO admitted that the software they had introduced earlier "had so many bugs, it was terrible." As a result, the company had to replace the earlier version with a completely new and far better version. But, he explained, "We had to design the first version in such a rush that we couldn't pay any attention to the software quality." Time to market is truly a critical measure for software product firms.

This emphasis on speed, in fact, was confirmed in our worldwide survey. When we asked what companies put more emphasis on—time to market or fully implemented product features—64 percent of the successful software companies focused on time to market, versus only 45 percent of the less successful ones.

But there are limits to the benefits of speed. Introducing an incomplete or bug-ridden program can be a serious mistake when the product is not "just" a word processor, but a mission-critical system. A few years ago, for instance, one of Germany's largest industrial companies purchased an electronic truck weight measurement system for its steel plants. Suddenly, due to software bugs, the weighing system stopped working. There was no emergency backup, the plant had to be shut down for two days, and the losses amounted to millions of dollars.

But even if the timing and quality of software are right, even if globalization, sales efforts, advertising and PR are done well, and even if the first goal, market leadership, is reached: The next challenge is often even greater—*keeping* one's leading position over time.

SUSTAINING MARKET LEADERSHIP

In 1994, IBM decided to win back the market for PC operating systems from Microsoft, its former ally. The weapon would be the new IBM system, *OS/2 Warp*. An advertising budget of $40 million was approved for the last three months of 1994 alone.[52] Development and marketing costs for this, and the previous versions of *OS/2*, came close to $2 billion.

A year later, and exactly two weeks before the launch of the new Microsoft *Windows95* operating system, David Barnes, a top *OS/2* manager, conceded that the "war" was over. "Let's not kid ourselves," he said to the German weekly journal *Wirtschaftswoche*. "I will install *Windows95* on my home PC as well."[53]

Microsoft had to fend off a $2 billion attack.

Four months later, Barnes's home PC was one of 18.8 million worldwide running *Windows95*. *OS/2 Warp*, in comparison, shipped about 5 million units during the entire year.[54] By 1996, Dataquest reported that the new *Windows95* held 70 percent of the PC operating system market, the older *Windows 3.1* still held 11 percent—and IBM's *OS/2* held 2 percent.

Microsoft successfully defended its market leadership of PC desktop operating systems. How can other companies do the same?

Eating their own young: life among the cannibals

Market leadership is maintained by actively removing the chances for competitors to jump into a market leadership position. That defense calls for new products to be released at very close intervals.

As Microsoft's *Windows95* launch illustrates, software companies are willing to "cannibalize" their own products to stay ahead. Microsoft *Windows95* was introduced when *Windows 3.11* and *DOS* together still held *almost 85 percent* of the PC platform market.[55] Despite this comfortable lead, Microsoft decided to actively encourage its customers to replace *Windows 3.11* with *Windows95*. Continued market leadership and cannibalization closely correlate. Cannibalization, says Pierre Haren, CEO of Paris-based Ilog, "is a prerequisite for continuous innovation."

Nice Systems, a Tel Aviv, Israel–based voice-logging systems firm, also has cannibalization down pat. Despite its name, Nice products don't have a long life. Instead of cashing in on its products, Nice prefers to "eat" them. *NiceLog 1.0*, for instance, was introduced in 1994 as a digital audio software and hardware system for telephone record-ings. A revised edition came shortly thereafter. Additional revisions followed. Two years later, the *fifth* release was already for sale. This version received "Product of the Year" by *Call Center Magazine*, but never mind—within a year it was consumed by a vastly changed ver-sion, *NiceLog 7.0.*

Nice proves that product cannibalization can be profitable: From 1994 to 1997, the company grew from $9 million in revenues to $69 million, an annual growth rate of 97 percent. Margins were about 14 percent during these years of continuous product self-cannibalization. Our global survey emphasized the importance of cannibalization. *In fact, the cannibalization rate was one of the strongest and most distin-guishing differences between successful and unsuccessful companies.*

More than half of the lower-performing companies waited beyond the growth and the cash cow phases, until the downsizing phase, in fact, to replace their old products with new ones. In stark contrast, *80 percent of the successful companies introduced a new product during the growth phase of the previous one.* This made the previous one obsolete—"eating" up its market to a great extent.

SAP has been another advocate for "leaving the old behind." At the end of the 1980s, the company had a near-total hold on the mar-ket with its *R/2* package, and soaring revenues. Still, in 1992, SAP came out with *R/3*, a completely new software product. The result? Sales shot from less than $500 million in 1992 to $1.5 billion in 1995.

Playing on fear: convincing your customers, again, that the next upgrade is key

Of course, competitors will always try to shoot down a significant upgrade, like SAP's or Microsoft's. "There are two ways to market a product," said Sun Microsystems CEO Scott McNealy. "Either I excite our customers with our new technological innovations. Or I practice the deodorant trick: I act as if the customer smells, and imply that he's nasty if he doesn't buy my product."[56] That, he added, was exactly how he believes some software companies succeed. "The customer is made to believe that the future will pass him by if he does not migrate over to the next program version."

The deodorant trick may work for some, but the greatest fear tactic in software is to tell a customer that the software he or she owns won't be able to communicate with newer software versions. Furthermore, full customer support often comes only with the latest release.

To sustain market leadership, software players must make certain that customers purchase upgrades, for two reasons: For one, it gives the company an important revenue source, of course. But at least equally important, it is a "guarantee" that the customer won't switch over to a competitor's products.

Upgrade discounts give customers more "factual" persuasion for moving to the latest upgrades. **Upgrades are intended to raise user switching costs.** *Lotus Notes*, for example, offered 30 percent upgrade discounts in March 1998, in its fight to protect its world market leadership in groupware software. At the time, Lotus held an installed base of more than 20 million copies. However, the market leadership ratio in installed seats over competitor *Microsoft Exchange* had already largely decreased: from 5:1 at the end of 1996 down to 2:1 in the spring of 1998.[57]

Besides cannibalization, playing on fear, and offering carrots and sticks to defend market share against competitors, there are also ways to keep new competitors out of the market entirely. Advertising and PR are strategic tools for this job.

Advertising as a threat: announcing products before any code is written

When they try to *build* market leadership, software companies often sell incomplete products, and even some with known errors. But to *sustain* market leadership, many successful market leaders have gone even further—they sometimes *announce and promote* new products so early that not a single line of new code has been programmed.[58] The reason, of course, is to maintain the appearance of being a step ahead of the competition.

In 1987, for example, RTI, an Oracle competitor, announced a new feature for its database product, *Ingres*. The feature was a breakthrough that enabled users to make "distributed queries," thus finding information that was scattered among different networked computers.

Once the feature was announced by RTI, Oracle's customers demanded the same. In response, Larry Ellison, Oracle's CEO, ordered his marketing crew to launch an ad campaign announcing a similar feature, this time named *SQL*Star*.[59] Programmers were assigned to develop the feature around the *same* time the ads were prepared. Fortunately, by the time the ads were printed, the feature was ready.[60]

Premature promotions were an integral part of the early computer age to the extent that in 1973, IBM was told by U.S. Federal District Judge Sherman Christensen to stop its frequent use of early promotions and to make the details of new products known as soon as IBM announced them.[61] He also told IBM that if it announced a new product, it had better ship it within 60 days.[62] The courts had recognized early announcements as a powerful way to keep customers from buying competitive products. After all, users tend to wait for quite some time for a new product from their current provider rather than switching to a newer technology from a competitor they do not know.

> **Oracle announced *SQL*Star* to the public while simultaneously assigning programmers to develop it.**

Our survey showed how significant early product promotion is to the industry. Successful larger software companies we interviewed started promoting their products very early. Some start at about 50 percent of the development phase; others when they have just *started* the programming phase; and even some *before* they have started programming. This is a truly aggressive move: to promote products when the program features have been designed, but not coded yet.

Smaller companies, however, generally wait longer to announce their products—until they are about 70 percent through development. Intershop, for example, waits until about 85 percent of the development time is complete before beginning promotions. Why? Because, a very early announcement of a new product could be detrimental to a small firm: It can attract bigger companies that have the resources to take the market by brute force.

CEOs as media celebrities

Those companies that try to *sustain* market leadership need PR just as much as players trying to build it. But the purpose is different, and approaches differ as well. The goal is to *manifest* the image of market leadership—the clear pole position. Top companies that are well known in their markets are usually led by well-known persons as well.

Many successful software players profit from the media's interest in their CEOs. Bill Gates, for example, went to see a class of 20 junior high school kids in California in 1997 to discuss the "future of technology." Gates sat down with the students, chatted and surfed the Web with them, while media cameras captured the event.

Executives in other marketing-intensive industries we spoke to widely admired software companies for their capability to build celebrities. "The way Bill Gates markets himself like a magic figure, as a guru, a brand, a cult for young people, is truly impressive," said Herbert Brenke, former CEO of E-Plus, a large German cell phone service company. "He has understood one thing, and that puts him one step ahead: He is not selling tangible products like sneakers, but imaginary, untouchable products. And those take more imaginary marketing, more fantasy, more image building. Gates does that in an unbelievable way."

SAP also makes sure that its top managers produce stories for the press. In 1994, for instance, cofounder Hasso Plattner strapped on a

guitar and performed on stage at the SAP Sapphire user conference in Orlando, in front of 4,400 IT experts from 31 countries.[63] Officially it was supposed to be a "Technology Update," not a jam session. **"Let others do PR for you."**
But the media loved it. "Let others
do PR for you," summarized SAP's director of corporate marketing, Guenther Tolkmit. SAP leveraged its market leader position so that the press *reported* on SAP: Not only cheaper than advertising, but much more credible.

Software CEOs also collaborate to make sure that "external PR" occurs. For example, Oracle's CEO Larry Ellison has frequently sailed competitively against SAP's Plattner. Of course, the press was alerted to the fact that Plattner personally wrote the navigation software for his *Morning Glory* ship and that special simulation programs, using Cray supercomputers, had calculated the optimum shape for the boat.

In reality, Ellison's *Sayonara* may have won more of the races so far, but in terms of PR, both Oracle *and* SAP have struck gold.

PR IS NECESSARY because attackers are almost continuously waiting in line to break the leader's pole position. "It is fear that every evening makes me read the trade press reports on competitors' new developments," said Andy Grove once.[64] "It is fear that gives me the will to listen to Cassandras when all I want to do is cry out, 'Enough already, the sky isn't falling,' and go home."

BREAKING THE MARKET
LEADERSHIP OF ANOTHER PLAYER

In 1990, there was no doubt as to who led the word processing software market: WordPerfect. The Orem, Utah, company had held about 46 percent of the total $1.5 billion word processing market for years—at least a third more than Microsoft, whose share reached little more than 30 percent at the time.

Two years later, the winner and follower were reversed. Microsoft *Word* held 46 percent, and *WordPerfect* held 31 percent.[65] In 1997, *WordPerfect* had tumbled to 17 percent.[66]

Was this win made possible through the sheer market strength of Microsoft alone? No, size alone was not accountable. In fact, since 80 percent of WordPerfect's revenues were derived from the word processing software, versus 20 percent of Microsoft's, WordPerfect arguably could have been able to better concentrate on the word processing market.

There were other reasons for Microsoft's success: WordPerfect had failed to realize the importance of one major technological change and of one major marketing change.

Windows 3.0, which offered graphical user interfaces, was introduced as a new operating platform in May 1990. By July, Microsoft added *Word for Windows.* Despite the challenge, WordPerfect took about 14 months to respond to the technological change. By then, Microsoft had captured 53 percent of the Windows market. Bill Gates summarized what could have been the epitaph: "We've seen many, many examples of companies that weren't open-minded," he told *Fortune* magazine. "We saw companies like . . . WordPerfect ignore the graphical user interface. They could have afforded to put five people on the thing—even if their CEO thought it was stupid."[67]

Unfortunately, WordPerfect stumbled again—this time in marketing: In 1990, Microsoft added several features to *MS Office*, one of the many product suites with several applications in one that became popular at the time and that clearly offered advantages to consumers. WordPerfect waited until 1993 to offer a similar suite, but adding a database package from Borland. It took Microsoft less than a month to include a database package in *MS Office* as well.[68]

WordPerfect was sold off to Novell in late 1994 and resold to Corel in 1996. Corel's SEC report stated in early 1998 that its quarterly sales had decreased 44 percent "primarily due to decreased aggregate unit sales." Microsoft had managed to break WordPerfect's market leadership.

Interestingly, Japan's largest software product company, Justsystem, is currently defending its *Ichitaro* word processing system against Microsoft *Word* as well. In 1995, Microsoft held less than 10 percent of the market. *Ichitaro* held about 70 percent. But following the introduction of *Windows95* and an improved Japanese language version of *MS Word*, the two companies are about even and still without a clear winner.

Attacks on the market leadership of established players are frequent in the software product business.

In our global survey, we found players trying to break the market leadership of a competitor in multiple cases: Raptor, holding 15 percent of the firewall security market, was up against Checkpoint with about 30 percent; Intellicorp tried to catch up with IDS Scheer, which holds about 25 percent of the ERP installation tool market for process modeling; Microsoft competed against Lotus in groupware and messaging software, a battle where Lotus's advantage has dwindled from five-to-one in 1996 to two-to-one in 1998. In addition, Microsoft was also engaging in the well-publicized battle with Netscape in the browser market. And Sun and Oracle were confronting Microsoft in the battle for operating system standards with the Java-run NC.

When to break a standard?
And when not to break a standard?

Attempting to break a standard is a major effort. Not all battles end in favor of the attacker, as in the case of *Word* versus *WordPerfect*. IBM did not manage to establish *OS/2* against *MS-DOS* and *Windows,* as mentioned earlier.

When is it favorable to attack the market leader then? A simple principle: There must be a large upside potential *for the company* and relatively low entry barriers.

LARGE POTENTIAL FOR THE COMPANY ITSELF. For Microsoft, the Web browser was not just another product; it offered an extremely high upside, *especially* for Microsoft.

Strategic importance in product portfolio. The browser did not promise large revenues by itself, as most users received it for free. But it was the gateway to the Internet. "Like the PC, the Internet is a tidal wave," Bill Gates wrote in a *New York Times* article.[69] "It will wash over the computer industry and many others, drowning those who don't learn to swim in its waves." Microsoft realized that having a popular browser was the key to swim in those waves. Its own browser would ensure links without gateway tolls to future Microsoft applications placed on Internet servers.

> "Like the PC, the Internet is a tidal wave."

Like the browser software, *MS Word* was also a key asset in Microsoft's product portfolio: How could they become the leader in packaged office software, after all, without being the leader in text software?

True technology advantage to sell. While the browser competition offered relatively few opportunities for Microsoft to achieve a clear differentiation in technology, the text software, *MS Word*, did: *Word* operated with a graphical user interface; *WordPerfect* did not. It was the key reason for the attacker to win.

Large or growing market. Text software had made *WordPerfect* a soaring $550 million star company in the late 1980s. Browsers had the same potential. Early on it became clear that browser technologies would become vitally important. Netscape, the first company in the browser mass market, saw its stocks soaring from $25 a share in mid-1995 at the time of its IPO, to $80 in the beginning of 1996. And despite major challenges from Microsoft, Netscape's market cap was still at more than $2.7 billion in early 1998. AOL then paid $4.2 billion in stock for Netscape in November 1998.[70]

RELATIVELY LOW BARRIERS. Several factors facilitate breaking market leadership.

Completely new technologies. Browsers were completely new software products when Netscape took its browser to market. It was not only a technology shift but a new technology as well. Netscape took a chance. Similarly, the change from *DOS* to a *Windows* environment offered a good chance to jump in the driver's seat: The *WordPerfect* example again shows how technology shifts facilitate shifts in market leadership.

Low user-switching costs. Browsers are relatively easy for users to switch to and from, as comparatively little learning is involved in using the program. That helps the attacker. Switching database products, or even enterprise solutions software, in contrast, takes significant retraining.

Weakness of the leading player. *WordPerfect* lacked the speed to keep up with technology and consumer needs. Microsoft used this weakness to jump in. Small size may also be a weakness when trying to compete in a highly attractive market segment. Netscape made little more than $500 million in fiscal 1997 when it tried to sustain market leadership in the browser segment. While being big may not in itself be enough to break a standard, of course, it may help.

BUT EVEN LARGE players do not always succeed in breaking a standard: The Intuit *Quicken* versus *MS Money* story clearly demonstrated that. A variety of actions help the attacker win the game.

How to break the market leadership?

Sometimes buying a company is the answer. When Baan, the large Dutch enterprise solutions company (with $680 million 1997 revenues), realized that Aurum Software, a much smaller newcomer, was setting a new standard in customer interaction software, it simply bought the company for $275 million. At other times, alliances work to reach market leadership: Baan, again, formed a close alliance with Hyperion, a Stamford, Connecticut, software company, because Hyperion was being acknowledged as the market leader in budget management software.

Size helps. But even for big players, purchases and alliances may not be options. In the case of Intuit, for example, the Federal Trade Commission intervened when Microsoft wanted to acquire it.[71] Other strategies must be put to work.

PUSHING PRODUCTS INTO THE MARKET. When one company is the market leader, it often takes creative marketing approaches to get consumers to *at least try* another program. Great new features alone won't work. A better strategy is through preinstallations—for example, Intuit's *Quicken* has been preinstalled by many PC vendors.

LOWER USER-SWITCHING COSTS. Convincing the customer that the new software is compatible with what he or she has used previously is also critical. In 1997, for instance, Microsoft positioned its new *Money 98* product against Intuit's *Quicken Deluxe 98*. To convert *Quicken* customers, Microsoft included a booklet explaining how *Quicken* files could be converted simply and seamlessly into *Money 98*.

Price also counts. Microsoft introduced *Access*, its database product, for $99 in 1992. That was about two-thirds cheaper than existing products, such as Lotus's product *Approach* or Borland's *Paradox*. Price obviously made a difference here: Within three months, Microsoft sold 700,000 copies of *Access*.[72] The total database market in 1992 was only 1.2 million units.

OFFERING FACTUAL ADVANTAGES FOR SWITCHING. Once customers switch products, lower prices alone are not enough to keep their business. The product really does need to be better. The *MS Office* suite, for example, was, in fact, superior to the combined suite of Borland and *WordPerfect*. Unlike the others, its spreadsheet, word processor, and database offered well-functioning interfaces to exchange data. Good customer service can also offer advantages for an attacker, if the leading player provides poor customer service.

CHALLENGING THE COMPETITOR'S BUSINESS MODEL. Netscape was under attack from Microsoft early on. But the real threat to Netscape arose when Microsoft supplied not only free browsers to private users—as Netscape did—but also gave away the server software, called *Microsoft Internet Information Server,* to companies for free. The server software was a major source of income for Netscape. "That certainly puts a motivation and impetus behind Microsoft's adoption as opposed to Netscape's," said industry analyst Martin Marshall of Zona Research.[73]

PROVIDING OR BUILDING ON NEW PLATFORMS. To compete against Microsoft's market leadership in PC desktop operating systems, Sun announced the network computer (NC) and Java, the platform-independent programming language. "The Internet belongs to nobody—especially not to Microsoft," Sun CEO Scott McNealy said in a recent magazine interview. "When a software author has published a few successful Java programs on the Internet, millions of computer users around the globe will wait impatiently for the next version—like Stephen King fans waiting for the next thriller."[74]

JOINING FORCES. Against strong market leaders, big firms often choose to become allies. Netscape, IBM, Oracle, and Sun joined forces against Microsoft to promote the CORBA standard (Common Object Request Broker Architecture) using protocols different from

Microsoft's standard DCOM (Distributed Component Object Model).

MARKETING IS *the* key to success in the software product business. It builds market leaders, sustains them, and even lets aggressive upstarts attack the current leaders. As Mr. Ramachandran of Ramco Systems told us when we visited him in India: "Once we get the status, the revenues will fall into place."

7

PROFESSIONAL SOFTWARE SERVICES

EXPERTS AT MARKETING TRUST

In Paris, eight streets (one of them the Champs Elysées) run from the Place de l'Étoile in the shape of a star. This is one of the finest addresses in Paris, next to one of the most well known landmarks in the world, the Arc de Triomphe. And it is here that one of the world's most renowned software services companies, Cap Gemini, is located. As a visitor approaches the entrance, security cameras swivel and make an examination, before permitting entrance to the offices within.

Cap Gemini's headquarters speak volumes about the difference in marketing strategies used by software product makers—including both mass-market product and enterprise solutions firms—and those used by the purveyors of software services. After all, software product makers aggressively push their message to customers through every medium they can find, from the Internet to gigantic user conferences. Software services companies strive, instead, for understatement. Their calm demeanor, and even their muted dress, suggest investment banking rather than software services.

The reason they maintain this image is that software service providers build their businesses on one-to-one relationships with their clients. Their primary marketing goal is to win the trust of these clients, to hold onto their faith—and their project orders—for as long as possible.

Faith is not the wrong word, incidentally. "The act of hiring a professional is, by very definition, an act of faith. I must, inevitably, believe a promise,"[1] says professional services expert David Maister. For unlike software product makers—whose software code often arrives shrink-wrapped in a box—software services first *promise* to solve a client's problems. Then, after much time and effort, they finally produce the software code. "Unfortunately, you cannot try software services before you buy them," explains Julie Schwartz, vice president of research of the Information Technology Services Marketing Association. "That makes personal trust a much more important factor." That sentiment is echoed by the CIO of a European stock exchange. "Honestly," he said, explaining how he chose between several vendors for a $70 million contract, "we had to go with the company with the better reputation."

A service firm's reputation is vitally important to customers—and not without reason. The risks involved in software projects are enormous. The Denver airport's problems a few years ago are telling.[2] Software bugs caused the luggage routing system to misbehave, sending suitcases everywhere. Before the problem was fixed, the city of Denver and the airlines had lost some $500 million. The Denver airport was not a singular example. In fact, failing projects are more the rule than the exception: When Malaysia's new airport opened in 1998, check-in services and escalators shut down abruptly. The reason: The new $167 million network system and its software had crashed before it ever started working.[3]

It doesn't take an airport to illustrate project failures, though. Individual companies, with much smaller systems, undergo the same problems. FoxMeyer Drug, formerly a $5 billion drug distribution company, decided to install new systems in 1994. Top management signed off a budget of $10 million for a server system, $18 million for a robotic warehouse, and $15 million for the software *intended* to make the system work. It never did work correctly, though, and in fact spewed out so many erroneous shipping orders that FoxMeyer lost about $15 million in unrecovered excess shipments. Losses were so high that FoxMeyer eventually had to file for bankruptcy. Lawsuits swirled afterward for years.[4]

But what happened at FoxMeyer is not unusual either. In a study conducted in 1997 by RONIN, a high-tech research group, 76 percent of 500 IT managers interviewed in the United States and the United Kingdom said that they had experienced at least one *complete* project failure in their career. And nearly half the managers admitted that getting projects right on the first try would be "alien" to most of their IT suppliers.[5]

Of 500 IT managers interviewed, 76 percent had experienced at least one complete project failure in their careers.

"If you want a safe bet, go to Las Vegas and play the slot machines," wrote software expert Steve McConnell.[6] "But if this sounds too tame, software might be just the right gamble." He added: "Software projects include a glut of risks that would give Vegas oddsmakers nightmares: shifting user requirements, poor schedule estimates, unreliable contractors, management inexperience, bleeding-edge technology failures—just to name a few."

THE TRUST BUILDERS

The software project business is a highly risky environment. Nevertheless, some service firms have won the trust of their clients and have been highly successful.

Getting potential clients to meet each other

A recent survey of 200 Fortune 1,000 companies, conducted by the Information Technology Services Marketing Association (ITSMA), revealed that the single most important factor in selecting IT services providers, besides knowledge of specific projects, is the decision makers' interaction with his or her peers.[7] Indeed, recommendations and references from colleagues from other companies very strongly influence the decision maker. "Exchanging information with peers can help CIOs make better business decisions," says Jim Ware, executive director of Berkeley's Fisher Center for Management and Information Technology of the University of California in Berkeley. "It's not like the old days, when the decisions were as easy as 'Buy IBM and you won't get fired.'"[8] But how can a software services company interject itself into the discussions between IT decision makers—and make use of it?

CIOs' purchasing decisions are heavily influenced by discussions with their peers.

SPONSORING HOT-TOPIC IT CONFERENCES. One of the most successful techniques, in this respect, is to sponsor IT conferences.

American Management Systems (AMS), one of the largest IT services companies, has this kind of event down pat. Last summer, for instance, it held its annual "AMS Telecommunications Executive Forum" in San Francisco. Don Tapscott, cyber-guru and author of *Growing Up Digital: The Rise of the Net Generation*, spoke, as well as Jack Boyle, vice president of AMS. "We put a real investment in this channel," says Michael Markovic, senior principal of American Management Systems. "People find it to be very credible, but it also gives telecommunications executives the chance to meet each other and exchange their experiences."

Small companies use the same strategy. Etnoteam, a small software services firm in Milan in northern Italy, for instance, organizes an annual conference on quality software engineering. "We want to position ourselves as the quality leader in our country," explained Alberto Cazziol, marketing manager. Considering that Etnoteam has only 300 employees and annual revenues of $40 million, this is a huge event. In 1997, the three-day conference—held at the Cavalieri Hilton Conference Center in Rome—attracted 1,600 attendees, 35 journalists, and 220 speakers, from such companies as Digital, Finsiel, INet, Microsoft, PLATINUM *technology*, and Etnoteam.

INVITING SELECTIVE SMALL AUDIENCES TO "DISCUSSION CIRCLES." On the other hand, Cambridge Technology Partners aims at small, intimate gatherings. One gathering, which the company calls a "Lycea" event, was held recently at UCLA's Andersen Graduate School of Management. "We find the academic environment and facilities to be extremely conducive to sleeves-rolled-up, soul-bearing working sessions like this one," Tim Mead, vice president of strategic marketing, said.

Sometimes clients will help sponsor events. Cambridge Technology Partners, for example, helped Twentieth Century Fox to bring together about 40 IT and business executives from 20 organizations—ranging from CBS Broadcasting to Procter & Gamble—to discuss and learn more about strategic IT planning. These small meetings work, says Mead, noting that 6 of the company's 18 top clients were signed up through such events.

BUILDING ONLINE WEB COMMUNITIES. The Internet can also serve as a meaningful place to meet. In 1996, for instance, Cambridge Technology Partners founded the Cambridge Information Network (CIN), the first Internet-based service that provides an "online community" designed specifically for senior IT executives. Here, CIOs share best practices, debate strategies, and discuss general trends with their peers—all without leaving their offices. The secret of the club's success is its exclusivity. "If you meet people in a virtual community, trust is even more important than in the real world," says Paul McNabb, founder of CIN. "So we put strong emphasis on the quality of our audience."

Web communities are an innovative services marketing tool.

There is no fee for gaining entry, but members must be CIOs or other senior-level IT executives. Of the 1,600 members in 1998, as many as 500 executives were using the site for about 20 minutes a week, McNabb told us. One of those, Roger Jones, senior VP of IT at IBP, Inc., a meat processor in Sioux City, Iowa, had this to say: "The real value of the online discussions is relating common problems and experiences. I can get specific answers to specific questions, such as how to implement a particular technology."[9]

So members get a lot of valuable information for free. But what's in it for Cambridge Technology Partners, considering that only about 20 percent of the CIN members are their current customers? The average IT budget of the members is about $15 million each, and the total purchase power of the frequent users alone reaches more than $5 billion a year. "To reach that kind of audience with traditional advertising or PR would cost huge amounts of money," says McNabb.

But at the end of the day, professional services companies not only have to talk with their potential clients, they also have to convince them of their competence.

Creating a trustworthy image

The most successful service companies in our global survey applied a whole range of approaches to building their image as experts—from carefully preparing their employees for customer presentations, to publishing articles in trade publications, to selling solutions packages.

MARKETING THE FIRM'S TOP CONSULTANTS. The software services business is a people business, and nothing sells a company better than the quality of its people. Dr. Susanne Berendes, director of IT at steelmaker Thyssen Krupp Stahl AG, agrees: "In choosing a software services provider," she says, "the most important factor is the quality of the person who will be responsible for the project."

This is especially true when new technology is involved. When American Management Systems was invited to make a presentation to a company that was looking for a next-generation customer care and billing system, the firm decided to bring along Chris Polman,[10] an 18-year veteran with the company who had extensive experience as a pure technologist and systems architect. "The client company didn't seem very interested in us at first, so we were very lucky that we were invited for the presentation," recalled Susan Culler, director of marketing and product development at American Management Systems (AMS). "But Chris talked for three hours and really fascinated the people—and this was a hard, tough senior audience."

After the presentation, AMS was invited for further talks, and finally won the contract, worth $15 million. "Without Chris, we would have never made it," Culler says. "He is one of the very few people who can talk at any level in both technical and business detail. I have a great deal of difficulty finding technical guys who can speak like that. I wish I had more like him."

Like other software firms, American Management Systems has decided to invest in the communications skills of its key technologists. When the company finished developing a new customer care and billing system, for instance, it prepared its key technical presenter carefully for the road show that would take him to more than 35 major telecommunications companies in North America and Europe. Furthermore, the company created test audiences, with three to five people, for the presenters to work with. Then they brought in managers from marketing, sales, and public relations to evaluate the progress. Altogether, the presenter had to run through his presentation about 40 times before he hit the road.

> **The key technical presenter had to run through his presentation 40 times before he hit the road.**

PUBLISHING THE FIRM'S SUCCESS STORIES. Articles in prestigious publications are another way to win client confidence. But the software firms are less interested in the big, mass circulation press than they are in client-specific publications. In the telecommunications industry, for instance, magazines like *Telephony*, *Billing World*, *International Communication*, or *Wireless World* are where it counts. "If we can get some ink on a project we did for a particular client, that story may cause the phones to start to ring, with other companies calling us to help," says Michael Markovic, senior principal at American Management Systems. "They'll tell us that they have the same kind of problem that we solved for the other company and could we come and work with them."

Software services firms also use IT articles to highlight specific strength areas. Colin Stringer, director of EuroTransformation Services of Cap Gemini Consulting in the United Kingdom, for instance, has helped his company attract work through his writings about currency conversion in Europe and its IT consequences. He not only wrote a book titled *EMU—An Analysis of How UK Companies Should Prepare* but also published articles in such industry-specific journals as the *Steel Times* and the *Chartered Banker Magazine*.

Other companies attract attention by posting their technical white papers on the Web. Computer Sciences Corporation, for instance, offers *CSC PERSPECTIVES* on its Web site, a place where experts within the company discuss management and technology issues affecting specific industries. Recently, the company had 25 articles to browse through, ranging in subject matter from supply-chain management and data warehousing to partnerships in manufacturing.

Some companies publish their own magazines, where experts from within and outside the company can publish articles. Andersen Consulting, for instance, has its award-winning, bimonthly magazine *Outlook,* which is available on paper and on the Web. Similarly, American Management Systems educates its staff and clients on emerging technologies with *AMS Insight,* a journal that is published by the AMS Center for Advanced Technologies (AMSCAT). At this research facility, more than 250 employees in 30 locations worldwide research new technologies and publish their findings.

But it's not just knowledge that the services try to make more tangible. It's also their specific services.

PACKAGING THE FIRM'S SOFTWARE SERVICES. "Years ago, most software services firms argued that they didn't need products, and didn't have any," said Julie Schwartz of the ITSMA. But the world has changed. Most of the high-performing companies we talked to "productize" at least part of their services. In other words, they develop methodologies or solutions that effectively can be reused in individual projects for other clients.

Computer Sciences Corporation, for instance, has developed solutions in electronic commerce and supply-chain management. "These solutions allow clients to take advantage of our learning experience very quickly," Kirk Arnold, vice president, strategic services and marketing of CSC Consulting & System Integration explained. Companies even name their solutions: CSC's core methodology, for instance, is *Lynx.* Cambridge Technology Partners, meanwhile, actively markets its *Rapid Application Development* methodology. The names help the solutions seem more tangible.

> Software services firms "productize" their services.

BUILDING ONE SUCCESS ON TOP OF ANOTHER. "The most credible argument you can make to an executive is that you have solved the problem before for another company," Michael Markovic, senior principal at American Management Systems told us. That was certainly the case in the winning of a contract to provide software for the German stock exchange. After evaluating several companies, the exchange's CEO, Dr. Werner Seifert, cut the race to two finalists. Although both had excellent reputations and similar products, one company—Andersen Consulting—had already developed software for another stock exchange. Mainly because of that convincing reference case, Andersen won the multimillion-dollar contract, which meanwhile resulted in the very successfully implemented electronic trading system *XETRA*.[11]

Proving the trustworthiness

But proving one's competence is not enough for some service companies. They go one step further and address one of their clients' key concerns in software projects head on: They reduce their risks of project failure.

We found that while the less successful service companies take almost any business that comes their way, the high-performing companies reject more than 40 percent of their potential business. To minimize risk for both themselves and the potential customer, some companies activate a structured process to determine at a very early stage if a potential engagement is worthwhile or not.

High-performing companies reject 40 percent of their potential business.

The Consulting & System Integration Group, a unit of CSC, which is one of the largest global software services companies in the world, uses a structured process called *Pioneer. Pioneer* forces them to ask four basic questions: Is there an opportunity? Can we compete? Can we win? Is it worth winning? "Most of the time, the project leaders are very much engaged with the details of a project," explained Kirk Arnold. "*Pioneer* forces them to get out of the trees and look at the forest."

One American city, for instance, asked the company for help with its Year 2000 computer problem. Through the evaluation, CSC came to two conclusions. One, they were not sure if the client would ever decide to move forward with a contract. Two, they were not sure if they could satisfy the city's comprehensive needs with the resources they had available at that time. "We believed that the risks for both us *and* them were way too high," says Arnold. "We explained why we thought it wasn't a good match, and they accepted it." In fact, after these discussions, the company continued its discussions on smaller city matters, which enabled the firm to continue its relationship with the important organization.

Some companies will even share risk with their clients. According to the ITSMA, software services companies are increasingly willing to share risks with their clients. Indeed, more and more projects are negotiated for a fixed price or a price based on results.[12] Malcolm Frank, senior vice president of marketing at Cambridge Technology Partners, is a firm believer in sharing risks. "We are the experts, so why should the client take all the risk?" he says. His company, in fact, is one of the very few service providers that offer all their IT projects at a fixed price. To do so, the company breaks projects into pieces, or phases, that are negotiated separately. To start, the company might offer a client a three-week "Rapid Solution Workshop," for instance, which is independent of the following project. Such a workshop, Frank says, may cost about $100,000.

Compared to a complete project, which could run into the millions, this is comparably inexpensive, says Frank, and no more than the client would spend to analyze requirements and develop a software prototype. Following the workshop, the customer can continue with Cambridge or take what has been done thus far to another software services company.

But the workshops can be powerful convincers. Frank says that on one occasion, the CEO of a client company came to the presentation that followed the three-week workshop. At the end, the executive was so impressed that he stood up. "My CIO told me a couple of weeks ago that Cambridge's services are pretty strategic and expensive," he said. Then he took his wallet out of his pocket and threw it on the table. "After seeing this, I really don't care how much it costs. Let's start Monday!"

CLIENTS FOR LIFE

If gaining the trust of new clients is a challenge, so is the building of relationships over time. The software services companies we met devote a great deal of effort to deepening customer loyalty, satisfaction—and the opportunity to win more and more business. "The issue in marketing IT services is not growth per se; it is finding the right kind of growth. It is growth with the right kind of customers at the right level of profit," David Munn of the ITSMA told us. "For that reason, companies are increasingly tending to aim for more revenues with fewer customers." David Maister, author of two books about professional services firms, agrees: "Marketing in a professional firm is (or should be) about getting better business, not just more business."[13]

Less competition, larger projects

There are good reasons for that. The deeper the relationship with an existing client, the more likely the service firm will be to win a new project without a lot of competition. "If you look at our strategic long-term clients, on average, we win more than 50 percent of our business with them without competition," explained Kirk Arnold. This can make a big difference. "A competitive bid can cost us up to 10 percent of the total revenues earned with the project," she said. Tata Consultancy Services in India concurs: If they have to compete, they'd spend on average 4 percent of the final project contract to win the business. "If we *don't* compete and win a project due to our superior customer relationship, our initial costs are less than 1 percent," said Lal Singh, senior vice president of sales and marketing. But costs are not the only reason.

In a client relationship, often as the level of trust increases with every successful project, so does the project volume. In 1995, Tata Consultancy Services, for instance, started to serve one of the largest banks in South Africa. Initially, the relationship began with a small project worth $250,000. Two years and seven projects later, a typical contract size with this important client was about $5 million. "This is the typical evolution of a successful client relationship," Singh explained.

Deepening customer relationships

Computer Science Corporation is a company that values and studies customer satisfaction. At CSC, five different client relationship levels are identified: vendor, credible source, solution provider, trusted advisor, and finally partner. The goal is to become a partner with most of the clients.

TRACKING CUSTOMER SATISFACTION. In CSC's *SatisfactionPLUS* program, during and after every single project, clients are interviewed as to how they evaluate projects with CSC. After some analysis of their responses, customers are rated, on a scale from 1 to 5, according to their satisfaction level. "With a rating below 2, we classify them as terrorists," laughed Jerry Materella, vice president of sales. "They really can harm our business. Ratings between 3 and 4 are classified as opportunists. Although they are satisfied with our work, they are not jumping up and down; they will continue to look for other services providers. What we really want are loyalists that rank higher than that. They usually stay with us for years."

> Customer loyalty is key for professional software services.

Materella explains that with business as usual, it's almost impossible to get a client from level 4 to level 5. "That's why we started *SatisfactionPLUS*," he says. He explains that at least every quarter, CSC surveys the satisfaction within each project and organizes meetings with clients to discuss possible differences between their initial expectations and their project experiences. The assessments, he says, affect how the customers are treated.

GOING THE EXTRA MILE. In 1996, for instance, CSC was asked to create a donation matching system for a big nonprofit organization that also did work in Honduras. The contract initially was worth more than $5 million. "Everything started out very nicely, and we had no problems with the technology," Materella explained. But at their first review, CSC realized that the client wasn't as happy as they had thought they would be. While the client was satisfied with the work per se, they felt that CSC didn't really understand the business and financial constraints of the nonprofit organization. The highest client satisfaction level was yet to be reached.

Responding, CSC sent a couple of the developers to Honduras to learn more about the client's situation in that country. "After my team had experienced all the constraints in this country, they had a much greater empathy for the people." They took all efforts to address the constraints. In the following quarter, for instance, they realized the project actually had to be extended to complete it successfully, as more functionality—and thus more budget—was required. With the trip to Honduras in mind, though, they applied new processes to reduce costs, while still ensuring some of their own profit. "For instance, we developed parts of the software in India, something we've never done before," Materella explained. "The effort paid off. Today we get all the business they have."

BEGGING CLIENTS FOR CRITIQUE. In India, Tata Consultancy Services (TCS) assesses customer satisfaction in a much more informal way—but not without the care and investment of CSC. Lal Singh, vice president of worldwide sales, for instance, travels the world constantly, meeting customers. "Getting feedback through questionnaires does not work. It has to be through personal meetings because people are usually afraid of putting things down in writing," Singh told us. He says he personally cares for about 60 top clients—and meets the top management of these companies usually every three months. He spends more than a third of his time outside of India for this reason, but he also invites clients to India to have a look at the research development center or other development locations. And every month, they come for a visit. In fact, one core client, a large bank in South Africa, has sent about 15 people in the last two years to see Singh's operations in India.

> **"Getting feedback through questionnaires does not work.**
> **It has to be through personal meetings."**

APPOINTING RELATIONSHIP MANAGERS FOR EACH CLIENT. Additionally, TCS invests in client relationships by appointing account managers, or "relationship managers," to each important client. The managers try to develop clear communications between the companies. "Account managers have a dual role. Not only do they serve as ambassadors to our clients, they also represent our clients to our organization," Singh explained.

GIVING TOUGH LOVE ADVICE TO CLIENTS. Although one would think that always pleasing the customer is the best way to increase customer loyalty and improve long-term customer relationships, our interviews offered a different view. Overall, successful professional services providers treat their customers very rigorously, not only in terms of pricing but in terms of accepting their wishes as well. Often software services companies, for instance, are faced with additional customer wishes that they feel are

> **Successful companies bid aggressively, demanding the highest prices they can get.**

truly unnecessary. Our data reveal that successful companies reject many more of these customer requests than their less successful companies—even if the customer is paying for those additional requests. This is because they are looking beyond short-term business, and they feel that they need to serve the customer on a long-term basis. Successful companies, our survey shows, also bid aggressively, demanding the highest price they feel they can get, while less successful companies base their pricing more on actual costs or the prices of competitors.

SOME OF THE QUIET GUYS
ARE GETTING LOUDER

If they advertise at all, the professional services companies do it carefully, and with a sense of restraint. The Web page of Andersen Consulting, the largest software services provider in the world, for instance, presents the company as "a global leader in support of the arts."[14] Indeed, Andersen recently announced that it will sponsor an exhibit at the National Gallery of Art in Washington, D.C., entitled "Van Gogh's Van Goghs: Masterpieces from the Van Gogh Museum, Amsterdam."

The German software services company sd&m has a different ploy. The company advertises only in magazines read by IT managers in Germany, like *Informatik Spektrum* and *Computerwoche*. One series of six newspaper advertisements used images from nature to draw parallels with software engineering. One page, titled "Reliability," had nothing but an egg shell with a hole in it and two paragraphs: one describing the reliability of an egg shell in performing its function in life, the other describing the company's performance in terms of software engineering quality. "It's about creating a positive public image," says Ernst Denert, founder and CEO. "Since we do not have any finished products, we focus on general characteristics of the way our company performs in projects."

"What do you mean—advertising?"

When we asked several services firms about their advertising budgets, several indicated that they didn't understand the question. Nearly a third of the companies we talked to, in fact, did not allocate a budget for advertising at all.

Some services firms say advertising is irrelevant. "In our business, market share is not important," says Malcolm Frank, vice president of marketing at Cambridge Technology Partners. "It is all about mind share. As many IT decision makers as possible have to be aware of our capabilities and really believe in us." Frank knows that standard

> **"In our business, market share is not important. It's all about mind share."**

product marketing approaches do not work in professional services companies. "Mind share cannot be achieved by broad advertising campaigns alone," he reminded us.

But if the software services world has been a quiet and restrained one, that world may finally be changing. In fact, several companies are already breaking the old rules.

Moving to more provocative tones

The most prominent of those companies starting to break the traditional rules is Andersen Consulting, which employed more than 50,000 people in 1998. It is the first software services firm among its peers to advertise so actively not only in newspapers but also in TV. The New York advertising agency Young & Rubicam has been developing a worldwide image campaign in 24 countries for Andersen Consulting, one costing about $30 million. The ad itself is highbrow—art figures dancing in a museum as a voice intones, "Imagine the potential of your organization if all the different talents play together in harmony"—but it has been effective. In Germany, for instance, awareness of the Andersen Consulting "brand" increased by nearly 300 percent after the spots were shown on TV.[15]

In 1998, Andersen went even further—revealing a global branding strategy with new logos and a fully rebuilt site on the World Wide Web. The company is even sponsoring the PGA Tour's new World Golf Championships and the Williams Grand Prix Engineering Formula One car racing team. "Our new brand identity is intended to be instantly recognized around the world and to sharply differentiate our firm in the marketplace," said James Murphy, global managing director of marketing and communications. "In an increasingly noisy and cluttered environment, we want to ensure that Andersen Consulting's messages rise above the crowd."[16]

Going on the air

Other companies also see the advantages and are starting to follow Andersen's example. Keane, for instance, launched its first image campaign with the slogan, "We get *IT* done," which wound up in *CIO* and *InformationWeek* magazines as well as in 31 airports in the United States.

Keane is even going on the air on National Public Radio's *Morning Edition* program in all 170 markets across the country. "NPR's listener demographics are of high interest to Keane; a lot of them are highly educated top managers," explained Larry Vale. And most surprisingly, Keane has sent 3,700 direct-mail packages to IT executives around the United States. Each box included a personal letter, a gift item, an executive brief, and a response card to send for white papers and further information. "A similar mailing campaign in 1994 proved to be very successful for us. At a cost of a quarter of a million, it generated business for us worth more than $25 million," said Vale.

Cutting through the clutter via advertising

"For 30 years, I've believed that customers buy from us based on trust alone," said Keane CEO and president John F. Keane. "But now I see that we have to use marketing. With an increasing number of competitors, a brand image is more and more important. Advertising is what cuts through all the clutter," he said. Then he excused himself: Keane needed to get to San Francisco, where the company was sponsoring its first-ever golf tournament.

Professional services may never again be as quiet, or as subdued.

RADICALLY DIFFERENT MARKETING APPROACHES, YET ONE TEAM

Overall, the key differentiator between software product companies and professional services firms is their marketing approach—as this and the previous chapter described.

While the race for market leadership rules the game at product companies, software services firms strive for building personal, one-to-one relationships based on trust. All their marketing activities focus on exactly that, from establishing mini-discussion forums with highly selective groups of invited CIOs, to service sales experts traveling four months of the year around the world to hold *personal* meetings with clients.

Successful professional services companies are experts not only in establishing trust with their clients but also in deepening it over time. Better business with clients for life is their goal. As different as product and services firms are, however, they are absolutely dependent on each other. In fact, in many instances they are the strongest partners.

8

GROW YOUR PARTNERS TO GROW YOURSELF

In January 1998, 500 strategic allies and sales partners of Baan Company, one of the world's large enterprise solutions software providers, gathered at the Sheraton Hotel in Washington, D.C.

As the group settled into their chairs and turned their attention to the podium, they were given great news. "Our goal is to reduce our own share in the total value of worldwide Baan installations to about 20 percent," announced Graham Sharman, then president of Baan Investment (now professor of supply chain management at Eindhoven University).[1] "The other 80 percent will go to you, our partners." That represented a significant change from earlier practices for the $680 million software company. Now it was clear that partners were a crucial part of Baan's strategy.

That night, Baan's partners were courted with even greater intensity than before. Chairman Jan Baan and President Tom Tinsley mingled at the buffet with representatives from Andersen Consulting, KPMG, IBM, HP, Oracle, Microsoft, Compaq, and many smaller companies. During the following dinner, Baan's top executives divided themselves up among the tables, making sure that all the invitees felt as if they were among Baan's key strategic allies.

"I couldn't believe they'd spend so much time with me," the president of one small software integrator company told us, noting that Doug Sallen, then head of Baan's Japanese office, spent more than 20 minutes with him, emphasizing the importance of their new partnership.

Two months later, Jan Baan arrived at another important company function, with another important partner. This time it was the industry's top leader: Bill Gates. Eight months earlier, Gates and Baan had formed an alliance, planning out several collaborative projects. Now, before 3,500 Baan customers, Gates promised the crowd that together, Baan, Microsoft, and their partners would create "a digital nervous system" for the world's business.[2] "Enterprise customers clearly benefit from this relationship," said Gates, "by lowering their cost of ownership, increasing interoperability, and accelerating their measurable return on investment."[3]

That sentiment was echoed by Professor Graham Sharman. "In this industry, you do not simply deliver a product yourself to the customer," Sharman explained. "You deliver a product together with two or three other parties. And together, the group determines whether the product will ultimately be useful to customers. Partnering is absolutely fundamental to the success of a software company."

And so partnering has reached a truly new level in the software business.

PARTNERING IN A NEW DIMENSION

Around the globe, software companies have realized the critical importance of partnering. Indeed, in our survey, we found that successful software companies openly admit that they cannot win alone: They rated the importance of partners for their flagship product almost 30 percent higher than less successful software companies did. In fact, partners help fill gaps in technology, speed time to market, and increase market penetration. Software firms even form new organization structures they call *partner webs* that can consist of thousands of informal, yet highly performance-driven partnerships.

Successful companies, we further discovered, realize that they must not only have strong partners but many of them. In fact, successful companies have on average four times as many partners, we found, as the less successful ones. Microsoft's Richard Roy, general manager of the $700 million[4] German subsidiary, told us, "More than 50 percent of our success is due to partnering." He's not alone in that opinion. In the *New York Times* recently, Cisco president John Chambers noted, "No one can do it by themselves anymore. The companies that do not understand how to truly partner will get left behind."[5]

Exceptional efforts to build partnerships

Reaping the benefits from partnering is not left to chance. Successful companies train and nurture their partners carefully. In 1996, for instance, SAP launched the "SAP Partner Academy"—the first "international institution of higher education" of its kind. Here, SAP consultants from *external* partner companies attend five-week training courses. The academy is truly global, with classes held around the world. In the Far East, for example, courses are offered in six different countries, with topics ranging from financial accounting to accelerated SAP implementation. At the end of the classes, the "students" take a demanding "SAP certification" examination.

SAP is not alone in helping train its partners. In our survey, we found that the successful software companies spent an average 1.4 percent of their revenues on training their partners, *75 percent more* than the less successful companies. In 1997, for instance, Microsoft had invested $600 million *annually* on training, certification, and support of partner developers, according to a report by the U.S. securities firm Everen.[6] That was more than 5 percent of Microsoft's 1997 revenues. In Germany alone, Microsoft plans to train *110,000* of its software and hardware partners, development partners, and customers in 1999, we were told by Richard Roy, general manager of Microsoft Germany.

> **Successful companies spend 75 percent more on training their partners than less successful ones do.**

If training partners is important, so is "pampering" the most important ones. Great Plains Software, the $100 million enterprise solutions company in Fargo, North Dakota, for instance, flies its top partners to the annual "Great Plains Inner Circle Retreat" at a luxury resort in the mountains of Idaho.[7] There, they enjoy four days of golfing, hiking, sunbathing, and dinners combined with a professional program.

Very large partner clubs

In addition to the quality of a firm's partners, the quantity is also important. In fact, important differences between successful and less successful software firms often pivot on the numbers of partners: *The successful companies had, on average, more than four times more partners than the less successful players.*

During 1997, Baan was signing up partners so fast that one day in April, a notice appeared on the bulletin boards announcing *twenty-seven* new global business partners, including such big names as Cap Gemini, Ernst & Young Technologies, Bell Canada, KPMG, and Star Solutions. The notice began with an almost humorous, "Today's partners include . . ."[8]

SAP, meanwhile, had grown to several hundred software, hard-ware, technology, and consulting partners by 1998. Microsoft had more than 600 of the leading software vendors as certified logo part-ners, and hundreds of hardware partners, adding up to more than 1,000 altogether.[9]

Smaller software firms also value partners. Start-up Intershop, for example, counted almost 600 allies at the beginning of 1999, includ-ing Sun, HP, Coopers & Lybrand, and Silicon Graphics.[10] Great Plains Software, meanwhile, had more than 1,000 implementation partners.

Equality of partners

In the automobile industry, it would be almost unthinkable to imagine customers deciding who would make the brakes or the seats for their new automobiles and who would finally assemble it. But the software business is different. Many of the partners hold *direct* relationships with their customers. That is much different from traditional supplier-manufacturer relationships.

In enterprise solutions installations, for example, customers have a range of choices not only among the software *makers*—SAP, Baan, Oracle, Peoplesoft, and others—but also among the software *imple-menters,* companies like Andersen Consulting, Ernst & Young, Ori-gin, KPMG, and CSC. If a customer chooses enterprise software from Baan and implements the software with KPMG, then both Baan and KPMG have established direct and largely equal relationships with the end user.

THE STRATEGIC IMPERATIVE OF PARTNERING

In 1997, personal finance leader Intuit faced a crisis. Its stock had plunged from more than $80 at the end of 1995 to less than $25 a share in July 1997. Founder Scott Cook decided the company needed to redirect itself from a stand-alone software company to an Internet software provider.[11] To achieve that, Cook decided to form new partnerships on all fronts.

In the first five months of 1998 alone, Intuit allied itself with 12 companies.[12] Most were companies that could pour information toward Intuit's new online services—companies like the *Financial Times,* with investor news, or Standard & Poor's, with company and market research. Intuit also signed up dozens of banks. By mid-1998, nearly 80 banks had established partnerships with Intuit to provide links to the online software version of *Quicken.* The banks made it possible for Intuit users to handle money transactions and bank account activities remotely via PC.

Further deals were struck with America Online for electronic commerce applications, CNNfn for financial news, and the Web browser company Excite. In the Excite partnership alone, Intuit invested $40 million dollars in equity in June 1997, to seal the seven-year partnership contract that would program and distribute a new online financial service.

"We've had to sublimate our ego and become part of somebody else's business," said the newly designated CEO, William Harris, Jr., in a *Business Week* article in 1998. The magazine commented, "It was either partner or perish."[13]

"It was either partner or perish."

For Intuit, the partnerships showed their first payoffs. More than 2 million users visited Intuit's Web sites in April 1998, up 60 percent from the previous October. And by June 1998, Intuit's stock had almost tripled to more than $60 a share.

Intuit is not a singular case. In 1995, Software AG, a German database software company with $550 million in revenues, faced substantial losses, and serious threats to its existence. "The most significant shortcoming of Software AG in the early 1990s was that no partner network was built," the new CEO, Dr. Erwin Koenigs, told us.

"In the 1980s, having few partners didn't hurt us. *Adabas,* our database, was in the marketplace years earlier than comparable products," he continued. "But in the 1990s, living alone in the software market is impossible. Our lack of partners was the main reason we didn't sustain the market penetration required." When the company installed a new board, it quickly created an "Empowered Partner Program" that heavily involved partners in sales strategies for the first time.

Apple is the most well-known example of a company that suffered from a "go-it-alone" strategy. In 1997, Apple's share in the PC operating system market had decreased down to about 3 percent, from almost 10 four years earlier.[14] For fiscal 1997, ending in September, Apple posted a loss of $1 billion—on sales of $7 billion.

Apple's existence was threatened. Cofounder Steve Jobs, who eight months earlier had returned to the company as interim chairman, made two major announcements on August 6, 1997. First, he formed a new board of directors. Two new key members would be Larry Ellison, CEO of Oracle, and Bill Campbell, then-CEO and afterward chairman of Intuit. Campbell reconfirmed that Intuit would continue to provide its flagship product *Quicken* for the Macintosh platform.[15]

Second, Microsoft would take a $150 million stake in Apple. Jobs himself had initiated this bold move, which made an ally of one of Apple's biggest adversaries. Said Jobs in a *Time* magazine interview: "Apple has to move beyond the point of view that for Apple to win, Microsoft has to lose."[16] Later, Gates announced that Microsoft would keep developing future *MS Office* suite versions and other tools for the Macintosh platform. "Microsoft has millions of customers who rely on Macintosh technology, and they can be assured that Microsoft products for the Mac will continue to be available," Gates said.[17]

Three powerful allies had expressed their support for Apple. The stock market reacted immediately. Despite Apple's poor financial performance, its stock price rose from $12 in July 1997 to almost $23 in September 1997.

The fast-growing software and Internet companies are mostly true partnering experts. Yahoo!, the Santa Clara, California–based

Internet company, for example, was founded in 1994. By 1998, it provided the most frequented Internet search engine with more than 2 million users per day. How was that possible? Only one year after its start-up, the two young founders, David Filo and Jerry Yang, started cooperating with Netscape, running their Internet search engine on Netscape's server platform.[18]

That was just the beginning, for they soon formed partnerships with dozens of other companies. In February 1998, for instance, Yahoo! formed an alliance with Visa for electronic commerce over the Web in order to reap benefits beyond portal advertising, for example, from transaction commissions. It offered Web browsers the opportunity to shop for anything from clothes to cigars over the Web—searching for items with the Yahoo! portal and paying for them with the "virtual Visa card."[19] In March, Yahoo! announced its next big partnership: "Yahoo! Online powered by MCI." All U.S. customers who applied for Internet access through the long-distance phone carrier MCI would automatically receive a Yahoo! Online Web home page from then on.

Yahoo! has since remained a master in partnering, with many additional deals.

Closing crucial gaps

Market leadership is crucial in the software business, as described before. To build and sustain market leadership, volume power, fast marketing, technology lead, and a complete product solution have to be maintained at all times—despite the fast changes in the software industry.

No matter how large, no one software company can achieve market leadership by itself. Gaps in product portfolio, market penetration, and R&D expertise spring up all the time. "Very often, the fastest

Gaps spring up all the time that only partners can fill.

way to fill skill and competency gaps is with the capabilities of strategic allies," experts Yves Doz and Gary Hamel wrote recently.[20]

FOCUSING ON KEY COMPETENCIES. "We only focus on those issues that we know," Lars Carstensen, application coordinator at Navision Software, the Danish ERP company, told us. "Partnering is absolutely essential for us to provide a complete product." Carstensen said that for instance, the company received its retail backoffice management software from Naviplus, an Icelandic company. Distribution and logistics modules for the software, meanwhile, came from Lanham and Associates, based in Atlanta.

Competencies in other software segments. Even the largest software players focus strictly on their core competencies. Databases for SAP's *R/3* systems, for example, are often provided by Oracle—a fierce competitor of SAP in the enterprise resource planning software area but in databases, a close partner. Why? One motivation for this has been SAP's desire to remain open for various database platforms; but the other reason is that SAP's main focus and expertise is the "electronic mirroring" of business processes, *not* the development of database software. Its partnerships with database suppliers, then, let SAP maintain its rigorous focus on its core competencies.

> SAP's partnerships with database suppliers enable it to focus on its core competencies.

Competencies outside the software business. Software companies generally are not skilled in hardware manufacturing; therefore, they must find hardware partners. Justsystem, Japan's big application software provider, and Sony formed such a technical partnership in 1998. The partnership works both ways. "It is difficult for Sony to develop all the products and technologies for the digital network," said Sunobu Horigome, president of Sony's Digital Network Solution Company. "Certainly, there is a need to have help from outside software engineers."[21] Justsystem's President Kazunori Ukigawa stated in return that Sony made an excellent partner because it had the expertise in the hardware market.

ACCELERATING THE TIME TO MARKET. Nice Systems, the voice record-ing systems software and hardware company that we met in Tel Aviv, partners with several companies, including Siemens, Lucent, and IPC, the American telecommunication equipment manufacturer, which has special ties to the financial markets. "Our partners have been critical for our extremely fast market penetration," David Ben-Ze'ev, senior VP of strategic planning told us—noting that the part-nerships helped Nice to market six new versions of their software in two years and helped Nice grow from $9 million in 1994 to $69 mil-lion in 1997.

Partnerships also help companies launch products earlier. Klaus-Michael Vogelberg, head of software development at Sage KHK, a German ERP systems provider for small businesses, told us: "Since we are one of the strategic partners of Microsoft, and are committed to making software that is Microsoft-compatible, we receive their software several months early—so we can build our applications faster on it." Vogelberg added that he held meetings with top manag-ers from Microsoft to discuss new "beta-version" software that was coming down the pipeline.

Such "beta-version partnerships" are common worldwide. In India, Mr. Ramadorai, CEO of Tata Consultancy Services, India's largest professional software services company, explained that beta versions give them a head start not just in training the 4,700 develop-ers on his payroll on new technologies earlier but also in developing customized software that links to the beta versions.[22] So partners cre-ate substantial first-mover advantages.

INCREASING MARKET PENETRATION. In the months before Christmas 1995, Scott McNealy, CEO of Sun Microsystems, traveled from soft-ware giant to software giant, trying to make friends for Java, his new programming language that would run on multiple computers "inde-pendently" from the operating platform. McNealy convinced Ora-cle—then Netscape—then IBM to use the new language and to promote it throughout the industry. Slowly, a critical mass of partners formed.

Then, on December 6, 1995, a fax arrived at Sun's headquarters in Palo Alto—sent by none other than Senior Vice President Roger Heinen of Microsoft, Sun's key competitor.[23] Heinen wrote that Microsoft would also license Java from Sun.

Partnering allowed Java to grow quickly and exponentially.

Three years later, the jury was still out on Java's future, but more than 750,000 developers worldwide were already programming in Java, according to IDC Research. By then, the language ran on 70 million computers worldwide. By partnering, McNealy was able to leverage the law of increasing returns, in which increasing usage of a software product fuels even greater usage.

Many start-up companies have also realized this point. Rather than face the "Goliaths" of the industry, the software "Davids" often seek partnerships with them. Intershop, the German start-up, is a good example. While Microsoft's 1997 backoffice software *Site Server Commerce Edition* represented some degree of competition to Intershop's virtual shopping software, CEO Stephan Schambach found ways to avoid head-to-head competition with Microsoft: "We build our software on the Microsoft NT platform. And that product segment is much more important to Microsoft than the backoffice site server segment." The olive branch helped form a good relationship, Schambach told us. "Furthermore, we moved our strategic focus slightly away from the mass segment that Microsoft is in, and towards more complex business implementations," he told us.

Microsoft wasn't the only partner Schambach courted. Within two years, the start-up built a network of 20 core partners and 500 sales partners. Among them were Sun, Coopers & Lybrand, Silicon Graphics, Siemens, CyberCash, and Hewlett Packard. "We lacked standard electronic commerce technology. Intershop was one of the early movers in this segment," Ulrich Modler, Hewlett Packard's European program manager for electronic commerce, told us. "We met them in November 1995 and were impressed with the flexibility of the management team. Two months later, we gave Intershop our first order, and a year later we also entered a comarketing agreement with them." For Intershop, the big names represented key market boosters. "These partners built our image in the marketplace," Schambach told us. "It showed others that the big players believed in us."

So partners create market volume, shorten the time to market, and allow focus on the key competencies of the software company.

But isn't that just like a traditional supplier-manufacturer relationship, the kind that car makers have had for years?

Not quite.

BEYOND WELL-KNOWN
SUPPLIER RELATIONSHIPS

Imagine the day when you could walk into an automobile showroom and custom-pick the car you want, choosing, for instance, an engine by BMW, seats by Recaro, shocks by Monroe, and brakes by Knorr.

While ordering a car like this is possible, according to experts, it is a rather futuristic vision.[24] But in the software business, that's how the market works today. In fact, it makes software partnerships radically different from classic supplier-manufacturer relationships.

New market approach: Customers pick a combination of partners

The invitation booklet for SAP's 1998 *Sapphire* user conference in Madrid listed *104 SAP partners*. Among them were the fiercest competitors in each business segment:

- ► ERP implementation consultants such as Andersen Consulting, Coopers & Lybrand, and Ernst &Young
- ► Database manufacturers such as Oracle and Informix
- ► Software implementation tool providers such as Intellicorp and IDS Scheer

➤ Document management software companies such as iXOS, FileNET, and Documentum

➤ Hardware manufacturers such as Compaq, Dell, and IBM

These competitors cosponsored the same event for thousands of SAP end users. Why? All these companies were jockeying for the favor of SAP's end users. "With the SAP Partner Program, customers have the clear benefit of choice based on individual needs," stated SAP's Web site in 1998.[25] Customers can choose between Andersen Consulting *or* Coopers & Lybrand *or* Ernst & Young *or* another consultant for managing the implementation of SAP's *R/3* software. The same in the hardware part of an *R/3* installation—users could choose Dell *or* Compaq *or* IBM *or* Siemens Nixdorf *or* any other hardware vendor.

Said Marty Hollander, former vice president of marketing and business development at Intellicorp, "We increasingly focus on the end users in our marketing activities, so that they specifically *ask* the IT consultants to use *our* tools for *R/3* implementations. This 'pull effect' from the end user makes us less dependent on the IT consultants' favor."

End users can assemble their favorite combination of partners.

So, end users increasingly assemble their favorite combination of partners for the implementation of the entire software solution.

It is a new level of partnership in the real sense of the word.

A new level of equality between partners

When we asked Professor Graham Sharman (formerly with Baan) what makes software partnerships exceptional, he explained that if you study, for instance, General Motors, you will notice that they keep their parts suppliers under tight control. Even the dealerships that sell the cars are tightly controlled. But in the software business, he explained, players depend largely on independent partners who are not controlled or owned.

This lack of control has its downside, of course. For example, if Andersen Consulting does not implement a Baan solution to the satisfaction of the end user, then both Andersen *and* Baan have a problem. An *implementation failure* of the Baan product makes the Baan *product itself* look like a failure as well.

"The value that your product gives to the ultimate customer is fundamentally dependent on the way in which the partners perform," Sharman explained, adding that perhaps 50 percent of Baan's perceived performance at the customer site is controlled by the partner. So the lack of control over independent partners involves a substantial risk of failure to software companies. Nevertheless, software executives are enthusiastic advocates of this system. "Entrepreneurship cannot be kept up exclusively in-house or in too-close alliances; there is also not enough management and inovation capacity available in most young companies to do everything themselves," Sharman explained.[26]

Software partnerships take place in many forms along the chain. But they have one point in common—an astonishing level of equality among the partners.

R&D PARTNERS: TEACHERS BECOMING STUDENTS. Big software manufacturers are ready to learn key lessons about their *own* customers from their partners. To extract this crucial know-how from them, a new degree of intensity in early involvement of partners in R&D has developed in the software business. This is especially true for enterprise solutions software firms and professional software services companies.

The joint efforts of SAP and Andersen serve as an example. In 1998, SAP and Andersen Consulting agreed to work together in creating new SAP solutions for the global utilities business. To facilitate the cooperation, they even opened "solution centers" in St. Petersburg, Florida, Cincinnati, Ohio, and Walldorf, Germany. These centers were staffed with software design and development experts of both parties. "Having Andersen Consulting's real-world experience readily available to our developers will accelerate the advancement of our product set," stated Peter Kirschbauer, program director of SAP's Industry Business Unit Utilities & Telecom.[27] Part of the partnership was also a direct software development assistance for SAP, according to Andersen Consulting.

Our survey verified the importance of partner involvement in R&D. The successful software companies we met rated their partner involvement in R&D as almost twice as intensive as the less successful companies did.

COMPLEMENTARY PRODUCT OR SERVICE PARTNERS. Autodesk, the San Rafael–based CAD software company, is among many of those firms that seek partners for additional products and services as part of their own solution. Robert Carr, former vice president in the AutoCAD market group, explained that the company seeks such partners when development is still at the 50 percent stage. "The early release of interfaces makes it possible for our partners to create complementary architecture design tools at the same time we do," he said. "So, shortly after our design phase is completed, our partners have their products ready as well."

Our worldwide survey showed that successful software companies *in general* announced their Application Program Interfaces (APIs) very early, while many of the less successful companies waited almost until the end of their development phase to announce the interfaces.

Professional service companies also partner with other service firms. TCS, the largest IT consulting company in India, for instance, formed alliances with such consulting partners as EDS, IFS (an ERP consulting partner), and Ernst & Young. Lal Singh, former senior vice president of marketing and sales at TCS, told us that Ernst & Young often provided the reengineering recommendations in consulting projects, while TCS offered the skills to implement

> **Successful companies announced their APIs very early in the development phase.**

the IT side of them. The successful cross-consulting partnerships have become a key project acquisition driver for TCS. "An entire 45 percent of our new customers are due to contacts via the partner consultants," said Singh.

MARKETING PARTNERS: MUTUAL APPEARANCE IN THE MARKETPLACE. The Sapphire conference in Madrid in June 1998, with its 104 SAP logo partners, was only one of many examples of comarketing in the software business. Another was the Yahoo! alliance with Visa, one that equally cobranded the "Yahoo! Platinum Visa Card." The multiple marketing efforts have paid back with an impressive 42 percent of U.S. households who were familiar with the Internet brand name "Yahoo!" in 1998, according to a study by NFO Research.[28]

Intershop, the virtual shopping software start-up, also used the logos of its big partners Sun, Hewlett-Packard, Silicon Graphics, and Coopers & Lybrand for promotions in the marketplace. Likewise, the big names have used their relationship with Intershop to indicate the breadth of their product portfolio.

Partnership marketing makes sense, the global survey showed: Successful software companies rated the intensity at which they involve partners in making product marketing decisions, almost 30 percent higher than the less successful ones.

IMPLEMENTATION AND MAINTENANCE PARTNERS: CRUCIAL FRIENDS DOWN THE VALUE CHAIN. External software implementation partners act as sales multipliers for product companies—especially for companies producing enterprise solutions software. Those ERP product companies that try to implement alone, in fact, often substantially limit their growth.

> **Companies that try to implement alone often substantially limit their growth.**

At a small German enterprise solutions provider we met, its regional subsidiaries both marketed and implemented the product alone—no external implementation partners whatsoever existed. Although the market was large, and some competitors grew into big companies, this particular firm was still at $18 million in revenues in 1997, after 14 years in business.

In contrast, look at SAP. By the early 1980s, SAP had started to outsource the system integration services, creating an alliance with Ploenzke—at the time a small German consulting company that is now part of the software service giant CSC. In 1982, SAP started another alliance with local provider Plaut, which was to support the accounting side of the *R/2* package. Both Plaut and "CSC Ploenzke" were still partners 16 years later. But in addition to that, the world's largest IT consulting firms had *also* become SAP partners, including Andersen Consulting, Cap Gemini, Coopers & Lybrand, EDS, Ernst & Young, HP, IBM, Deloitte & Touche, KPMG, and Price Waterhouse.

In the 15 years of SAP's existence, the number of its partners has grown from a handful in 1980 to several hundreds. At the same time, SAP's revenues grew to $3.3 billion in 1997, although—or *because*—it had not developed and implemented the software all by itself.

THE NEW ORGANIZATIONAL CHALLENGE

The true experts of software partnering have taken it to a new level. SAP counted more than 2,500 attendees at the second "International SAP Partner Congress" in Berlin in early 1998. Among them were representatives from about 50 key global partner firms in consulting, technology, and hardware; plus hundreds of smaller, more specialized or more regionally focused partners.

SAP does not necessarily maintain direct, regular relationships with these smaller partners once they have become independent "certified SAP consultants." These expert consultants serve clients during implementations of SAP software, as part of independent IT consulting firms, and largely remote from SAP itself. In 1997, there were about 20,000 of those independent consultants around the world—that was almost 50 percent more than the total number of internal SAP employees in the same year.[29]

But SAP is only one example of this new dimension of partnerships, centered around its *R/3* enterprise solutions software platform. Other software companies that also provide basic software platforms attract hundreds, or sometimes even thousands, of partners as well. Examples are Oracle and Baan, the SAP competitors, with their ERP platform, and Microsoft with its *Windows95* and *Windows NT* operating systems. Microsoft counted 225,000 developers worldwide in 1998.[30] They are individuals who write software under *Windows*, receive software tools from the Microsoft Developers Network, and who have acquired the "Microsoft Certified Professional (MCP)" title at Microsoft's Authorized Technical Education Centers.

Even small companies can have massive partner organizations. Navision Software, the midsized Danish ERP company, has 600 certified solutions center partners in 20 countries. Together they implemented 3,200 solutions for Navision in 1997, notes Lars Carstensen, application coordinator of Navision. Great Plains, the $60 million revenue enterprise solutions company in Fargo, North Dakota, has taken the partnering network to even larger dimensions. In 1998, Great Plains counted more than 1,000 smaller, localized IT consulting companies as implementation partners.

New management task

Virtual communities expert John Hagel III named these relationships *business webs*.[31] Baan publicly started to use the same term and named their partnership system the "Baan web."

How are webs with dozens, hundreds, or even thousands of partners managed?

But the large number of partners in the "Baan web" also posed a completely new organizational management challenge to Baan that any "organizer of webs" would face: How are webs with dozens, hundreds, or even thousands of web participants "managed"? How are the partners retained? How are new partners attracted? How is good performance of the partners ensured?

The short answer is: Software webs function not through partner contracts and control but rather through *incentives* for partners to join, to stay, and to act in the interest of the "organizing player."

Creating incentives to join the web, with increasing returns

When thousands of companies have to play together, they need a uniting force. The most effective uniting force is not control but a *common interest* on the part of the partners to pursue a mutual goal. Microsoft has been largely successful at offering value for other players to support its own goals.

Only a few years after Microsoft launched its object-oriented Visual C++ programming language in 1993, the company had become the largest provider of object-oriented languages.[32] Microsoft's simple, but convincing success recipe was to offer strong incentives for thousands of developers to support Visual C++.

INCENTIVES TO SUPPLY NEW SOFTWARE. Among other things, Microsoft laid open some of the source code of interfaces for the C++ tool kit to all development partners. That was an incentive for the Visual C++ developers to use the basic software and create their own programs that interfaced with it. In addition, the developers were encouraged to post their own programs—"classes"—on the Microsoft Developer Network (MSDN) for free use to other developers. The supply of programs increased dramatically. For developers, it meant a personal satisfaction to *post* their own classes on the site. "All my friends were proud when they placed their first class," said Dirk Anders, a Visual C++ developer at a small German software company. [33]

INCENTIVES TO DEMAND EXISTING SOFTWARE. For the developers, the "open web forum" meant an amazing ease of work, as it offered a large range of ready-made tools. In addition, Visual C++ offered a simple way to produce graphical user interfaces for the first time, with the visual tool *AppWizard*. "Our one core message at the 200 press conferences around the world was, 'It is easy to get started with Visual C++,'" Jim McCarthy, the former marketing director of the Visual C++ group at Microsoft, told us. The demand for Visual C++ soared because C++ was easier to use than nearly all other competing programming languages available at the time.

SIMPLE, YET POWERFUL PRINCIPLE OF SOFTWARE WEBS. The more players to join the "Visual C++ web," the higher the value became for everybody else—another example of the law of increasing returns: For users, the Visual C++ language became more attractive, as more programs were available for it. For suppliers of new programs, posting them on the developer network became more attractive as the audience (the users) grew. And for Microsoft, of course, the number of *Windows* applications increased as the number of Visual C++ developers grew who wrote software for *Windows* with Visual C++.

> **The more consulting partners there are, the more end users are convinced to purchase the central software.**

number of Visual C++ developers grew who wrote software for *Windows* with Visual C++.

So as each player tried to optimize his or her own success, he or she thereby supported the overall growth of the web as well—"invisible-hands economics." A similar example is the SAP web: The more consulting partners SAP has, the more users are convinced to purchase SAP software. And as the number of customers increases, it becomes more and more attractive to other software companies to join the SAP web and supply software applications compatible with SAP.

For the "kick-start" of webs, however, a "basic platform" for all partners is required.

A common platform as the center of a greater value proposition

The center of a web is usually a common technological platform. Partners can build their value proposition "on" it. SAP's $R/3$ enterprise solutions system resembles a typical web platform in two aspects. First, SAP offers opportunities for software product companies to link up to $R/3$ via standardized Application Program Interfaces (APIs). iXOS, the midsized document management company, is one of those product firms. It links its software directly to SAP's $R/3$ system.

Second, the $R/3$ software platform requires significant implementation efforts. This offers great incentives for the professional software services companies to join the SAP web.

As for Microsoft, thousands of web participants produce software that runs on the *Windows95/98* or *Windows NT* operating platforms. Some of these players, such as Sage KHK, the German enterprise solutions company, fully commit to the Microsoft web. Other players—over 600 companies in 1998—have less direct links. They hold logo partnerships with Microsoft ("Designed for *Windows98*"), but they often also serve other webs. Intuit is such an example, providing personal-finance software both for *Windows* and for the Macintosh.

Still others are "remotely affiliated partners" of Microsoft, producing software for the platform but without any established contracts or direct contacts. Netscape, for example, has not held a logo partnership with Microsoft for its Internet browser *Navigator* beyond the early program version 1.2, although it runs under the *Windows* environment.

Such loose relationships are typical of the software business webs. Intershop's CEO Stephan Schambach told us, "Our best partners are often those that we have no formal contract with at all—for example Silicon Graphics and Cybercash."

But despite those few formalistic control mechanisms, a strong performance focus exists among the players. Why? Because within the web and against other webs, only the best succeed.

SOFTWARE WEBS: FRIENDS AND ENEMIES IN ONE

As we contemplated the delicate balance between competition and cooperation in the partner webs,[34] we found a similarity in the animal world. "In a pride of lions, in which there are up to 20 members, its clearly a mixture of teamwork and competition," Dr. Pat Thomas, a biologist at the New York Bronx Zoo, told us. "By and large, the males are extremely tolerant of each other. They team up to protect their females and their prey against *outside* prides or outside males."

> **Within the web and against other webs, only the best succeed.**

Nevertheless, *within* their pride, lions also become adversaries: "Male lions *do* compete for the largest share of their resources *in* the pride, such as food and females," said Thomas. The competition goes so far that when a younger lion becomes too strong, it is kicked out of the pride by the adults. Similarly, the weakest lions in the pride can actually starve during times of food shortage, because they are not able to compete. It's Darwinistic: only the fittest survive.

Stiff web intracompetition spurs web success

Do software partners behave like lions? This story from the animal world is much closer to the software industry than the reader might expect. In fact, web partnerships function quite similarly. Webs are among the most competitive forms of cooperation. While all the web partners cooperate very closely in providing elements that promote a "larger software solution," they do compete against other software webs for the same customers and revenues in many cases (web inter-competition); and they also compete for the largest share of the "value pie" within their web (web intracompetition) at the same time.

Take the midsize companies IDS Scheer, based in Germany, and Intellicorp, based in the Silicon Valley. Both companies participate in the SAP web, offering process-modeling tools for *R/3* implementa-tions. By providing a critical element of SAP's overall solution, IDS and Intellicorp obviously both promote the SAP web, against compet-itors such as the Peoplesoft web and its solution ("web intercompeti-tion"). But at the same time IDS Scheer and Intellicorp are also competitors—battling for the business of the same end users ("web intracompetition"). "It's strange, but true," said Intellicorp's presi-dent, Ken Haas.

Price Waterhouse and Andersen Consulting are carrying out simi-lar competitions. While they are both SAP partners, they still battle for the end-user markets, as described in the *Global IT Consulting Report* article "SAP Battle Brewing between Andersen Consulting and Price Waterhouse" in November 1997. In 1997, Price Water-house was leading the U.S. market for SAP implementation services, while Andersen Consulting was leading the European market. And both firms were going after the worldwide leadership position among independent providers of implementation services within the SAP web. "The battle for global superiority will occur over the next three years," the article concluded.[35]

The intra-SAP-web competition is seen as generally positive: First, the SAP end users can choose among several process-modeling tool suppliers, and second, the intra-competition spurs performance and customer orientation. Says Intelli-corp President Ken Haas, "The com-petition with IDS has certainly pushed us in our performance,

Stiff intracompetition in software webs makes them intercompetitive.

because the better one wins. And it has also pushed us in our cus-tomer and partner orientation." He adds, "Since IDS is German, and

SAP is German, for example, we've also hired Germans and sent them to SAP's headquarters in Walldorf, Germany, to cater to our key partner's needs."

Projecting this principle to the entire web, such stiff intracompetition of partners helps sustain the web's strength in the "intercompetition" against other webs—in this case, for example, the "Baan web" or the "Peoplesoft web." Until 1997, SAP managed to hold 33 percent of the total enterprise solutions market, far outdistancing any other web, according to Advanced Manufacturing Research, Inc.

Microsoft and Intel, called the "Wintel" web, have also been successful by offering competing players the chance to write software for the *Windows* operating system. For instance, in the database segment, such fierce competitors as Oracle, Informix, and Sybase all offer their software for the *Windows NT* platform.

Two key roles to play in the web: shapers and adapters

Within the internal and external web competition, software companies take on different roles.

WEB SHAPERS LAY THE FOUNDATIONS. SAP (with its *R/3* software), Microsoft (with its *Windows* operating systems), and Sun (with its Java language platform) are all "web shapers," as author John Hagel called them.[36] Shapers establish these basic software platforms and control their key components. More or less intentionally, platform shapers such as SAP often establish new large webs with many followers who build their value proposition on these platforms.

WEB ADAPTERS BUILD ON THE FOUNDATION AND EXPAND THE WEB. Follower companies, or "web adapters," are attracted to webs for a share of the web's "value pie." If the value pie of the shaper's web is estimated to be potentially large at a later point, then adapters are often attracted in amazing numbers—even if the shaper is still very small and its future yet unproven. Take, for example, the web-shaping attempt by Pandesic, the SAP/Intel joint venture that started offering a unique e-commerce platform for small- and midsize businesses. Less than a year after its founding in 1997, the small venture attracted big followers, including Citibank, UPS, Cybercash, and Compaq.[37] Director of Partnering and Alliances Bruce Schechter "complained" half-jokingly, when we met him at the Internet Expo in Silicon Valley in February 1998, that "at each fair we go to, twice as many companies approach us wanting to be our partners as those wanting to be our customers."

Professional service companies Andersen Consulting, Ernst & Young, and others are generally web adapters because they provide services to implement a platform, but not the platform itself. Hardware manufacturers such as Hewlett-Packard or Digital provide the equipment in the software web. And additional software product companies often offer products that are complementary to the software platform, such as Oracle with its databases or iXOS with its document management software for SAP *R/3*.

BOTH SHAPER AND ADAPTER ROLES ARE ATTRACTIVE. Our worldwide survey revealed that the shaper role is *not* a much more attractive choice for software product companies than the adapter role. In fact, 41 percent of the successful product companies we interviewed chose the web *adapter* role (versus 50 percent web shapers). A good example is the SAP web adapter iXOS, a midsize German document software provider, founded in 1988.

> Being a shaper is not necessarily better than being an adapter.

iXOS faced severe competition from large U.S. competitors such as Documentum and FileNET. Revenues stayed below $10 million per year. In 1992 and 1993, iXOS received a partnership with SAP and developed an archiving module that links business documents with SAP's *R/3* system. iXOS revenues grew by more than 50 percent in the following four years. "The partnership with SAP was definitely the key point of take-off for us," Eberhard Faerber, the CEO, told us.

SOME PLAY BOTH SHAPER AND ADAPTER, BUT IN DIFFERENT WEBS.
Our worldwide survey also showed that successful companies often
play in multiple webs, being an adapter in one and a shaper in
another. Pandesic, for example, adapted to the SAP web in principle
by promoting SAP-based solutions for small- and midsize users. But,
by adapting the existing technology from SAP, along with technologies
from Intel, Citibank, Digex, and others, Pandesic also aims at shaping
a new e-commerce web platform for smaller clients, attracting such
adapters as HP and UPS.

SAP, meanwhile, is a shaper of software applications with its *R/3*
enterprise solutions software—but simultaneously is an adapter who
links into the "operating system webs" of *Windows NT* and *Unix* and
complies with Internet protocol standards as well. Thus, almost all
shapers also play the role of adapters, depending on the IT system
level.

But what does it take to play the shaper and adapter roles successfully? Which *actions* make a successful shaper or adapter?

Successful shapers give away a large share of the value pie to their adapters

"The growth of the company is determined by the growth of the web
around it. Without the web, market leadership cannot be built or
sustained," Professor Graham Shar-
man, then president of Baan Investment, stated.

ERP players give away up to 80 percent of their total revenue value to their partners.

That was the insight that convinced Baan to target 80 percent of
the total revenue value of the Baan
web for its partners. "There is a
takeoff point for webs, in which the whole web ignites and takes off to
success. This point, I think, is when partners hold about 50 to 60 percent of the share," said Sharman.

Over the course of four or five years, then, Baan guided more and more value share to its partners. While Baan did not shrink its own consulting work in terms of revenues, it *did* hand the bulk of the additional (and growing) consulting work to external players, to focus fully on the Baan ERP product development. IT professional services companies, such as Cambridge Technology Partners, Andersen Consulting, and Cap Gemini, are core Baan partners today. Additional software that was outside the core scope of the *Baan IV* software package, such as management reporting tools, was also provided by partners—for example, from Hyperion.[38]

"The key issue in successful partnering is a mentality issue. It's about having respect for the partners' skills, versus doing it all on your own," Graham Sharman told us.

GIVING AWAY A SHARE OFTEN PAYS OFF BIG. SAP, like Baan, also received only about 20 percent of the revenues created in a typical SAP *R/3* installation in 1998, a McKinsey analysis showed.[39] The other 80 percent went to partners, and with good reason: SAP's world leadership in the enterprise solutions market and its growth rate of 53 percent between 1993 and 1997 were largely reached through partnering.

In the 1996 publication *Global Strategies of SAP*, Dietmar Hopp, then CEO and now chairman of SAP AG's supervisory board, confirmed that it was the leveraging of its partners that built SAP's growth. Hopp explained that key goals in building the SAP partnership web were to "expand our market through the relationship network of partners," via an "increase in the range of the SAP product and service offers through the partner know-how."[40]

The video game market offers another example of successfully giving away share. A few years ago, Sony was far behind in the battle with Nintendo for the game market. Nintendo had a faster, more sophisticated machine. To tilt the tables, Sony decided to permit thousands of independent programmers to develop games for Sony's *PlayStation* console, even offering 4,000 software development tools and higher royalties to programmers.[41]

The result of Sony's partnering incentives? In the Japanese $6 billion game software market alone, more than 1,300 game titles appeared for the Sony *PlayStation*—in comparison to less than 100 for Nintendo's (faster) *N64* machine. Nintendo's president Hiroshi Yamauchi tried to discredit Sony's web strategy, stating that Sony would kill off the industry with all of "its garbage" products.[42] Up to 1997, however, customers seemed to have liked much of the "garbage." Sony posted record revenues of about $5 billion for its *PlayStation* in 1997, head to head in competition with Nintendo's results. *Business Week* reported in 1998 that Nintendo of America Chairman Howard Lincoln admitted its 64-bit machine had lost some market share in the United States.

The race between the two game producers was still on in 1998—but at least in terms of competing against a technologically faster Nintendo machine, Sony had successfully applied its "give-away-share" strategy, with incentives for developers to join the Sony web.

It can be extremely harmful to withhold significant market share from partners.

But those platform shapers that decide *not* to give away share, and *not* to offer market opportunities to partners, can indeed make webs falter entirely.

FAILURE TO GIVE AWAY ENOUGH VALUE IS OFTEN DETRIMENTAL. Take the example of the Apple web versus the Microsoft web. In 1993, Apple had revenues of $8 billion—twice those of Microsoft ($3.8 billion). But by 1997, the situation had reversed. Microsoft reached revenues of $11.4 billion, while Apple made $7.1 billion. To be sure, the figures are, of course, not directly comparable because Apple was largely a hardware company. But one trend was nevertheless very clear: Both companies used to be the stars of the PC business. Apple had fallen behind, while Microsoft had taken off. What had happened in those four years between 1993 and 1997?

Up to 1995, Apple revenues climbed up to $11.1 billion. But after that, revenues declined down to 1997's $7.1 billion. The decline began exactly when Microsoft issued its *Windows95* operating system. From then on, Apple's share in PC operating systems decreased from 10 percent in 1993 to less than 3 percent in 1997.[43] Heavy promotions were a reason for the success of *Windows95*. But another was Microsoft's policy of *giving away share to web adapters*—thus attracting those who would produce application software or preinstall the operating system on PC hardware.

Analyses of Dataquest, IDC, and Apple data showed that by 1993, Microsoft took less than 10 percent of its total web size of $66 billion for itself. This generous share, taken by partners, has not changed recently. Richard Roy, general manager of Microsoft Germany, told us in August 1998: "96 percent of the total value in our web goes to our partners that make PCs, microprocessors, and other application software."

In comparison, Apple owned about 80 percent of its $10 billion web in 1993, and it gave away only 20 percent to partners. It produced the operating system for its Macintosh computers, *and* the computer hardware, *and* even some of the printers and monitors. Since Apple did not give away much share to web partners, there were few allies fending off the attack by Microsoft's *Windows95* operating system either. Thus, Apple lost share in the operating system market, and since each operating system that was not sold meant one Macintosh computer not sold, Apple's hardware sales declined as well.

IBM's *OS/2* operating system also proved the necessity for followers joining the "web." *OS/2* continuously lacked applications from independent software developers. *OS/2* never took off as a real platform competitor to Microsoft *Windows*, and in 1996 it had less than 2 percent market share.[44]

Java is a more recent case. In 1998 some of Sun's partners began to complain that Sun was about to take control too tightly of the Java language development. In March 1998, Hewlett-Packard broke its Java partnership with Sun for that reason.[45] "Java can be a contender—if Sun lets it," *Business Week* commented in April 1998. Ruthann Quindlen of Institutional Venture Partners commented: "Java has stalled as a computing platform because Sun has less experience than Microsoft in supporting thousands of independent software vendors."[46]

In response, Sun went to great lengths to attract new programmers and promotion partners, greatly enlarging its list of existing adapters. At the JavaOne developer conference in San Francisco in March 1998, Sun's top executives, including CEO Scott McNealy, spoke extensively about the potential of a "mutual platform" Java. To lightheartedly prove that Java would have a future in many different applications, Sun executives even produced a coffee machine that could brew *Java coffee* based on *Java programs* that ran and controlled the machine.

So web success of shapers is heavily dependent on strong followership by adapters, which in turn requires "giving away value." Slow growth in the number of adapters leads to slower market penetration, lower speed of innovation, or bypassing of new technologies.

Slow growth in the number of partners is one key threat to shapers—and so is losing the most important partners.

Retaining key partners takes clear commitments

While webs often consist of many loose relationships without explicit contracts and much intracompetition among partners, it can be advisable for shapers to bind their important, difficult-to-replace partners closely to the web.

When Sony's *PlayStation* wanted to grab market share from Nintendo, they lured key personnel away from Nintendo's ranks. Yuji Horii, developer of the Nintendo success game *Dragonquest*, for instance, joined the Sony web in 1997, and made *Dragonquest*, version 7, for the *PlayStation* instead.[47]

Successful companies learn how to keep their best partners satisfied. Great Plains, the Fargo, North Dakota–based company, brings partners to its "Great Plains Inner Circle Retreat" for a long weekend at a luxury resort.

SAP also knows how to bind partners closer to itself. It starts with giving key partners the best booths at its big Sapphire User conferences. SAP is also willing to invest in its best partners. In April 1996, four months after Intellicorp began partnering with SAP, SAP took a 14 percent stake in the company.[48] Similarly, when IDS Scheer, which had worked primarily with SAP for 12 years, wanted to strengthen the alliance, SAP took a 25.2 percent stake in the company. "The new basis for cooperation will give both companies further impetus for the development of innovative information systems," stated Hasso Plattner, SAP's cochairman and CEO.[49]

SAP had invested in another key web partner and, by doing that, also bound the partner closer to itself.

Trust in key partners is good—sampling their performance is even better

For Microsoft, monitoring the performance of its *Windows* web partners is hardly necessary. In most cases, Microsoft can rely on the incentives within its web to produce good software and good revenues and on the intracompetition within the web, which allows only the good performers to prosper. Remote web partners, who may produce lower-quality software without the Microsoft logo on the box represent little direct threat because they are not connected by end users to Microsoft.

Successful companies monitor their closest web partners.

For web partners that are close allies, and especially those that might perform a critical piece of the value proposition, selective sampling of their performance is critical. The successful companies in the global survey professionally sampled the performance of key partners, ensuring that the *overall* value proposition from all partners remained strong, for example, in enterprise solutions. There were astonishing differences in this regard between successful and less successful software companies.

CUSTOMER SURVEYS ABOUT PARTNERS. We found that 75 percent of the successful software companies we interviewed continuously went back to the users and asked them in surveys about their level of satisfaction with their sales partners. This was almost *four times more* than the less successful software companies.

Great Plains, for example, saw these surveys as "a key driver of partner performance," as Don Nelson, who is responsible for partnership development at Great Plains, told us. "The *very existence* of these surveys is already a strong 'impulse' so that our partners continuously focus on superior performance," he said.

"CERTIFIED PARTNERS." Navision Software, the Danish enterprise solutions company, also certified its key partners. For software implementation, they held relationships with "Certified Solution Centers" and, for additional software, with certified development partner companies. Navision also takes samples of their key partners' performance. "We have software tools for testing the partners' software and graphical user interfaces, to make sure that they reach the quality standards necessary for the total Navision solution," Lars Carstensen, application coordinator at Navision Software, told us.

The global survey reflected the importance of certifying key partners, to ensure performance in a mutual IT solution. Seventy-one percent of the successful companies we met certified their key partners, compared to only 40 percent of the less successful ones.

Microsoft, for one, makes certification of its *closest* partners a priority. In 1998, Microsoft counted 13,000 "Certified Solution Providers" (MCSPs), as special distribution and product partners.[50] All of these partner companies were carefully screened because as Microsoft's close partners, they were also going to represent Microsoft in the marketplace. Selection to "MCSP Partner" status required companies to have several "Microsoft-certified professionals" on staff. In addition, Microsoft demanded "demonstrated expertise with Microsoft products, a significant commitment to Microsoft, established sales and marketing skills, and proven contributions to the success and sale of Microsoft products," according to the Microsoft partner Web site. "Only Microsoft field representatives can nominate MCSP Members for consideration as MCSP Partners," it added.

PRODUCT EXPERTS PARTICIPATING IN THE IMPLEMENTATION TEAMS. In early 1998, SAP announced "fundamental changes in the way SAP and its partners relate to each other."[51] This "Team SAP" approach increased the involvement of SAP in *R/3* implementation projects, including "partners' coordination and management of implementation time." In other words, while external IT consultants would still perform major implementation tasks for end users, SAP would provide one or more experts for the implementation team, in hopes that they would enhance quality and speed.

When shapers threaten the business of their adapters

To sustain growth, shapers continuously need to grow into new business arenas. Two growth directions are possible. First, they can grow *outside the current web*. When Microsoft expanded between 1994 and 1998, it either partnered with, acquired, or invested in nine companies in the television, cable, news, and movie business.[52] These new Microsoft segments obviously did not represent immediate threats to the current adapters of the Microsoft PC software-hardware web. Microsoft's partner and investment list included DreamWorks SKG, the movie studio of Spielberg, Katzenberg, and Geffen; NBC, the U.S. TV company; Comcast, the fourth-largest U.S. cable operator ($1 billion cash investment by Microsoft); and WebTV Networks, a company producing TV set-top devices for Internet access.

Second, shapers can grow *within the current web*. Expansion within the current web often means threatening the current adapters, sometimes cannibalizing them altogether. Take the famous *Lotus 1-2-3* case. Lotus was an adapter in the Microsoft web because the *1-2-3* application ran on *MS-DOS*. In 1987, Lotus still held more than 70 percent of the $500 million spreadsheet market.[53]

But then, Microsoft became attracted to the market and decided to compete against its adapter. In October 1987, after Microsoft had introduced its new *Windows* platform, it launched its spreadsheet software *Excel for Windows*. Four years later, IDC reported *MS Excel* had conquered 63 percent of the *Windows* spreadsheet market, versus only 27 percent for *Lotus 1-2-3*. And another five years later, *Lotus 1-2-3* had become a brand name for spreadsheets of the past. A more recent case has been the well-known browser war—Microsoft's *Internet Explorer* versus Netscape. The browser market became strategically important to Microsoft's own business. That caused severe problems for *MS Windows* adapter Netscape.

While the attack is not always so intensive, web adapters are aware that an attack *might* happen at any time. In that case, which strategies help web adapters win despite potential attacks from shapers?

PLAYING IN MORE THAN ONE WEB. Participating in several webs is a powerful way to diversify risk—and increase sales potential.

A good example is IDS Scheer. Despite SAP's minority stake in the company, IDS Scheer still intended to continue cooperation with other ERP vendors. The company's general manager Alexander Poc-say announced in an interview with *Information Week* in July 1997 that "we are also continuing to negotiate with Peoplesoft and Oracle about interfaces to their modeling tools."

Playing in more than one web can diminish risk.

Many other software product companies have played in several webs simultaneously, by offering their software products on *Windows, Unix*, and Macintosh platforms. Even Microsoft has offered *MS Office* for Apple computers. And in 1998, Intuit decided to continue making *Quicken* for Macintosh platforms.

Professional software services companies also play in competing webs. For example, the three biggest competing enterprise solutions webs—SAP, Baan, and Peoplesoft—are all served at the same time by the biggest IT implementation consultants—Andersen Consulting, Cap Gemini, Coopers & Lybrand, CSC, Deloitte & Touche, Ernst & Young, IBM Global Services, KPMG, and Price Waterhouse.[54]

BUILDING PRIVILEGED RELATIONSHIPS IN A SUBWEB. Close partner relationships, once established, can help protect adapters from the shaper's attack. For instance, Intuit has formed its own personal finance service subweb within the Microsoft *Windows* web. Between 1997 and 1998, Intuit built the more than 80 alliances with banks— such as Bank of America and BankBoston, and with other players like CNNfn. Although Intuit has been clearly an adapter in the Microsoft web, with the majority of its applications running on *Windows*, it has still maintained the market leadership against Microsoft—despite the fierce competition from Microsoft's *Money* software. Intuit's key strategic focus has been on leveraging the new relationships—in building its own personal finance web.

Professional services companies follow a similar approach. Keane, the Boston IT consulting firm, believes in leveraging customer contacts. "The customer contact is critical for us. From a strategic standpoint, it defends us from simply being replaced, for example, by enterprise solutions vendors against other IT consulting firms," Ed Longo, senior vice president of Keane's Information Services Division, told us. "The relationship with the customer stays long after the ERP installations have been completed. And when customers then ask broader questions concerning IT, they are right back at Keane."

PARTNERING IS TRENDY

Partnering in the software industry is likely to increase. New alliances will be built across national borders and even software components themselves, so that many partners can contribute small pieces to a larger software solution.

As Professor Graham Sharman, then at Baan, told us: "Partnering must indeed be in the DNA of your company."

9

THE
LANDSCAPE
OF THE
FUTURE

After traveling more than 2 million miles, and speaking with more than 450 senior software executives, we began to see the software industry not only as it is today but as it may be in the decade ahead. We saw not so much trends, but tendencies that will shape the software industry as it enters into the twenty-first century.

First, we see the industry benefiting from *enormous growth,* arising from new products and applications as well as further geographic expansion into new markets. In particular, we see the increasing presence of overseas companies in the U.S. market, as U.S. participation becomes a prerequisite for their success.

Second, we see *productivity gains* throughout the whole industry. The main sources of these gains will come from the continuing adoption of component technologies; outsourcing opportunities afforded by low-cost countries like India and China; and the use of fully digitized business systems, enabling close integration of suppliers, customers, and partners.

Third, we may see the emergence of a single customer interface, one driven by the need for simplification and easier integration. We will see a "productization of services," made possible by component technology, and, similarly, a "servicization of products," through the availability of networking services. Both will significantly speed the race for a single customer interface. Eventually, we will see *a new balance of power between product and service companies.* We may even see new players like Internet portals or telecommunications firms entering the software game and threatening the traditional software companies.

Fourth, we will see an *industry consolidation*, bringing further market concentration. But unlike other industries, where consolidation may stifle innovation and start-ups, the promise of acquisition will encourage software entrepreneurs (even more than the lure of IPOs) to jump into business, and out again, at the right price. Furthermore, as the industry matures and consolidates, we will see a reduction in complexity and increasing government regulation.

FUTURE GROWTH: NO LIMITS IN SIGHT

The software industry is already growing by leaps and bounds. From 1996 to 1997 software revenues jumped by 20 percent, led by top players like Microsoft and SAP (which scored revenue gains of 38 and 62 percent, respectively). Many smaller software players, meanwhile, grew at more than 100 percent.[1]

Between 1996 and the end of 1997, investor confidence had pushed the market cap of the top 10 software companies up 38 percent, to \$340 billion.[2] Almost all of this value was created on the basis of "intangible assets" rather than hard book value. With an average market-to-book ratio of 16, the top 10 software players reflected more investor optimism than almost any other industry. And the software CEOs agreed. Finding new growth

> **Managing — not just finding — new growth is the challenge.**

was not a major challenge for them, but more than 40 percent mentioned managing growth as a major challenge during our interviews.

Two major sources of growth

The software industry will see growth emanating from two primary sources: growth from new products and services and growth from geographic expansion.

According to IDC, an IT market research firm, the Internet value-added services era[3] that we have recently entered will create a huge demand for more powerful and flexible software. Over the next decade, as millions of multimedia Web sites are launched, new areas of functionality and value added services will emerge.

When this comes to pass, bringing with it virtual business systems, embedded software for thousands of common devices, and other innovations, the focus of the IT industry may move from dealing with platforms to making software products and services that will permeate everyday life.

NEW PRODUCTS AND SERVICES. New products, particularly those associated with the Internet and embedded software, will continue to expand the size of the software industry.

Internet applications. The growth leaders in the software industry today are suppliers of electronic commerce products and services. Initial emphasis had been on business-to-business transactions. But these products are already addressing business-to-consumer markets as well.

According to virtual communities expert John Hagel,[4] the numbers of intermediaries will continue to increase—ranging from Internet portals like Yahoo! and Infoseek and "transaction aggregators" like Auto-by-Tel or CompareNet. These new electronic commerce players represent a growth opportunity for software companies as well, which will provide the new generations of software as required.

The products will range from encryption software that ensures secure Web transactions, to agent technology that seeks and finds consumer information on the Net, based on personal preferences. The new software will better help companies track consumer behavior on the Web and even reward consumers for surfing to specific Web sites.

The Net also is the staging ground for the convergence of the "four C's": computers, consumer electronics, communications, and content. Microsoft, for instance, in its 1997 acquisition of WebTV Network, has taken an early stake in consumer-oriented access devices and access services. Siemens, meanwhile, recently reorganized and established an Information & Communication division combining $30 billion of business across the four C areas.

Embedded software: The "next unbundling." Embedded software, the kind found in TV sets, digital alarm clocks, and washing machines, is familiar. But today, the software is "hard-wired" into machines in specific integrated-chip circuits. They don't run on standard software platforms like *Windows*, and most cannot be upgraded or changed once "installed."

Artificial intelligence: Smart products will be the next object of software developers.

But hang on. The new generation of embedded software will run on standardized operating systems that soon will be available on a variety of appliances. These standard operating systems will attract innumerable software entrepreneurs, who will write the code that makes everything from toasters to refrigerators act with some measure of intelligence. Best yet, most of this software can be written for common software platforms, thereby allowing it to run on multiple devices. This will give software entrepreneurs vast markets for their innovations.

Embedded software, in fact, is the next "unbundling" of software from hardware, similar to the unbundling in 1969 of software from computers. Experts agree that this new unbundling has an even greater growth opportunity. Gartner Group predicts that the embedded software market will "literally explode over the next several years."[5] In fact, six times more high-end hardware devices with 32-bit processors than regular desktop computers were produced in 1998—more than 100 million in all.[6]

Consumers will benefit from these developments, of course. The new software will have easier-to-use interfaces, frequent feature updates, and a choice of applications. Higher quality and lower costs will arrive with more competition.

Setting the standard for these new operating platforms is a race that is already underway. Microsoft has been pushing hard to establish *WinCE*, a special version of *Windows* for devices with embedded software, as its next platform. Software applications like speech recognition and other functionalities are beginning to run on this platform. The importance of embedded systems for Microsoft was demonstrated at the company's 1998 annual sales meeting, when Bill Gates spent a third of his time speaking to his staff about embedded software. This was a bold gesture, considering that Microsoft had yet to produce significant revenues in the field.[7]

Microsoft's German headquarters recently displayed a prototype of one of these new devices, the Clarion AutoPC. While looking like a regular car stereo, it actually incorporates a computer that runs the *WinCE* operating system as a standard platform. Based on that platform, the radio offers customized traffic information and navigation systems, a wireless PC data sharing system, and even e-mail connectivity. All the features are controlled by speech recognition.

Many other companies are competing for standard operating systems for embedded software, including JavaSoft, Lynx Realtime

Systems, and British computer maker Psion. In October 1998 Psion formed Symbian, Ltd., a joint venture with Ericsson, Nokia, and Motorola. The three telecommunication giants who together account for more than 70 percent of global sales of mobile phones, will use the Psion operating system *EPOC* as the basis for new smart phones. Microsoft reacted immediately and built *WirelessKnowledge*, a joint venture with U.S. wireless manufacturer Qualcomm.[8]

Software companies once again reinventing themselves. While embedded software brings opportunities to conventional software companies, it also poses risks.

Who will own the customer relationship for embedded software? The hardware vendor or the software company? For the CarPC, Microsoft suggested an OEM model, which would give the car manufacturer ultimate control over which software is being used. Co-branding initiatives, or "Intel Inside"–like advertisements, could arise.

> **Who will own the customer relationship for embedded software?**

Currently, software companies frequently partner with other software vendors, services providers, and hardware vendors. But new embedded software will bring new partners into the market. The time horizons and management practices of automakers from Daewoo to DaimlerChrysler are vastly different from those of most software firms. The automakers, for instance, generally take three years to develop new products, rather than six months or less, as is common in the software industry. To address these cultural issues, Microsoft has established special partner programs for embedded systems.[9] Other companies will inevitably follow.

GEOGRAPHIC EXPANSION, ESPECIALLY TO THE UNITED STATES. Geographic expansion is the second crucial factor in future software growth. A strong global presence is already a strategic imperative for product companies. But for professional services companies, this will also become increasingly important as they seek to sustain their growth.[10]

U.S. vendors have been leading the global software industry from the beginning, both in product and professional services, as described in Chapter 2. Examples of U.S. leadership abound, from IBM's market share leadership position in mainframe operating systems, to Novell's in LANs, and Microsoft's in desktop operating systems. On the other hand, leading European players, like Germany's SAP, are still an exception. Out of the top 10 global software product companies, 8 are based in the United States; similarly, out of the top 10 professional software services firms, 7 are U.S. based.[11]

There are several reasons for U.S. dominance: U.S. software initiatives began earlier than in Europe, encouraged by government-sponsored projects like the *SAGE* air defense project, which was the largest software project undertaken in the 1950s. Later, U.S. software vendors were aided by America's creative and entrepreneurial business culture, an aggressive venture capital industry, ready access to the huge U.S. market, and the English language itself.

Today the U.S. market still holds some key advantages. Most important, the United States is by far the largest market for software and services. Americans outspend the rest of the world by a factor of more than 2 in terms of software and services spending per capita.[12] This is because the United States already has many more software-intensive service industries. It also has deregulated markets and a willingness to invest in new technology before productivity gains can be "proven."

> **Americans outspend the rest of the world by a factor of 2 in software and services per-capita spending.**

Overseas firms, in order to globalize, must penetrate the U.S. market. Professional services companies will increasingly follow their existing customers into new sales territories, whereas product companies will rely more strongly on partners with established operations and customer relationships in the new markets.

U.S. software companies, of course, will also have to continue to globalize. Interestingly, U.S.-based software companies are more aggressive than their European counterparts in exporting their products. The speed at which international language versions are made available by typical U.S. software product companies is 40 percent higher than that of most European players.

FUTURE QUALITY AND PRODUCTIVITY GAINS

A quarter of all CEOs and CTOs we interviewed said that quality and productivity are two areas where they seek substantial improvements. This includes general project management improvements as well as specific improvements in such areas as software module reuse and the use of componentware. Furthermore, managers we spoke with said that the fully digitized business system will probably deliver substantial productivity gains.

The fully digitized business system: an operational imperative

At last, the "paperless office" is approaching, although not in the same sense as it was envisioned a few years ago. The paperless office will mean more than simply avoiding paper. It will mean that digital data will be employed for partner and supplier integration, information storage, and customer relationship management—all carried out via digital channels, intranets, extranets, and the Internet.

For the software industry, which already deals with digitized products, digitized business processes will offer multiple advantages.

At Cisco Systems, many customers are wired into Cisco's electronic business network. More than 70,000 of these customers were registered users of Cisco's Web site in early 1998. Here, online users can place orders, view the most recent documentation, and contact product experts. In addition to providing higher customer satisfaction, the system also offers economic advantages. According to Pete Solvik, CIO at Cisco, more than 70 percent of Cisco's customers' product and technical questions are handled online.[13] The remaining 30 percent, which are typically more complex inquiries or situations, takes 800 network engineers to handle.

> **At Cisco, 70 percent of customer service transactions are handled via the firm's Web site.**

In 1997, Cisco Systems handled more than $2 billion of its $6.4 billion in revenues via the Net. In 1998, the amounts increased drastically again to about $6 billion.[14] Meanwhile, sales-force productivity has risen by 10 percent through the use of the Web, estimates Solvik.

Internally, Cisco benefits greatly from its digital business system. Cycle times and processing costs are lowered via the Net. And because Cisco has a special link with Stanford University, employees can even take courses online.

Figure 9-1 shows other uses of a fully digitized business system. Customers could become part of a company's "value chain," for instance, providing feedback on new product design. Marketing of software products could be more efficient, meanwhile, by reaching customers directly. The marketing could even take into account the personal tastes and requirements of the buyer, and software could be bought and delivered immediately via the Net. Customer services, ranging from fixing software bugs to maintaining software, could also be handled remotely via the Net.

In addition to customers, partners of all kinds will eventually be integrated into the business system, so that they can obtain current company information, submit change-of-order requests, contact product specialists, and alert the company early on to the presence of bugs. Development partners could be integrated "virtually" into internal development processes, submitting their part of the work via the

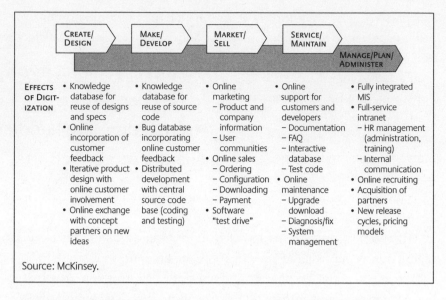

	CREATE/ DESIGN	MAKE/ DEVELOP	MARKET/ SELL	SERVICE/ MAINTAIN	MANAGE/PLAN/ ADMINISTER
EFFECTS OF DIGIT- IZATION	• Knowledge database for reuse of designs and specs • Online incorporation of customer feedback • Iterative product design with online customer involvement • Online exchange with concept partners on new ideas	• Knowledge database for reuse of source code • Bug database incorporating online customer feedback • Distributed development with central source code base (coding and testing)	• Online marketing – Product and company information – User communities • Online sales – Ordering – Configuration – Downloading – Payment • Software "test drive"	• Online support for customers and developers – Documentation – FAQ – Interactive database – Test code • Online maintenance – Upgrade download – Diagnosis/fix – System management	• Fully integrated MIS • Full-service intranet – HR management (administration, training) – Internal communication • Online recruiting • Acquisition of partners • New release cycles, pricing models

Source: McKinsey.

Figure 9-1. The fully digitized business system for software product companies

Net and participating in team discussions via Net-integrated video-conference systems.

Fully digitized business systems will also help many companies boost their knowledge management, providing a key competitive advantage. "Imagine the richness of our corporate memory," said Ernst Denert, CEO of professional services firm sd&m, "and the potential it has if fully distributed throughout our company."[15] In fully digitized business systems, with digitized business processes, it will indeed be much easier to track corporate knowledge, store it, and make it widely available.

> **Fully digitized business systems will facilitate a company's corporate knowledge base.**

In their book *Sense & Respond*, Stephen Bradley and Richard Nolan sketch a completely new value-creation model with a highly flexible and dynamic sensing of business parameters and changes, plus an immediate response to those signals—enabled only by digitization.[16]

Offshore outsourcing: productivity gains in India and other low-cost countries

Digitized business systems will also facilitate global operations. Outsourcing of development tasks and entire projects to low-cost countries like India, Russia, and China will be possible.

India has been the main country of choice for such offshore outsourcing, and with good reason: In 1997 the cost per function point of software for an average-size development project was about $895 in the United States, and $1,150 in Germany. In India, in contrast, the rate was $90.[17] Although this initial 90 percent cost advantage is reduced by travel and project management costs to 40 to 60 percent, this is still a significant potential.[18]

> **In the United States, the average cost per function point in 1997 was $895; in India, it was $90.**

Harvesting this potential isn't easy. Intellectual property disputes, bureaucratic governments, infrastructure limitations, and the difficulties of project management are common obstacles. If not addressed properly, these problems can obliterate favorable cost advantages and make an outsourced project even more expensive than an in-house project.

Nevertheless, global software companies are tackling these challenges. In 1998, about 160 of the Fortune 500 had already outsourced parts of their global software development activities to India, notes Dewang Mehta, executive director of the Indian National Association of Software and Service Companies. Companies such as IBM, Microsoft, Siemens, SAP, Baan, and Cadence have set up operations in India.

Ironically, India's software success has diminished one of its main advantages—low cost. Indeed, high demand for Indian software developers in and outside the country is reducing the cost advantage by 10 to 20 percent every year.[19]

Despite rising costs, however, India remains attractive, and it will remain viable for software companies in the future, if for no other reason than that the supply of talented programmers is so small elsewhere. After all, India has the world's second-largest English-speaking developer pool, with more than 200,000 software developers today and 50,000 new graduates every year.[20]

Other low-cost offshore suppliers include China. China has over 90,000 software developers, and the costs per function point were $74 in 1997, almost 18 percent lower than in India. Several new "computer science universities" are expected to boost China's software graduates to 200,000 a year.[21] The Philippines and Malaysia also offer alternatives and are catching up in terms of quality. Russia, the Baltic states, and Hungary are also enjoying more demand, although their software production costs are about twice as high as India's. Still, they offer a unique talent pool with specific technical and language capabilities.

Outsourcing opportunities will continue to grow rapidly, and Western software companies will need to learn how to harvest their benefits.

NEW BALANCE BETWEEN PRODUCTS AND SERVICES

Product and services firms depend on each other. Chapter 8 has explained how professional services firms like Ernst & Young implement software from enterprise solutions providers like SAP and how mass-market product firms like Microsoft use partners to market their software to millions of consumers. The importance of a balanced "partner portfolio" will remain in the future. However, the balance of power among the partners will become more complicated.

Driven by the customer's need for reduced complexity and less trouble with implementation, an increased demand for one-stop shopping is developing. Thus, product and professional services companies will enter a race for becoming this one shop. And new players like processing services providers, Internet services providers, and telecommunications giants line up for that race as well.

Two important events will affect the outcome of this competition: first, the adoption of componentware leading to a "productization of services"—the replacement of costly integration and custom programming by standardized reusable components.

Second, the importance of outsourcing services provided directly or via networks will increase. This will lead to a "servicization of products"—the replacement of product sales with subscription contracts for "all-in-one" service packages.

Together these events will have significant impact in shaping the future landscape of the software market.

One-stop shopping

Today, a complete software solution involves several players. This is especially true in the enterprise solutions segment, where vendor-independent professional services providers implement software products and build custom-specific networks. Large product players like SAP or Baan have hundreds and even thousands of these professional services players supporting their solutions.

Customers are demanding solutions from a single supplier, however. "Customers often want one single provider because it decreases complexity and gives them one company to blame if something goes wrong," said Kerry Lamson, Oracle's former vice president of applications product marketing.[22]

Software companies are responding to this demand. Some product companies, like Oracle and IBM, have built large professional services capabilities. In fact IBM's services arm, IBM Global Services, was the world's second-largest professional services provider in 1997.[23] In 1998 Computer Associates placed a $9 billion bid for CSC, the world's fourth-largest professional services company (with 1997 total revenues of $6.3 billion), but the bid failed. Instead, Computer Associates formed a new business unit, "CA Global Professional Services," and began building services capacities via internal growth and the acquisition of smaller players, companies like Reallogic, a Cleveland-based professional services firm.

Meanwhile, professional services providers are entering the product field. CSC, for instance, acquired Hogan, a provider of banking applications products, and Continuum, a provider of insurance applications, both with revenues of several hundred million dollars. Companies like SAP and Baan, which still rely on their outside partners, are also increasingly complementing this with their own services.

If customers increasingly demand a one-stop shopping solution, who will provide it? If product companies own the customer interface, they could tightly control professional services companies and even force service providers into exclusive contracts. They could say, for instance, "If you implement Baan ERP for clients, you cannot implement SAP *R/3*." Some key ERP companies seem to have the necessary market clout to establish such powerful webs. On the other hand, large professional services providers could use their existing customer relationships to gain leadership. Once they own the customer interface completely, they would be able to freely choose among various products.

> **Who will provide the one-stop shopping solution?**

The outcome of this race is still unclear and will be strongly affected by two important trends in application development and delivery: componentware and network services.

Componentware: productization of services

Componentization, the use of standardized components, will significantly change the dynamics of the software game. Like many other

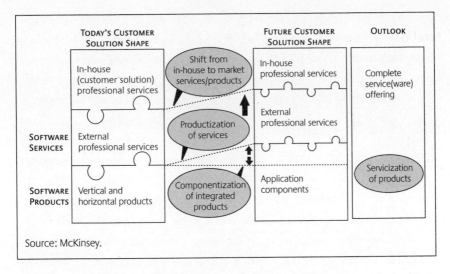

Figure 9-2. The shape of a customer's solutions over time

industries, the software industry is experiencing a "slicing" of labor, a disaggregation and disintegration of the value chain.[24] Componentware makes that slicing possible. With componentware suppliers can plug in software components piece by piece rather than purchasing a single, complete program from a single source.

PRESSURE ON ENTERPRISE SOLUTIONS COMPANIES TO MAKE PRODUCTS MORE ACCESSIBLE. SAP, Baan, Peoplesoft, Oracle, and other suppliers of integrated enterprise solutions see the monolithic and proprietary part of their business under increasing pressure. They realize that they must make their products more accessible and more easily combinable with other components. Most of them are already addressing this challenge. SAP, for example, plans to split its *R/3* system into 170 single components that will facilitate the customization and integration of its legacy systems and third-party components. Baan is doing the same with its *Baan Series*, changing it so that its core ERP functionality can be complemented seamlessly by its own and third-party components.

THREATS, BUT ALSO OPPORTUNITIES FOR PROFESSIONAL SERVICES FIRMS. Professional software services providers will have to look at componentware as both a threat and an opportunity. Their traditional tasks of intense customization, integration of legacy systems, and new developments will become less significant and even face obsolescence. Customized additions to a standard product, for instance, will be replaced by the addition of an extension product as a new component. Thus, the professional services business will become somewhat "productized."

> Componentware presents both a threat and an opportunity.

On the other hand, componentware could provide external professional services providers with a unique opportunity to improve their competitive position against in-house IT departments. Since external professional services firms usually move much faster than in-house resources, they can realize productivity gains earlier. Eventually, however, these productivity gains may have to be shared with or largely transferred to the customer.

"COMPONENT BROKERAGE" AS A NEW BUSINESS OPPORTUNITY. As an interesting side effect of these developments, a new genre of component integrators could spring up. With the wide adoption of component technology, custom-developed components could be marketed to other companies with similar needs. It is not clear yet who the component brokers will be. ERP companies are clearly best positioned for components that extend their own solutions, but professional services players or completely new entrants could compete as well. CrossWorlds, CrossRoutes, and Componentware, companies that provide additional *glueware* or *processware* for linking software with components, could play a bigger role.

The final impact of componentware will depend greatly on the emergence of component standards.

WHO WILL SET THE COMPONENT STANDARDS? In addition to technical standards, componentware needs "content standards." For instance, an accounting component needs to "know" *which data* it can expect from an order entry, and not just the technical format in which the data will arrive. Leading ERP providers like SAP and Baan, of course, are keen to establish their own standard and create a partner web around it.

Recent moves, like Baan's integration of third-party components into *Baan Series*, are strong indicators of that trend. Hyperion, a Stamford, Connecticut–based software company, for example, provides its budget management software to Baan. The ERP providers then "certify" the components, thus guaranteeing their compliance with the original ERP product. Altogether, this represents one significant step toward a single-source solution for the customer.

The dynamics of the componentware race are comparable to the race for the various operating systems standards. If a proprietary standard for an "operating system for businesses" emerges, its owners will probably benefit tremendously. This would give a major power base to the standard owners, at the expense of professional services companies and smaller enterprise solutions companies. And it would greatly help establish a customer interface for one-stop shopping.

Another approach is being pursued by IBM and its partners. Instead of extending a single ERP vendor's solution by other components, IBM is trying to build a new web of independent software vendors. Together with Swedish ERP provider IBS, IBM has developed the *San Francisco* project, presented first at CeBIT 98. *IBM San Francisco* is a "starter kit" with components for business applications development based on the Java standard and tools for the development of new components. It targets small- and medium-size software companies that do not want to develop *all* the general functionality of business applications but would rather focus on their specific core competencies.

By the end of 1998, hundreds of small software companies had licensed *San Francisco*, and several thousand others were evaluating it. The components they are building with the *San Francisco* tool kit comply with the same standard and can be reused by other companies. Thus, a powerful web of smaller companies is arising, embodying a functionality comparable or even exceeding that of today's ERP giants. IBM as a "standard keeper" seems to get higher acceptance than do ERP providers because the smaller companies do not fear competition from IBM in the applications business. "IBM only provides the tools," emphasized Stephen Ladwig, general manager of network computing and software at IBM. "We will not enter the applications business." The large ERP providers, on the other hand, do not give any guarantee that they will not enter the small companies' space sooner or later.[25]

> *IBM San Francisco components comply with one standard, so that they can be reused by other companies.*

Although owning the component standards does not necessarily mean winning the customer interface, it may well be a deciding factor in that competition.

In the same way that componentization will change the way applications are built, outsourcing via network services will change the way applications will be delivered.

"Servicization" of products

In the future, as broadband networking services become available, a re-intermediation of software providers by networking services providers becomes a real threat. A good example is the traditional outsourcing model, which partly displaces software companies by providing services to corporate IT directly in combination with software products. Networking services could do the same—with a much broader range than is available from traditional outsourcing providers.

OUTSOURCING: THE ULTIMATE ONE-STOP-SHOPPING SOLUTION? Outsource services providers do not sell a specific product or a custom-made solution. Rather, they take over parts of the client's IT operations and run them for their clients. In doing so, they bundle everything from hardware sales and maintenance to software integration, custom development, and maintenance. This is "classic" IT outsourcing.

Customers are increasingly turning to IT outsourcing. This tendency toward one-stop shopping will substantially affect the future shape of the software industry.

Services companies that are not providing outsourcing services face a real threat.

Services companies that are not providing outsourcing services face a real threat. They risk being intermediated in their customer relationships, becoming a subcontractor to an outsourcing services provider—or even being replaced. Thus, most of the larger professional software services players like CSC, EDS, or IBM also offer outsourcing services.

Software product companies can also lose their direct customer access to outsourcers and systems integrators. Most product companies, as a result, have learned to arrange themselves with these players in mutually beneficial partnering pacts.

BUSINESS PROCESS OUTSOURCING SERVICES. Business process outsourcing takes the outsourcing concept a step further and thus, offers greater implications. Here, the outsourcing provider not only handles the IT operations but also the complete business process, including administration tasks.

In the United Kingdom, the national passport agency has turned over its passport production function to Siemens Business Services (SBS). Application forms, signatures, and photographs are scanned by SBS into a database. The data pass electronically to the U.K. passport agency and, after scrutiny, transfer to a private, secure printing plant. In the United Kingdom, SBS has devised a processing system that could develop into a global market for passport production. For the passport agency, the benefit is that it can concentrate on its core competency: deciding who is eligible to hold a passport.[26]

This is mostly new territory for both the customers and the service providers. Quite often *business process outsourcing* (BPO) is offered by the same players as IT outsourcing. Perot Systems, which already since late 1991 has been handling the whole metering and billing process administration for a major utility in the United Kingdom, can be considered the pioneer of these new BPO services.[27] The fundamental idea of BPO, however, is about as old as ADP, which invented outsourced payroll when it began in 1949.[28]

BPO is an interesting option for vertical and horizontal software package providers as well. PMSC and Continuum have offered this quite successfully for insurance services. PMSC, for instance, offers BPO print services to insurance companies. This includes same-day printing of insurance policies and mail services, electronic archival access, and immediate-reprint capabilities on any archived document.

A CHALLENGE TO THE LICENSE-BASED BUSINESS MODEL. The most profound changes in software products and services may come as a special kind of outsourcing from a new blend of networking and application services. PC hardware is already being combined with software applications, as in a recent Dell offering, which offered consumers for a few dollars per month the "rental" of a personal computer that comes bundled with an Internet service package. Similar to outsourcing services, this is the basis for an attractive and lasting customer relationship. Marc Andreessen, founder of Netscape, said at a recent conference on the future of multimedia technology, "We are on a way towards free PCs and free consumer software. The money will be made with Internet services subscriptions and advertisement incomes."[29] Only a few months later this forecast turned into reality with free PCs being offered in a bundle with Internet service provisions.[30]

Thanks to Web technology, consumers can get software solutions without having to buy the software itself. "Call it serviceware," says Mark Gorenberg, partner at venture capital firm Hummer, Winblad Venture Partners. "It's software, but it comes to you as a service. We're looking at a number of companies that are implementing this business model. They may be keeping a database for you instead of your running it in your own facility."[31]

Network services provided via the Internet could be a serious threat to the established license-based business model. In taking on an intermediating role, they could mummify traditional software solutions as their "back end," thus capturing large chunks of the value. Traditional vendors are already reacting to that threat by offering their own network-based services.

Traditional product vendors provide their services via the Web. An example at the forefront is Intuit, which transformed their Web site into a service point, where customers can work on their personal finances online and even execute transactions. Currently, users need to buy a special version of *Quicken*, the personal finance software, in order to benefit from the new capabilities. But in the future there is no reason for Intuit to keep it that way. They might as well charge for the services rather than demanding an up-front payment in the form of a software purchase.

ERP players have also started to adopt this model. In August 1998 Oracle introduced a "rent-an-ERP" model delivered via the Web as a way to address small- and medium-size businesses. Oracle Business OnLine customers get the entire range of ERP applications together with product support and upgrades, data center services, network management services, and help-desk services—delivered via the Web. "For customers this means avoidance of initial hardware and software expenses involved in installing and hosting their own applications," said Don Haig, vice president of Oracle Business OnLine.[32] Other ERP vendors are joining the trend. Baan, for instance, took the first steps toward such a model with its combined ERP-*MS-Office* suite, starting at $99 per user per month (Fall 1999 prices).

Opportunities for Internet portals and telecoms to enter the market. Nontraditional players like Internet portals AOL, Excite, or Yahoo! might be very well positioned, too. Since they control the customer interface of the networking service, they could move beyond their current information and communications services to provide software application rental services of various types. Traditional and new telecommunications providers, who also control a customer interface (that of the basic network infrastructure access), also look at the market for software services provided via their networks as a future growth potential. A new breed of companies called application service providers is potentially transforming software from big, expensive, often nettlesome products into more affordable, easy-to-use services.[33] In this software services world, telcos may play a leading role.

ERP providers are well positioned as well. SAP, for instance, has 3 to 4 million individual users worldwide—users that log in every day. With that "eyeball-control," SAP is basically a portal itself and can harvest that potential, for instance, through multiple business community services offerings. The organization of a powerful procurement alliance through the linkage of small companies via their ERP system could be an intriguing example of this.

The servicization of products could rearrange the traditionally friendly relationships among the various software product, professional services, and processing services camps. Soon, some interesting constellations of product and services offerings may spring up, including a rich variety of IT and business process outsourcing services provided in conjunction with ERP providers. The ERP providers themselves are prepared for this through their strong brands and standards setting abilities.

INDUSTRY CONSOLIDATION AFTER ALL?

Of the top 500 software companies in the world, 137 acquired a company or product line in 1997, or merged with another company. Software M&A transactions in 1997 were up 30 percent from 1996, while the value of these transactions rose by 36 percent.[34] At the same time, the number of software IPOs in 1997 declined by 38 percent to only 80. These findings suggest that more companies are hoping to be acquired to build capital into their businesses rather than choosing the IPO route, which is seen as being more hazardous for many high-tech companies.

The ultimate implication of higher acquisition rates and fewer IPOs will be consolidation and increasing concentration.

In 1997 M&As were up 30 percent over 1996, and IPOs were down 38 percent.

According to Robert Strauss, CEO of Gedas, the software subsidiary of Volkswagen, the software industry will eventually consolidate similarly to the automotive industry. "Some 40 years ago there were 50 to 100 significant automotive suppliers. In the market as of July 1, 1998, there were 16," he said.[35] Looking at the software industry in the late 1990s, a similar development might be on the horizon. In fact, in certain segments where global leadership based on de facto standards exists, concentration is already extremely high.

Computer Associates acquired other companies rapidly in the 1980s, on its way to becoming a global leader. The acquisition list includes Capex Corporation in 1982; Sorcim and Johnson Systems in 1984; BPI Systems, Uccel, and Integrated Planning in 1987; ADR in 1988; and Cullinet in 1989—the latter alone for more than $300 million. Computer Associates continued to grow in size and performance, and it continued to pay heavy premiums for its acquisitions—for instance, it paid $1.78 billion for Legent in 1995. CA's biggest bid, however—its $108 per share cash offer for CSC in February 1998, totaling approximately $9 billion—has not succeeded.

Dutch enterprise solutions provider Baan also went shopping for rising stars and acquired, among others, Antalys, an order management software company, in November 1996. Baan also acquired Aurum, a sales-force automation software company, in August 1997. Compuware, meanwhile, refers to its many acquisitions in recruiting ads noting how the mergers have increased Compuware's size, performance, and resulting market clout.

However, acquisitions do not only hold growth upsides but carry major integration challenges with them. For example, "Baan focused on the logistics of harmonizing all its new acquisitions' different software systems. But melding the sales forces turned out to be the greater challenge." Meanwhile, by late 1998, Baan had announced workforce cuts of 20 percent, mostly sales staff."[36]

Higher industry concentration, more innovation

Rather than suppressing innovations, the consolidations seem to have the opposite effect among small vendors, notes Alec Ellison, a managing director with Broadview: "These people go into business to be bought. It's capitalism at its best. It's good news for customers. We're seeing such pace of innovation because of this," he said.[37] Some of these players do not focus on their own profits. "Creating revenue is a big distraction," said Arik Vardi, cofounder of Mirabilis, an Israeli Internet company, almost seriously.[38] Mirabilis was bought by AOL for $287 million in June 1998.

Acquisition activity makes new ventures want to set up shop—even if they normally could *not* compete with the big players. It's a contradiction of normal events, a paradox, that could lead to a unique form of "consolidation" in the software industry: a few large and powerful players, plus many small new players who *set up shop to be acquired* for their innovations. From a large player's perspective, this would essentially mean the outsourcing of R&D functions.

Less complexity, more government regulation

From a short-term user's perspective, concentration is advantageous: Since it tends to standardize platforms, it helps the user master the ever-increasing complexity of IT products. This complexity stems from the fact that most major technology platforms still exist and will continue to exist in the foreseeable future. Even the mainframe and the minicomputer will continue their life well into the next millen-

> **Concentration has its advantages: users need to master fewer IT products.**

nium. One obvious solution to mastering this technological complexity is to drop certain platforms, thus limiting the variety.

For the next few years, the user's choice seems clear: either accept the current highly layered system or increasingly move toward a more uniform, vendor-led enterprise environment. According to David Moschella,[39] users are choosing the latter: "Microsoft software is poised to take on the role within the corporate information systems organization that IBM's MVS/CISC/IMS had in the 1970s and early 1980s." Even though that does not seem like a bright outlook for the rest of the software world, it does open up opportunities for other players as well. Since "Microsoft's indirect [distribution and service] model does not allow for the close support that IBM always offered, . . . Microsoft will have to rely heavily on increasingly sophisticated partners," thus creating new opportunities for them. Whether or not customers will really go with a uniform Microsoft enterprise environment is not clear yet, though. The recent demand for Java and Linux environments may significantly alter what Moschella has predicted.

Responding to industry concentration trends and the need to "take care" of consumer interests, governments will increasingly become involved in the software business. Y2K legislation, the historic IBM and recent Microsoft antitrust suits, the debate on Internet taxes, and domain and privacy issues are all signs that regulation is finally hitting one of the supposedly least regulated industries.

The opportunities for success in this industry remain strong. But the pace of change brings new challenges and uncertainties. Neglecting these challenges could be a deadly mistake: falling behind in the software industry, after all, almost certainly means failure.

AFTERMATH

As we were writing about some of the trends in this fast-paced software industry, such as the digitization of business systems, they started to become a reality at a speed simply unprecedented. Internet penetration of business and homes seems to have taken off exponentially, and some of the wildest forecasts from our survey participants were "overtaken" in months instead of years.

Business @ the Speed of Thought by Bill Gates, published in March 1999,[40] is not science fiction. It's about a digital nervous system that is presumably as powerful as or even more powerful than the human nervous system. "Sense and respond" types of business systems,[41] which we consider to be the new operating modes for the 2000s, are already around, as Amazon.com, Yahoo!, Cisco, Microsoft, and Disney are demonstrating.

The revolution in interaction that several of our colleagues were predicting[42] is likely to happen sooner rather than later—"the 2000s will be about velocity."[43]

Given the amazing speed of change in the software industry at the turn of the century, is it worth studying today's secrets of software success? Will they provide any guidance and help in the future? We think so! Eventually, there will be "digital nervous system" infrastructures, "providing a well-integrated flow of information" and "distinguished from a mere network of computers by the accuracy, immediacy, and richness of the information [they bring] to the knowledge workers and the insight and collaboration made possible by the information."[44] We partially experienced this already throughout our research work. However, until corporations and consumers reach that stage, we envisage a continued need for skills like managing coexisting technology platforms and standards, handling data and information from different media, aspiring to unmatched levels of integration (the dream of almost every IT and business manager at least since the 1970s, yet most often reached partially at best), and accomplishing high integrity and reliability levels in information—a challenge that has increased dramatically with the increased use of the Internet.

10

STAYING
ON THE
BULL

So what is it— that secret of software success?

Many "small secrets" lie in the details mentioned in the previous chapters—from setting up global corporate partner training academies to PR-savvy sailing competitions on the high seas between the CEOs of the software giants.

Software leaders have become highly innovative in managing in an industry of extremes—where outstanding growth, wealth, and job opportunities are obtained by only a few real winners; where extreme uncertainty is intermingled with vast technological complexity; where talent is extraordinarily scarce; where low entry barriers constantly attract competitors; where product life cycles are among the shortest of all industries[1]; and where the law of increasing returns allows only the top-product companies to win.

All these "small secrets" are indeed key to mastering the industry's challenges. But beyond this, the more fundamental secret is in addressing all the multiple details simultaneously—not focusing too intently on one issue, not neglecting another.

The secret is in mastering a very difficult *balancing act*: Finding the right mix of actions *within* key management areas such as partnering and people motivation; finding the right level of management in each of the areas *relative* to each other. What is more important for software leaders to focus on, for instance: partnering or good software development processes? People management or marketing? Setting the right priorities is crucial.

STRIKING THE RIGHT BALANCE IN THE THREE SEGMENTS

Among the three software industry segments—professional services, enterprise solutions, and mass-market products—the importance of the seven main management areas (people management, assignment of human resources, software development, marketing, partnering, globalization, and service strategy) differs. Indeed, our global survey revealed that software leaders, depending on their particular industry segment, should put their emphasis on very different issues.[2]

Professional services companies: emphasis on people

Because of the scarcity of talent, managing people is crucial in the software industry. In professional services firms, this is even more the case because they involve people who not only develop software but who also go out and sell *themselves*—their competence, their ability to get the project done on time and on budget. It is no surprise, then, that

PROFESSIONAL SOFTWARE SERVICES			
Top Five Management Areas by Priority	Key Balances to Find within the Top Five Areas		
1 People management	Invest in developing and retaining individuals long term	versus	Focus on short-term profitabiliity by "utilizing people" efficiently
2 Human resource assignment	Spend time on future business and reputation building	versus	Ensure full capacity utilization
3 Development	Keep project schedules	versus	Deliver all features and top quality
4 Marketing	Invest in personal trust-based relationships and keep "professional touch"	versus	Invest in more aggressive brand building
5 Partnering	Tie up with many product partners and expand quickly	versus	Build up deeper relationships with only a few product partners, but slow the expansion
Source: McKinsey.			

Table 10-1. Key balancing acts of leaders of professional software services firms

our survey showed that people management had the most impact on the success of the surveyed professional services companies (followed by assignment of human resources, software development, marketing, and partnering strategy, as Table 10-1 shows).

PEOPLE MANAGEMENT: MENTORING INDIVIDUALS VERSUS UTILIZING THEIR SKILLS. *Within* people management, leaders must balance between utilizing their employees efficiently in the short term versus investing in opportunities for them to "grow" personally and to retain them in the long term. Top companies manage to grow and retain their *best* people. Their methods range from stock options and perks to the creation of an attractive culture.

HUMAN RESOURCES ASSIGNMENT: THE BATTLE BETWEEN SHORT- AND LONG-TERM PERSPECTIVE. Human resources assignment is the second key issue related to managing people in service firms. Of course, companies have to ensure that their people are assigned to revenue-producing projects. But they also must balance that with the need for their top people to market the company through attending conferences, writing articles, and conducting other public relations–related activities. Again, the balance must be struck between present and future performance.

> People management had the most impact on the success of professional services firms.

SOFTWARE DEVELOPMENT: BEING THE FASTEST, THE BEST, OR BOTH? Software development is the third key area for professional services firms. Better methodologies, team structures, and processes increase the quality of software products, reduce the time requirements for their development, and even reduce the costs. Examples range from simply investing time early in the design phase, to avoiding bugs later in the coding phase, to building team structures like those in hospital emergency rooms, to daily builds and software module reuse.

But even with better methodologies, software leaders must strike a balance between shortening time to market on the one hand, and delivering program features and the highest quality on the other.

MARKETING: FROM A PERSONAL TO A PUBLIC ISSUE. In the service business, leaders increasingly face another marketing-related balancing act. The question for leaders in the professional services segment is whether they should focus more on building personal trust-based relationships with clients or whether they should start building stronger company brands for better differentiation and faster regional expansion. Increasingly, service leaders are looking at building their brands with and beyond single customer relationships.

PARTNERING: FRIENDS ON THE OTHER SIDE. Service firms are also using partners to grow their markets—particularly partners that are product firms. Enterprise solutions companies, in particular, rely on such partner relationships. A decent balance between breadth and depth is another accomplishment.

Enterprise solutions companies: partnering imperative

The biggest enterprise solutions firms show most clearly that success is not achieved alone in the software industry. From SAP to Oracle to Peoplesoft, the market leaders have grown *through* their many partnerships. This includes giving away up to 80 percent of the value of their total solutions to their partners and by making them equal

> **Market leaders grow *through* their partners.**

allies in their customer relationships. It means involving them in everything from R&D all the way to software implementation and maintenance. Partnering is the most crucial management issue facing enterprise solutions firms in our global survey, followed by their service strategy, marketing, people management, and software development (as Table 10-2 shows). (The challenges for keeping balance in the last three areas are similar to professional services firms; thus they are not described again here.)

PARTNERING: MAINTAINING FOCUS VERSUS GROWING MARKET SIZE. In partnering, leaders must find the balance between giving away the optimal amount of power and revenues to their partners, while keep-

| ENTERPRISE SOLUTIONS | | | |
Top Five Management Areas by Priority	Key Balances to Find within the Top Five Areas		
1 Partnering	Grow the market, but share it with partners	versus	Focus on a smaller market, but "take it alone"
2 Service strategy	Grow revenues with products and services combined	versus	Maintain organizational focus on product business only
3 Marketing	Invest in brand and relationship building to reach market dominance	versus	Limit marketing expenses to raise profitablility
4 People management	Invest in developing and retaining people long term	versus	Focus on short-term profitability by "utilizing people" efficiently
5 Development	Shorten time to market	versus	Deliver all features and top quality
Source: McKinsey.			

Table 10-2. Key balancing acts of leaders of enterprise solutions firms

ing some for themselves. And more fundamentally, they must decide whether to build deeper quality relationships with fewer partners, which may limit their market size, or to share a larger market with many partners (while potentially offering implementation support to ensure quality).

SERVICE STRATEGY: GET INTO SERVICES OR STAY WITH PRODUCTS ALONE? The second key concern of enterprise solutions firms is their service delivery system. Enterprise solutions companies need customization and implementation services, and the question is, who should help customers implement solutions? Again, leaders face a balancing act between growing their revenues, yet risking the loss of organizational focus by going for both the product and service segment, versus handing of the service part to specialized professional services companies such as Andersen Consulting and Ernst & Young. Most successful enterprise solutions players outsource the bulk of services. But those that don't at least manage to strictly separate the two businesses internally, in order to address their substantial differences.

Mass-market software companies: prime marketeers

Software firms must grow themselves into ever better high-speed, high-impact marketing experts. They must often surpass the skills of traditional marketing-intensive consumer goods companies. In the product business in particular, where only *the* leading market players win, marketing excellence is the way to the top. In the mass-market product segment, companies must have the true marketing pizzazz—from staging impressive PR events, to advertising value propositions, to enforcing product cannibalization—to convincing millions of consumers to buy, now.

> **In the software product business, marketing excellence is *the* way to the top.**

The need for excellent marketing in mass-market software companies is followed by the need for excellent partnering, globalization, people management, and software development (as Table 10-3 shows). (Only marketing and globalization are discussed in detail here since the other three areas have already been discussed in this chapter.)

MARKETING: THE CHALLENGE TO STAY PROFITABLE WHILE INVESTING HEAVILY. Heavy marketing is key, especially for mass-market firms, but investing too much in marketing, to the exclusion of other neces-

MASS-MARKET SOFTWARE Top Five Management Areas by Priority	Key Balances to Find within the Top Five Areas		
1 Marketing	Invest in marketing to build dominance	versus	Limit marketing expenses to raise profitablility
2 Partnering	Grow the market, but share it with partners	versus	Focus on a smaller market, but "take it alone"
3 Globalization	Invest in fast international expansion	versus	Keep organizational focus and profitability
4 People management	Invest in developing and retaining people long term	versus	Focus on short-term profitability by "utilizing people" efficiently
5 Development	Shorten time to market	versus	Deliver all features and top quality

Source: McKinsey.

Table 10-3. Key balancing acts of leaders of software mass-market product firms

sities, has made companies fail. Striking the balance between profitability and marketing investments is a challenge for product leaders. The winners have found ways to address the challenge—for example, by having third parties do "PR for free" for their company, so they don't have to spend massive amounts themselves.

GLOBALIZATION: SPEED VERSUS COST AND FOCUS. Leaders in the product business must decide how fast to internationalize. This decision comes not after a few years of stable income but from the start of their business—literally in the first year or two. The race for market leadership, after all, is not local, but global. Globalization is costly, however; massive marketing and sales efforts are involved. Rapid globalization misses its purpose if financial performance deteriorates because of it. Thus, software leaders once again need to strike a balance between speed and profitability.

THE RIGHT STUFF

The task may seem daunting: finding multiple balances between and within management areas—balances that differ in various business segments and that have changing requirements over time.

With the advent of the Internet, the boundaries between the business segments have blurred: What clearly used to be software product offerings have suddenly become services over the Web, such as *Quicken*'s personal finance home page. As a result, management priorities are less clear and more capable of shifting.

> The Internet is blurring the distinctions between the three business segments.

Tackling the difficult task of finding the right management priorities and balances—despite all various obstacles—is a major challenge. It requires one particular asset—top people, from the CEO on down. Without them, winning strategies, from partnering to marketing, will neither be developed nor implemented. *Fortune* magazine recently noted that Silicon Valley's top talent is "widely thought of as the No. 1 factor in determining whether a company sinks or swims."[3] The people at the top must not only survive but thrive on uncertainty, speed, and talent scarcity. And their followers must make the (sometimes wildly optimistic) aspirations of their leaders happen.

> Those at the top must thrive on uncertainty, speed, and talent scarcity.

Together, top leaders and their followers must manage "riding the bull," as John Keane has described the software business.

TRANSFERRING INSIGHTS TO OTHER INDUSTRIES

Are all these management insights limited to the software industry? Or are there any principles that top executives in other industries could learn from the software industry?

Obviously, the findings are relevant for CIOs of larger IT user organizations in many industries—in fact, many of those IT organizations are as large as a sizeable software company. Yet, we believe the transferability goes much further.

When we talked to 50 top executives—many of them CEOs— from 10 different industries across the United States and Europe from the automobile, banking, insurance, retail, packaged goods, entertainment, telecommunications, pharmaceuticals and biotechnology, and petroleum industries, their answer was far beyond a vague "Maybe, why not." The managers emphatically said the software industry served as an outstanding model for them, with lessons that could be transferred to their own businesses.

Other industries are becoming increasingly knowledge based, like the software industry.

Why? Because as companies around the world become increasingly knowledge intensive, they find themselves facing similar challenges to those of the software industry.

Texaco's annual report, for instance, carried this telling quote from Peter Bijur, Texaco's chairman and CEO, on the cover: "I believe that the secret of adding value lies in energy. Not the kind that's buried deep in the earth, but that which is deep in our minds.

Intellectual energy is the force that fuels Texaco. And it is what makes us a true energy company."

That sentiment was repeated when we spoke with Roger Davis, managing director of Citicorp Securities' $1 billion global insurance banking business: "We are users and producers of information, the raw material of knowledge-based industries," he said, adding, "By definition, the software industry is one of the most knowledge-based industries. I would say there is a lot we can learn from them."

Indeed, a number of challenges that face the software industry are also critical to the economy at large. Attracting scarce talent is a good example. Dr. David Cole, from the University of Michigan's Transportation Research Institute, told us that car manufacturers were struggling to attract enough knowledge workers for the future more than ever—from top engineers to top software experts. Other industries expressed the same pressing concerns. "We are fundamentally a talent pool—we are dependent on very good people," Dave Vitale, vice chairman of BancOne, told us. "Software companies manage to get the best people. They build great organizations that attract excellent people, with their teamwork, flat hierarchies, and informal communication style."

Managing change was another concern. From entertainment companies to telecommunications firms, leaders looked to the software business for some guidance. Herbert Brenke, former CEO of E-Plus, the German cellular phone service company, said: "The ability to respond to change very quickly is vital for us as well, because the half-life time of services, products, and ideas in the telecom business has shrunk to six to nine months. Some software firms like Microsoft are excellent at managing this pace of change." Other statements mentioned partnering, rapid marketing, and effective team structures.

It gets down to the fundamental attitude driving many software leaders. "A key point about software businesses is that their executives manage for tomorrow, while we manage very much for today," Roger Davis of Citicorp said, and he added:

"You know, we often say 'Why?' and our friends in software say: 'Why not?' "

APPENDIX I.
THE SCOPE AND
METHODOLOGY
OF THE SURVEY

This book is the outcome of an extensive research project that lasted from October 1996 to July 1998. It is the final piece of a journey around the globe to more than 100 software companies. These visits produced 500 in-depth interviews that produced a large number of qualitative insights, a database with more than 200,000 quantitative data points, and hours of conversations with experts.

THE SAMPLE OF COMPANIES
AND PEOPLE INTERVIEWED

The companies and people interviewed and included in the research form three groups:

➤ We visited 94 software product and services companies for a full day and interviewed them in depth. A typical interview calendar encompassed about two hours each with the CEO, CTO, head of marketing and/or sales, and the head of human resources. All the quantitative data shown in the book are derived from these interviews unless quoted otherwise.

➤ Experts from academia, consulting firms, and 10 additional software companies (including Microsoft, already well covered in *Microsoft Secrets*) were interviewed on specific topics relating to the management of software projects and software firms. The main purpose was to collect qualitative data and deepen our understanding of the industry, its specific challenges and recent trends.

► Managers and experts from other industries were interviewed—including the automotive industry, pharmaceuticals, biotech, basic materials, retail, consumer goods, entertainment, banking, insurance, telecommunications, and the petroleum business, as well as academics in related fields such as growth theory. The purpose was to gain insights *from* other industries and to explore the transferability of insights from the software industry *to* other industries.

We hoped to understand the entire software industry through our research and travels. Therefore, following thorough analysis, we finally chose 94 companies to represent the main database.

The selection factors were:

► *Size.* In order to mirror the industry at large, we decided to look at both large and small companies. Large companies, of course, shape and form major parts of the industry. Small companies, however, provide lessons in innovation, growth management, and trends. And many of them have the potential to emerge as some of the big players of the future.

► *Geography.* Software is a global phenomenon—a worldwide industry. To reflect this, we chose software firms from around the world, and from 16 countries.

► *Industry segment.* We made sure to cover companies from the three main software businesses: professional services, enterprise solutions, and mass-market packaged software.

► *Performance.* In the software business there are of course many companies that are not as successful as Microsoft, SAP, or Andersen Consulting. To reflect this, we also sought out and interviewed less successful software companies. Only by looking at both ends of the success spectrum could we identify the differences between them and truly appreciate the best practices.

Taking all these factors into consideration, we visited companies in Austria, Canada, Denmark, France, Germany, India, Ireland, Israel, Italy, Japan, Netherlands, Luxembourg, Sweden, Switzerland, the United Kingdom, and the United States. Most of the companies were located in the United States, followed by Germany, France, and India (see also Figure A-1). Nearly half

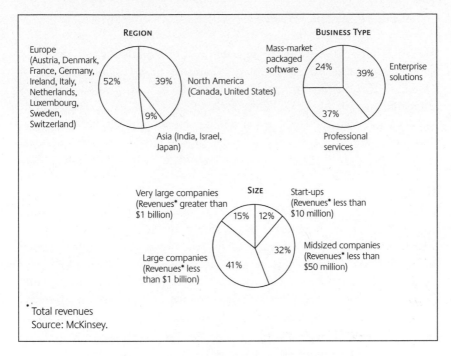

Figure A-1. Distribution of interviewed companies in the sample

the firms were based in such high-tech regions as the Silicon Valley, Boston's Route 128, Dallas, Munich, and Bangalore (India). Overall, we conducted interviews at companies in 32 different locations, traveling some 2 million miles.

Of the 10 largest software product as well as services firms in the world, 6 are included in the survey. Additionally, we interviewed 12 start-up companies, and a wide array of mid-size and large firms of the three main industry segments (see Figure A-1).

Interviews were generally conducted with the most senior-level managers. However, in order to compare data collected from smaller firms with larger ones, we often focused on specific strategic business units. Those units were either responsible for a particular software product (including strategic directions, development, marketing, and human resources) or offered services to a specific region or industry. Overall, we interviewed about 70 CEOs, 230 corporate senior vice presidents, 25 heads of strategic business units, 125 vice presidents of strategic business units and product managers, and, additionally, more than 50 experts outside these software firms.

HYPOTHESIS DEVELOPMENT AND DATA GATHERING

We began our research with the development of hypotheses and a preliminary questionnaire. After five months of research and an initial round of interviews with experts, we built a preliminary set of questions that was tested and only slightly revised thereafter.

Data gathering then followed, involving nine months of scheduling, traveling, and interviewing. Four major questionnaires, with different questions for software product and professional services firms, formed the basis of the interviews. They covered corporate strategy, marketing and/or sales, software development, and human resource management. The questionnaires included both open and multiple choice questions. Additionally, information was gathered about the internal cost structure of the company, the balance sheet, and its earnings and losses. Usually, two members of the team spent a full day at the company to perform four interviews with the appropriate people. Each of the interviews took about two hours. In addition, most companies gave us a tour of their research departments, "war rooms," and the like. At Tata Consultancy Services in India, for instance, we were invited to their modern development center, 20 minutes outside Bombay, in the midst of SEEPZ, the massive Indian technology park.

Overall, our questionnaire consisted of 200 questions that were developed on the basis of 80 hypotheses about successful management principles. Approximately 2,000 data points were collected per company. The overall result was a database with more than 200,000 entries.

In addition to the detailed interviews with 100 companies, some in-depth case studies were researched, and more than 50 expert interviews were conducted about hot topics, such as offshore development, componentware, and e-commerce. We also gathered information about the early days of the software industry. Furthermore, we tracked down several former CEOs who were no longer in business at the time of the interview simply because their software companies had gone bankrupt. This provided us with an opportunity to learn about sources of failures instead of success.

After more than nine months of data collection, we began to analyze what we had found and to synthesize some key insights.

DATA ANALYSIS

Our goal was to analyze the data to identify key factors for success—by determining what exactly distinguishes successful management practices in this industry from less successful ones. This led us to some important questions: What is success? When is a company truly successful? What is less successful? And how should success be measured?

Success measurement

After thorough evaluations, a decision was made to use a combined success indicator (common in many empirical studies). It included two individual success measurements, revenue growth and profitability:

- ▶ Compound annual growth rate of revenues between 1994 and 1996
- ▶ Average return on sales (before taxes) between 1994 and 1996

In other words, we decided that a successful company is one that had grown rapidly and had achieved a high net margin over a recent three-year period. On the basis of these two measurements, the companies interviewed were ranked according to their performance and were divided into three different groups: very successful companies (upper third), average successful companies, and less successful ones (lower third), as Figure 1-3 shows in Chapter 1.

In general, a very successful company in the sample grew more than 20 percent a year, with a net margin of more than 12 percent. The less successful companies, on the other hand, did not grow more than 10 percent annually, with a net margin lower than 3 percent.

A company could compensate for a lower margin, however, with a very high growth rate, and vice versa. If a young company, for instance, decided to sacrifice profitability in favor of higher growth, or if a larger company decided to aim for high profitability combined with controlled growth, they were classified as successful. In general, a company's overperforming in one criterion could compensate for weaker performance in other criteria.

But there were also companies in the sample that did not have to compensate for either growth or margin. Several of them, for instance, combined a growth rate of 40 percent with more than 20 percent return on sales. And, interestingly, such "outperformers" could be found in all three industry segments and on all three continents.

Test of hypotheses

After we classified the companies according to the three success categories, the top third were compared to the bottom third. Average companies were excluded from the analyses, so that the contrast between the successful and less successful companies would be sharper and less diffused by borderline cases.

Then the data were analyzed to test whether regional or industry segment differences, for instance, affected the results. For example, we asked the participating companies about their annual employee turnover rate. With this data, we first calculated the average turnover rate among the top-performing companies versus that of the less successful companies. We found that while a firm's turnover rate does not correlate with the success of the company or the business type, the turnover rate does correlate with the region. North American companies, for instance, had an average personnel turnover rate three times higher than that of European companies.

Hundreds of other data points were tested in a similar way.

APPENDIX II.
SOFTWARE HISTORY
AN OVERVIEW

It is surprising to realize that the history of software runs back 50 years—a half century of development that most of us assume is a modern-day phenomenon. Looking back, one can find the players that are still active today, and the roots of a business that is changing the way industries work around the world.

The software business has unfolded in stages: first, the big, custom-tailored software projects; second, the appearance of independent software products; third, the rise of the enterprise solutions players; and finally the rise of the "shrink-wrapped" software for the mass market (see also Figure A-1).

ERA 1: EARLY PROFESSIONAL SERVICES FIRMS, 1949 THROUGH 1959

Summary

The first vendor-independent software companies were professional software services that developed tailor-made solutions for individual customers. In the United States, this development was facilitated by several big software projects underwritten by the U.S. government and later by several large U.S. corporations. These megaprojects provided important learning opportunities for the first independent U.S. software services firms and gave the United States an early lead in the software industry.

The *SAGE* system, for example, which was developed between 1949 and 1962, was the first very large computer project, with a

1949 through
1962: The
SAGE air
defense
project

total cost eventually amounting to $8 billion.[1] In 1959, Rand Corporation established an independent company, System Development Corporation (SDC), to further develop the software that was estimated to need 1 million lines of code.

The *SAGE* software development program became one of the great "heroic" undertakings in the development of software engineering. At a time when the number of programmers in the United States consisted of about 1,200 people, 700 worked for the *SAGE* project.[2]

1954 through
1964:
Development
of the *SABRE*
reservation
system

In 1954, when American Airlines asked IBM to develop the *SABRE* airline reservation system, the first industry-sponsored software project was launched, one that employed about 200 software engineers and cost $30 million.[3] It was completed in 1964. The system has since grown to a network of over 30,000 travel agencies and 3 million online consumers.[4]

Early
supremacy of
the U.S.
software
industry

The *SAGE* and *SABRE* systems both became "universities for programmers." Afterward many of the programmers spread out across the country, starting their own companies with the knowledge learned at these big projects. As there were no comparable European or Asian equivalents of these big projects, they laid the foundation for the supremacy of the U.S. software industry.

Although mainframe computer manufacturers undertook major software projects for their biggest customers, they did not have the adequate resources to develop software for medium-size customers. It was this market vacuum that the first programming entrepreneurs rushed to fill.

The first
software
company

In 1955, at a time when the term *software* had not even been coined (it first came into use in about 1959),[5] two former IBM colleagues founded Computer Usage Company (CUC), considered the world's first vendor-independent computer software (programming) services company.[6] With $40,000 in start-up capital, they began offering software services for more than one hardware platform.

CUC's first
projects

CUC's first project, completed in 1955 for California Research Corporation, was a program that would simulate the flow of oil. They subsequently developed software for insurance and retail chain companies. All were custom-made for one customer at a time.

By 1959, CUC had 59 employees, and the following year it went public. By end of 1967, the company had 12 offices around the country and more than 700 employees.[7]

Soon afterward, other enterpreneurs followed the example of CUC. Computer Sciences Corporation (CSC), for instance, was founded in 1959 by Fletcher Jones and Roy Nutt. By 1963, CSC was the largest independent computer services firm, with revenues approaching $4 million. In 1997, CSC was still one of the largest software services firms worldwide, with total revenues of $6.3 billion.

Others followed soon afterward.

Other successful companies founded in this era were Applied Data Research in 1959; EDS in 1962; Management Science America (MSA) in 1963 (which shifted its emphasis to software products after a bankruptcy in the early 1970s); California Analysis Centers, Inc. (CACI) in 1962; and Keane in 1965. Most are still in business.

In the first half of the 1960s, the software services industry boomed. The speed, size, and number of computers had all grown enormously. This created a software-hungry environment in which computer manufacturers contracted out much of their own software development. CUC, for example, had a team of 20 programmers working on software for IBM's System/360, and CSC was a major software subcontractor to Honeywell.

Professional software services firms boom in early 1960s.

By 1965, there were about 45 major software contractors in the United States. Some employed more than a hundred programmers and had annual revenues ranging to $100 million.[8] Beneath them lay numerous small software contractors, typically with just a few programmers. In 1967, it was estimated that there were 2,800 software services firms in the United States.[9]

In Europe several major software contractors also developed during the 1950s and 1960s, but in general, years later than such development occurred in the United States.

Europe stays behind.

In France, for example, SEMA was formed in 1958 as a joint venture between the Marcel Loichot management consultancy and the Banque de Paris.[10] Early customers included the oil- and sugar-refining industries, the natural gas industry, the nuclear power industry, and defense agencies. The specialized local knowledge required in many of these applications, or the fact that they were defense related, effectively excluded overseas competition. By the early 1960s, SEMA already had some 120 employees.[11]

SEMA

In Britain, besides several computer services firms, two major software services firms were established in the 1960s: Computer Analysts and Programmers (CAP) in 1962, which merged in 1988 with SEMA into the Sema Group; and Logica in 1969, which was

CAP and Logica

involved in 1970 in a major project for the European end of a hotel reservation system being built in the United States by Planning Research Corporation. Both companies are active today.

ERA 2: EARLY SOFTWARE PRODUCT COMPANIES, 1959 THROUGH 1969

Summary

Ten years after the founding of the first independent software services firm, the first software products appeared. These were developed specifically for repeated sales to more than one customer. A new type of software company was born, one that required different management techniques.

First software products custom-made or offered for free

In the 1960s, the conventional wisdom was that no one could make money selling software alone. It had to be written specifically for each customer or given away by the manufacturer of the computer.[12]

IBM, for instance, had *CFO (Consolidated Functions Ordinary)*, a program for insurance companies that was included with its computer 1401. The *CFO* package gained widespread acceptance by 1964, actually becoming the most successful insurance software package ever.

Most computer executives believed there would never be a significant market for software products. But a few entrepreneurs disagreed. They believed that it was possible to write software for multiple reuse that could be sold *off-the-shelf* to hundreds of customers.

ADR, the first software product company

In 1964, hardware vendor RCA approached ADR, founded in 1959 by seven programmers, to develop a flowcharting program that would visually represent the logical flow of instructions in a program. Eventually, this piece of software became the first true software product that not only was sold off the shelf to many users over and over again but also resulted in a company that was organized around the development and marketing of software products.

Autoflow's success

Since RCA showed no interest in the program, ADR tried to get back the initial investment of about $10,000 by licensing it directly to the 100 users of RCA 501 computers. But only two users bought the program at its selling price of $2,400. Shifting its strategy, ADR then rewrote the program for the IBM 1401 and later again for the IBM /360 system. This was a success, and within a few years thousands of IBM computers used the ADR software.

In March 1962, three employees of Ramo-Wooldridge Corporation founded Informatics, a firm that became famous for the development of a software product called *Mark IV*. The new software was introduced in November 1967, selling for $30,000. Within a year, sales were over $1 million. Later it became the first software product with cumulative sales of more than $100 million.

The most successful software product for a long time: *Mark IV*

One of the major challenges faced by Informatics was determining what to include in the selling price. Influenced by IBM's policy to include a substantial amount of customer service in the price of its computers, Informatics initially provided free product maintenance and upgrades. After about four years, however, Informatics saw the real cost of these services and began to charge for them.

How to price a software product?

Concerned about unauthorized copying of the product, both ADR and Informatics searched for a way to protect their proprietary interests.

How to protect a software product?

Martin Goetz, product manager at ADR, decided to file for a patent for *Autoflow*; it became the first patented software product.[13]

The first software patent

Informatics, meanwhile, developed a licensing agreement which gave the customer perpetual permission to use the software—but ownership of the program code remained with Informatics. This became the model for the software industry, and, with very few exceptions, it is still used today.

The first software licensing agreement

These software pioneers of the 1960s set foundations that still exist today. They include the basic concept of a software product; its pricing; its maintenance; and its means of legal protection. Furthermore, they demonstrated that software projects and the software product enterprises are two very different businesses.

The software product business, however, was still in its infancy. In as late as 1970, software product sales were estimated to be no more than $200 million.[14]

IBM set the ground for a much larger software industry. In April 1964, it introduced the IBM /360 system, the first "family" of computers to use interchangeable software and peripheral equipment. Quickly it became the first stable industry-standard platform, with a consistent market share in 1969 to 1971 of about 80 percent.

IBM/ 360: The first industry-standard platform

Now a company could write a software program that would run on about 50,000 computers. It was also a big winner for IBM. The System/360 brought in a total of $16 billion in revenues and $6 billion of profits for the company.[15]

Despite this industry standard, most of the software was still developed by IBM—and was included free with the hardware.

ERA 3: EMERGENCE OF STRONG INDEPENDENT ENTERPRISE SOLUTIONS PROVIDERS, 1969 THROUGH 1981

Summary

IBM's decision to price software separately from its hardware rejustified the independence of the software business. In the following years, more and more independent software companies sprang up, offering new products for all sizes of enterprises—products that were seen as superior to those of the hardware vendors. Eventually, customers began to source their software from vendors other than the hardware companies and actually to pay for it.

IBM's unbundling decision

At the end of the 1960s, it was IBM that once again accelerated the development of the independent software industry. On June 23, 1969, the company announced that from January 1970 onward it would price its software and services separately from its hardware. While it has never been firmly established whether antitrust pressure or business strategy lay behind the decision, the impact on the emerging software industry was substantial.

Although software products had emerged well before 1969, IBM's "unbundling" made it easier for independent software companies to develop and market their products. After all, customers now had to pay for software, even if it came from their hardware vendor.

The applications market for insurance companies

The software applications market for the insurance industry was one of the very first to be changed by IBM's unbundling decision.[16] Before 1969, insurance companies either developed their own solutions or used IBM's *CFO '62* (*Consolidated Functions Ordinary*) that came bundled with its hardware. This left little room for independent software product companies. After IBM's unbundling decision, however, new software players arose almost immediately. Cybertek Computer Products, for instance, was founded in 1969 by a team that included a member of the IBM programming team of the *CFO '62*. Another example is Tractor Computering Corporation (TCC), founded in 1969, with its *Life 70*, a consolidated functions system that competed with IBM's product.

By 1972, numerous software packages were being developed by independent companies. As reflected in one software catalog in 1972, the majority of offerings consisted of software products for the insurance industry.

Still, most other industries still relied on software supplied with the hardware. The situation, however, was about to change.

Start-up companies offering insurance software products

ONE OF THE REASONS was the emergence of independent database companies. Database systems were technically sophisticated and required by nearly all industries. But since the systems offered by the computer manufacturers were considered lacking, the market was invaded by independent providers, making it one of the most active markets in the 1970s.

Early 1970s' database market as one of the most active ones

One of the first and most successful new firms was the Cullinane Company, founded in 1968 by John Cullinane, a former IBM database expert. The Cullinane Company was typical of the new software product entrants in that it was totally product oriented and did not diversify into software contracting or computer services. Typical of other new packaged-software firms, Cullinane was organized by technically sophisticated entrepreneurs with access to venture capital.

Cullinane Company

European companies also entered this market. In 1969 six members of the Institute for Applied Information Processing in Darmstadt, a midsize city south of Frankfurt, Germany, founded Software AG. The new firm developed and marketed its database system *ADABAS* (adaptable database system), a remarkably flexible database management system. By 1972, it had entered the U.S. market and soon thereafter, was selling it flagship product around the world.

Software AG

Other companies that played an important role in this market were Cincom Systems (founded in 1968), Computer Associates (1976), Oracle (1977), and Sybase (1984). In the early years, all

Other companies followed

these companies advertised their products exclusively in trade magazines and through direct mail.

Computer Associates

Of all those companies, Computer Associates had the most distinct and successful corporate strategy. The company, formed in 1976 by former University Computing Company executives, was one of the first major computer software firms to make a corporate strategy of growth through merger and acquisition. All Computer Associates' moves were aimed at acquiring "legitimate products with strong sales" rather than technological capabilities. Indeed, Computer Associates typically fired half of the staff of the companies it acquired.[17] By 1987, Computer Associates had taken over 15 companies, including the University Computing Company (then called Uccel), then the world's second-largest software company, for $629 million. Numerous other acquisitions followed, including ADR, Panasophic, and Cullinet. By 1992, Computer Associates was one of a few members of the traditional enterprise software suppliers to make the transition to the new market of personal computer software—and it did so by acquisition.

Need for standard enterprise applications

While the large software services companies continued to serve clients with custom-made applications, an increasing demand was felt for standard enterprise applications packages. Standardization meant that software developers would not always have to start from scratch when creating software for such common tasks as accounts receivables and payables, payroll, order entry, and materials management.

1972: SAP founded

The most successful of them was SAP (Systems, Applications, and Products), which was formed in spring 1972 by five former IBM colleagues. They believed they could develop software faster and less expensively by relying on a core product that could be used by many companies.

SAP's success story

Eight years later, SAP's revenues reached about $60 million, and it had 77 employees; furthermore, 50 of the top 100 industrial enterprises of Germany were SAP customers. Eight years later, when SAP went public, its revenues were about $200 million, and it had almost 1,000 employees. Today, with its *R/3* product, it is the clear market leader in this segment.

Baan

Baan, a Dutch consulting company founded in 1978 by two brothers, Jan Baan and J. G. Paul Baan, is a similar success story. The company shipped its first enterprise solutions products in 1982 and later invested heavily to build a non-European presence. In 1996, it had revenues of $388 million.

A third successful player, founded by Larry Ellison in 1977 as Relational Software, is Oracle.

During the 1980s and 1990s many enterprise solutions providers moved away from mainframe-only proprietary operating systems platforms onto new ones like *Unix* (1973), *IBM OS/2*, and Microsoft *NT*. This move often allowed them to boost profits by using their own proprietary software.

The shift toward newer operating system platforms enabled additional companies to enter the market. One was Peoplesoft, founded in 1987 by Dave Duffield and Ken Morris, two software engineers from Integral Systems, who saw the potential in PC-based human resources management systems (HRMS) software.

Peoplesoft was able to develop a number of vertical-functional markets beyond HRMS (such as health care and financial services) through acquisition, making itself a serious competitor to traditional enterprise solutions providers.

Most of the ERP players relied heavily on partners to implement and customize their products. These partners often realized two to six times as much in revenues per major installation as the ERP vendors did. Thus, both sides benefited from the great market growth since the early 1990s.

In the camp of the ERP partners, in particular, the large accounting firms, a quite active consolidation-concentration took place in the 1980s and 1990s. Both the KPMG merger in 1987 and the more recent Price Waterhouse/Coopers & Lybrand merger in 1998 seemed to signal an industrialization of professional software services on a global scale.

ERA 4: CONSUMER MASS-MARKET SOFTWARE, 1981 THROUGH 1994

The emergence of personal computers established a completely new type of software: PC-based mass-market packaged software. For the first time, software companies addressed the mass market with their products. This called for substantially different approaches to marketing and sales.

PARC sets the technological groundwork for the PCs of today.

The Palo Alto Research Center (PARC), created by Xerox in 1969, set the groundwork for the personal computer revolution with breakthrough innovations such as black-on-white screeens, bitmapped display, icons, laser printers, word processors, and networks (most notably ethernet). Some of the scientists who worked at the PARC later went to work for Apple and Microsoft or started their own companies.

The first personal computers

VisiCalc

In 1975, one of the very first "personal" computers, the Altair 8800, was introduced and sold through mail orders by Model Instrumentation Telemetry Systems (MITS), a tiny company in Albuquerque, New Mexico. Apple II, the computer that offered much more functionality, was introduced in 1977. In 1979 Daniel Bricklin and Bob Frankson developed *VisiCalc* for the Apple II, the first spreadsheet program, and the "killer application."

But both platforms failed to become the lasting standard platform for personal computers.

Introduction of the IBM PC

Rather, it was the IBM Personal Computer, introduced on August 12, 1981, that became the leading platform. With the IBM PC, a new software era was initiated.

The birth of a truly independent software industry

Microsoft

It was also the birth of the truly independent software industry and the introduction of shrink-wrapped, packaged software.

Undoubtedly, Microsoft is the most successful and most influential software company of this era. Founded as a partnership by William Gates and Paul Allen in 1975, Microsoft incorporated in 1981 and went public in 1986.

MS DOS

IBM's decision, in 1981, to outsource the development of the PC operating system by having Microsoft develop it laid the foundation for the tremendous success of the Redmond-based company. Ironically, Microsoft didn't even develop the product core—it was acquired from Seattle Computer Products, in the deal of the century, for a mere $50,000.

Microsoft's leadership

Microsoft's *MS DOS*, and later, *Windows*, became leading market standards and provided the company with the income to further strengthen its position in several PC software markets. Later Microsoft also entered the enterprise software business with its high-end operating system *NT*.

The new IBM platform attracted a variety of new software application start-ups. In fact, most PC software segments were quickly dominated by new entrants. Established vendors, on the other hand, only rarely managed a successful transition to the mass-market software market.

Some of the successful new entrants were Adobe, Autodesk, Corel, Intuit, Lotus, and Novell.

In 1982, Mitch Kapor started Lotus Development and designed *Lotus 1-2-3*, which made the IBM PC the choice of business users.

Novell, founded in 1983, launched the era of computer networking. In 1989, it introduced a *multi-thread local area networking system* that worked on major operating systems, including IBM's *OS/2*, *Unix*, and Apple's Macintosh.

Intuit was another new entrant to the market in this era. Founded by Scott Cook and Tom Proulx in 1983, it introduced its personal financial software *Quicken* in 1984, and it still leads the market with its product.

Overall, the 1980s saw dramatic, 20 percent a year, growth rates in the software industry. The annual revenues of U.S. firms had grown to $10 billion in 1982 and to $25 billion by 1985—10 times greater than the 1979 figure.[18]

Lotus

Novell: The leader in local area networking

Intuit

ERA 5: INTERNET VALUE-ADDED SERVICES, 1994 THROUGH 2008

The takeoff of the Internet, which provides universal networking capabilities, initiated a new era. While major parts of the software industry will further be challenged by the coexistence of many different standards and platforms, the software business might strongly be affected by new Web-enabled business opportunities and convergence trends.

The company that shaped the beginning of the Internet age more than any other company is probably Netscape.

James H. Clark and Marc Andreesen founded Netscape in 1994. Two years earlier, Andreesen had created the *NCSA Mosaic*, a Web browser whose graphical user interface radically simplified Internet navigation. The company grew nearly as fast as the new technology did. Just 16 months after its founding, it went public, another two years later it employed more than 2,000 people around the world.

Summary

Netscape

The *history* of this company very much represents the new pace of the industry. The Internet technology and easy-to-use graphical Web browsers provided radically new software applications and services opportunities. New companies popped up nearly every day.

New start-up companies offer e-commerce software

Companies offering software solutions for electronic commerce are a good example. Many entrepreneurs took the chance and founded new companies to offer this kind of software. BroadVision, iCat, Intershop Communications, Open Market, and Commerce Wave are some of the firms, to name just a few. Also young professional services firms took advantage of the opportunities.

Convergence trends

The Internet, however, is not just a software industry phenomenon. The telecommunications, media, and eventually consumer electronics industries will also be heavily involved. This brings a new dimension to the industry and may lead to the convergence of the software industry with other industries.

The coexistence challenge

ANOTHER PHENOMENON is and will be important throughout this era: the coexistence challenge. Today, several platforms, programming languages, and strong de facto standards coexist and often have to be managed in parallel. Some of those strong standards are *MVS* and *OS/390* for mainframe sytems, *Unix, NT,* and *Windows* for midrange systems and PCs, and Microsoft *CE* for embedded systems (introduced in 1996), to name just a few.

So far, no other era has experienced a similar high level of complexity from coexisting IT and communications architectures. Software companies often offer their products on several platforms, which has yet to be managed.

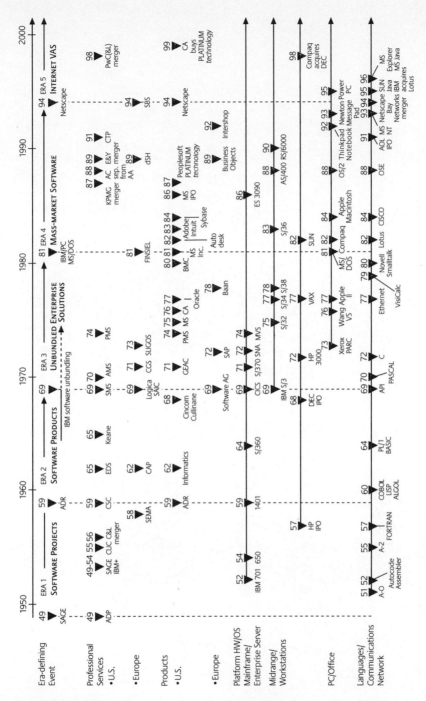

Source: McKinsey Research

Figure B-1. Software history eras (including foundation dates of selected major players)

NOTES

1. "It's Like Riding a Bull"

1. Thomas H. Marshall, *James Watt* (Edinburg: Leonard Parsons, 1925), 11–20.

2. Andrew Carnegie, *James Watt* (New York: Doubleday, 1905), 1–20, 39.

3. Marshall, *James Watt*, 36.

4. From personal interviews with Dan Bricklin on July 3, 1998, and from Paul Stranahan, "Dan Bricklin," *Jones Telecommunications and Multimedia Encyclopedia*, <http://www.digitalcentury.com/encyclo/update/bricklin.html>.

5. Margie Wylie, "The Man Who Made PCs Useful," *News.com*, 13 October 1997, 8.

6. Frank Delaney, *History of the Microcomputer Revolution*, National Public Radio, 1995, part 10, "The Killer Application."

7. Will Tracz, "Dan Bricklin Receives IEEE's Computer Entrepreneur Award," *International Conference on Software Engineering 1997 (ICSE 97) Proceedings*, <http://www.ics.uci.edu/~icse97/news/bricklin.html>.

8. Paul Judge, "For Net Writers, 'Hot Links' With Less Hassle," *Business Week*, 4 August 1997, 2 via Web.

9. Thomas McGibbon, Buddy VanDoren, and Terrie Clouse, "The 7th Software Engineering Process Group Conference," DACS Web site, <http://www.dacs.dtic.mil>.

10. Don Tapscott, *The Digital Economy: Promise and Peril in the Age of Networked Intelligence* (New York: McGraw-Hill, 1995), 143–147.

11. For example, in: *Business Week*, 24–31 August 1998, 10–11.

12. Robin Madell, "Human Genome Sciences: Genes As Tools to Drug Discovery," *Pharmaceutical Executive*, February 1997, 84.

13. Amy Cortese, "My Jet Is Bigger Than Your Jet," *Business Week*, 25 August 1997, 126.

14. According to the Forbes List, *Forbes Magazine*, June 1998. See also Eric Quinones, "Gates Tops Forbes Billionaires List," Associated Press, 21 June 1998.

15. According to interview with Tampa, Florida–based Payment Systems, Inc., 18 August 1998.

16. NYSE chairman Richard Grasso in the following article: Jens Wiegmann, "SAP: Debut On Wall Street," *Berliner Morgenpost*, 4 August 1998. See also *The Wall Street Journal*, 4 August 1998.

17. *Note:* Total revenues here include software licensing, maintenance, and support sales.

18. According to Datastream and McKinsey analysis.

19. According to Datastream and McKinsey analysis.

20. Anonymous, "The Importance of Being American," in the survey "A World Gone Soft," *The Economist*, 25 May 1996, 18.

21. Business Software Alliance, "Statistics," via Web site <http://www.bsa.org/statistics/index.html>, June 1998, 1.

22. Carolyn Veneri, "Computer Scientists, Computer Engineers, and Systems Analysts," in *1998–99 Occupational Outlook Handbook*, ed. U.S. Bureau of Labor Statistics (Chicago: U.S. Bureau of Labor Statistics, 1998), part: via Web <http://stats.bls.gov/oco/ocos042.htm>.

23. From: Diana Kunde, "Companies Get Creative to Lure Workers," *Dallas Morning News*, 5 January 1998, based on a study by the Engineering Workforce Commission of the American Association of Engineering Societies, National Center for Education Statistics, Information Technology Association of America.

24. Study by the Information Technology Association of America (ITAA) and Virginia Tech University.

25. Anonymous, "The Importance of Being American," 18.

26. According to the Voluntary Service Organization (VSO), a charitable organization, on its Web site.

27. Study by NASSCOM, "The Software Industry In India, A Strategic Review, 1997–98," 1–2; see <http://www.nasscom.org/indian.htm>.

28. According to the Gartner Group report *Computing in Small Energetic Countries*, 9 October 1996, 1.

29. Anonymous, "Making Waves: Is Information Technology Different From Earlier Innovations?" *The Economist*, 28 September 1996, 10.

30. 1990 figure: Kathy Rebello, "The Glitch at WordPerfect," *Business Week*, 17 May 1993, 56–57. 1997 figure: Dataquest.

31. Christian Deysson and Matthias Wulff, "Unter die Fittiche" (Under One's Wings), *Wirtschaftswoche*, no. 33, 10 August 1995, 53.

32. From speech at the *Manager Magazine's* 1997 Hall of Fame event in Germany, via team partner participation.

33. John Nesheim, *High-Tech Start-up*, self-published, 1992, 1–15.

34. McKinsey analysis of U.S. Census data from years 1992 through 1995, released in 1998 on request.

2. A NEW BUSINESS CALLED "SOFTWARE"

1. Elmer C. Kubie, "Recollections of the First Software Company," *IEEE Annals of the History of Computing* 16, no. 2 (1994): 65–71.

2. See Figure 2-2.

3. Martin Campbell-Kelly, "Development and Structure of the International Software Industry, 1950–1990," *Business and Economic History* 24, no. 2 (winter 1995): 84.

4. Campbell-Kelly, "Development and Structure of the International Software Industry, 1950–1990," 83.

5. Campbell-Kelly, "Development and Structure of the International Software Industry, 1950-1990," 82.

6. Campbell-Kelly, "Development and Structure of the International Software Industry, 1950-1990."

7. Luanne (James) Johnson, "A View From the 1960s: How the Software Industry Began," *IEEE Annals of the History of Computing*, 20, no. 1 (1998): 36–42.

8. Johnson, "A View from the 1960s: How the Software Industry Began," 39–41.

9. Stanley Gibson, "Software Industry Born with IBM's Unbundling," *Computerworld*, 19 June, 1989, 6.

10. Gerd Meissner, *SAP—die heimliche Software-Macht (SAP—The Secret Software Power)* (Hamburg, Germany: Hoffmann und Campe, 1997), 21.

11. Sourced from SAP's Web page (<http://www.sap.com>).

12. According to personal interview with Dan Bricklin, 14 July 1998.

13. Frank Delaney, *History of the Microcomputer Revolution,* National Public Radio, 1995, part 10, "The Killer Application."

14. Michael Busch and Stefan Spang, *SAP Implementation Lessons Learned,* internal McKinsey study, 1996, 16.

15. Information for the case sourced from SAP's Web page <http://www.sap.com>.

16. According to Dataquest.

17. *SAPINFO Magazine,* October 1998, via Web at <http://www.sap.com/press/magnews/regular/ma_1098e/ma_1098e.htm>.

18. Peter Pfister, personal interview, June 1997.

19. Kubie, "Recollections of the First Software Company," 69; Campbell-Kelly, "Development and Structure of the International Software Industry, 1950–1990," 90.

20. According to an estimate of Anne Griffith, research director at the Software Publishers Association (SPA). According to the data provided by other national software associations and trade departments, we estimate the total number of software companies (regardless of their size) to be at least 150,000 worldwide. Exact numbers, however, are not available.

21. According to an interview done by Jeff Ubois, published in *Internet World* magazine, vol. 9, no. 1, 1998.

22. Piper Jaffray Research, ed., *The Electronic Commerce Report*, August 1997.

23. Personal interview with Capers Jones, 17 July 1998.

24. Official price of a full version of *Windows95*. Street prices may be even significantly lower. See Stuart J. Johnson, "Win98 Nearly Set," *Informationweek,* 20 April 1998, 129.

25. According to *PC Data*, 1998.

26. Geoffrey A. Moore, *Inside the Tornado: Marketing Strategies from Silicon Valley's Cutting Edge* (New York: HarperBusiness, 1995), 44.

27. According to AMR research report, *ERP Software Market On A Global Tear*, 5, August 1997.
   Note: In IDC's August 1998 report *Worldwide "Enterprise" Applications*, the market was defined more broadly as "enterprise application software license and maintenance revenues." Under that definition, SAP reached a market share of "only" 15.6 percent, but that share was higher than the share of the four fiercest competitors *together*.

28. IDC, ed., *Information Access Tools: 1998 Worldwide Markets and Trends*, research report, 1998.

29. According to a telephone interview with *PC Data*.

30. Cost of revenue as a percentage of total costs.

31. According to an internal McKinsey study on software project and product economies in 1989.

32. U.S. Census data, 1992 through 1995, McKinsey analysis.

33. Refers to the share of Andersen Consulting's total revenues in McKinsey's total estimate of the global professional software services market in 1997 (of $115 billion). For some specialized services such as SAP *R/3* installations, Andersen Consulting's market share is likely be higher.

34. *Capacity utilization rate* is defined as billed days per total billable working days (260 days) of the regular project staff (consultants).

3. EXCEPTIONAL SOFTWARE LEADERS ARE THE RULE

1. Introduction story from Stephan Schambach, personal and telephone conversations with author, 1997 through 1998.

2. Frank Gessner, personal conversation with author, June 1997.

3. Gert Köhler, personal conversation with author, March 1997.

4. Gerd Meissner, *SAP—die heimliche Softwaremacht (SAP—The Secret Software Power)* (Hamburg: Hoffmann und Campe, 1997), 68–76.

5. According to SAP annual reports.

6. Joe Liemandt, telephone conversation with author, August 1998.

7. Anonymous, "List of the World's 400 Richest People," *Forbes*, via Web at <http://www.forbes.com/tool/toolbox/billnew/1998.asp>.

8. Joe Liemandt, telephone conversation with author, August 1998.

9. Henning Kagermann, personal conversation with author, November 1997.

10. Jim Sims, personal conversation with author, September 1997.

11. Juergen Homeyer, "Die Champions (The Champions)," *Wirtschafts-woche*, 5 February 1998, 45.

12. Pehong Chen, personal conversation with author, June 1998.

13. Andrew Filipowski, telephone conversation with author, June 1998.

14. SEC Filings and *McKinsey Computer Industry Database*, unpublished internal report, 1998.

15. Joshua Cooper Ramo, "Winner Take All." *Time*, 16 September 1996, via Web at <http://www.milligan.edu/Communications/101files/timebg3.htm>.

16. Richard Roy, personal conversation with author, July 1998.

17. Ramo, "Winner Take All."

18. Andrew S. Grove, *Only the Paranoid Survive: How to Exploit the Crisis Points That Challenge Every Company and Career* (New York: Doubleday, 1996).

19. John F. Keane, Sr., personal conversation with author, June 1998.

20. Tony Jackson, "Different Jobs, Same Problems," *Financial Times*, 16 June 1998.

21. Michael Zeitlin, telephone conversation with author, July 1998.

22. Bill Veber and Ron DeMott, personal conversation with author, June 1998.

23. Jon R. Katzenbach, *Teams at the Top* (Boston: Harvard Business School Press, 1997), 3.

24. Theo Schnittfink, personal conversation with author, September 1997.

25. Jim Sims, personal conversation with author, September 1997.

26. Rob Mundle, "Sydney Hobart," *Grand Prix Sailor*, 3 January 1997.

27. Tom Abate, "Oracle's First-Rate Second in Command Ray Lane Makes Larry Ellison's Visions a Reality," *San Francisco Chronicle*, 4 September 1997.

28. Edward B. Roberts, *Entrepreneurs in High-Technology* (New York: Oxford University Press, 1991), 348ff.

29. Roger Davis, telephone conversation with author, July 1998.

4. WINNING THE WAR FOR SOFTWARE TALENT

1. Saurabh Srivastava, president of IIS Infotech and of India's National Association of Software and Services Companies NASSCOM, telephone conversation with author, October 1998.

2. ITAA and Virginia Tech, *Help Wanted 1998—Second Annual Report on the IT Workforce Shortage,* unpublished study, January 1998, via Web at <http://www.itaa.org/workforce/studies/hw98.htm>.

3. Saurabh Srivastava, telephone conversation with author, October 1998.

4. Nico Fickinger, "Ruhelose Spezialisten für neue Aufgaben" (Restless specialists for new challenges), *Frankfurter Allgemeine Zeitung,* 30 May 1998, 51.

5. "Kampf um Köpfe" (Battle for brains), *Der Spiegel,* no. 36, 31 August 1998, 100–103.

6. Joachim Penner, *Neues "Highlight" für die Saar-Universität* in *Saarbrücker Zeitung,* 2 November 98, 6.

7. Roberto Polillo, personal conversation with author, June 1997.

8. Patricia Nakache, "Cisco's Recruiting Edge," *Fortune Magazine,* 29 September, 1997.

9. Marc Ugol, personal conversation with author, September 1997.

10. Ron Watson, personal conversation with author, September 1997.

11. Alex S. Vieux, "The Once and Future Kings," the *Red Herring* magazine, November 1995.

12. Anthony B. Perkins, "The Thinker—Interview with John Doerr, General Partner in Charge of Investments in Information Technology at Kleiner Perkins Caulfield & Byers," the *Red Herring* magazine, March 1995.

13. Pehong Chen, personal conversation with author, June 1997.

14. Nakache, "Cisco's Recruiting Edge."

15. ITAA and Virginia Tech, *Help Wanted 1998.*

16. Maria Seminerio, "Immigration Battle Looms on 'Imported' High-Tech Workers," *ZDNN,* 20 September 1998, via Web at <http://www.zdnet.com/zdnn/>.

17. Michael Hopkins, "The Antihero's Guide to the New Economy," *Inc. Magazine*, January 1998, 36–48.

18. Ann-Marie Westergaard (HR manager, Navision), personal conversation with author, September 1997.

19. Amy Cortese, "How IPOs Turn Pip-Squeaks into Players," *Business Week*, 25 August 1997.

20. Alan Sloan, "The Millionaires Next Door (If Your Neighbors Work for Microsoft)," *Washington Post*, 2 December 1997, DO3.

21. Stephen Baker, "Look Who's Bait Now, The Rise and Fall of a Software Legend (Baan)," *Business Week (European Edition)*, 28 December 1998, 21.

22. Marc Ugol, personal communication with author, September 1997.

23. Rob Goffee and Gareth Jones, *The Character of a Corporation* (New York: HarperBusiness, 1998), 97–122.

24. Andy Palmer, personal conversation with author, September 1997.

25. Saratoga Institute, *Human Resource Financial Report*, 1997, 187, 201.

26. See also Jeffrey Pfeffer, *The Human Equation* (Boston: Harvard Business School Press, 1998), 162.

27. Bob Hagman, telephone conversation with author, May 1998.

28. This high turnover rate is true for all software industry segments; however, turnover rates are significantly lower in Europe (7% compared to 20%).

29. Kerry Lamson, personal conversation with author, February 1998.

30. Aldy Duffield, personal conversation with author, February 1998.

31. Anne-Marie Westergaard, personal conversation with author, September 1998.

32. John Wookey, personal conversation with author, February 1998.

33. Christoph Filles, personal conversation with author, June 1998.

34. Peter Karmanos, personal conversation with author, June 1998.

35. John F. Keane, Sr., personal conversation with author, June 1998.

5. SOFTWARE DEVELOPMENT: COMPLETING A MISSION IMPOSSIBLE

1. Anonymous, "Chek Lap Kok—The Story So Far," *Airwise News,* via Web at <http://www.airwise.com/news/airports/hkg_hongkong2.html>.

2. "Boeing Changes Delta III Control Software," press release, 19 October 1998, via Web at <http://www.boeing.com/defense-space/space/delta/delta3/10-15.htm>.

3. The Standish Group, ed., *Chaos,* unpublished report, 1995, sourced from <http://www.standishgroup.com>. (Statistics covered 365 development organizations and 8,000 software projects in the United States.)

4. Capers Jones, *Applied Software Management* (New York: McGraw-Hill, 1996), 221, and personal conversation with author, August 1998.

5. Stephen Flowers, *Software Failure: Management Failure. Amazing Stories and Cautionary Tales* (West Sussex, England: John Wiley & Sons Ltd.).

6. Brad Cox, telephone conversation with author, August 1998.

7. Capers Jones, telephone conversation with author.

8. Jones, telephone conversation with author.

9. Kevin Carnahan, partner, Andersen Consulting Europe, personal conversation with team partner, June 1999.

10. Greg Baryza (former CTO Object Design), personal conversation with author, June 1998.

11. Stephen Bradley and Richard Nolan, *Sense and Respond* (Boston: Harvard Business School Press, 1998), 188–189

12. Baryza, personal conversation with author, June 1998.

13. Fred Brooks, *The Mythical Man Month,* 20th anniversary edition (Reading, Mass.: Addison-Wesley, 1995). Brooks is professor of computer science at the University of North Carolina at Chapel Hill.

14. Barry Boehm, telephone conversation with author, August 1998. (Boehm is TRW professor of software engineering at the University of Southern California and has more than 25 years experience in software project estimation. The database on his COCOMO model for cost and schedule estimation was calibrated with more than 80 projects.)

15. Steve McConnell, telephone conversation with author, August 1998.

16. Brooks, *The Mythical Man Month,* 14.

17. Brooks, *The Mythical Man Month.*

18. Brooks, *The Mythical Man Month,* 5.

19. Baryza, personal conversation with author, June 1998.

20. Robert Glass "IS Field: Stress Up, Satisfaction Down," *Software Practitioner,* 1 November 1994.

21. Boehm, telephone conversation with author, August 1998.

22. Jerry Popek, telephone conversation with author, August 1998.

23. Software Engineering Institute, *The Capability Maturity Model: Guidelines for Improving the Software Process* (Reading, Mass.: Addison-Wesley, 1995).

24. W. Wayt Gibbs, "Software's Chronic Crisis," *Scientific American*, September 1994, 86.

25. Popek, telephone conversation with author, August 1998.

26. McConnell, telephone conversation with author, August 1998.

27. Edward Yourdon, *Death March* (Upper Saddle River: Prentice-Hall PTR, 1997), 132.

28. Patrick Albert, personal conversation with author, July 1997.

29. Boehm, telephone conversation with author, August 1998.

30. Steve McConnell, *Software Project Survival Guide,* (Redmond, Wash: Microsoft Press, 1998), 30.

31. Steve McConnell, telephone conversation with author, August 1998.

32. Andrew Filipowski, telephone conversation with author, June 1998.

33. Brooks, *The Mythical Man Month*, 32.

34. Paul Humenansky, telephone conversation with author, July 1998.

35. Bradford Clark, *Effects of Software Process Maturity on Software Development Effort,* Ph.D. dissertation, University of Southern California, August 1997; conversation with Barry Boehm, March 1999.

36. McConnell, *Software Project Survival Guide*, 26.

37. James Herbsleb, et al., "Software Quality and the Capability Maturity Model, *Communications of the ACM,* June 1997.

38. Usability Research, Microsoft Web site at <http://office.microsoft.com/usability/about.htm>.

39. Michael Oneal, "Scott Cook Wants to Control Your Checkbook," *BusinessWeek*, 26 September 1994.

40. Bradley and Nolan, *Sense and Respond*, 192–193.

41. Blake Ives, professor of MIS at Louisiana State University, Empirical study.

42. Boris Anderer, personal communication with author, June 1997.

43. Brooks, *The Mythical Man Month,* 180.

44. Brad Cox, telephone conversation with author, August 1998.

45. Brooks, *The Mythical Man Month,* 5.

6. MARKETING GODS MAKE SOFTWARE KINGS

1. According to Raptor corporate information; see also <http://www.raptor.com/news/press/shaunceo.html>.

2. Details based on personal interviews with Shaun McConnon, 10 January 1998.

3. Anonymous, "Axent Technologies Buys Raptor," *The Wall Street Journal,* 6 February 1998.

4. Statistics in this paragraph stem from SEC filings.

5. According to Microsoft annual report and SEC filings.

6. Based on data from interview with Capers Jones.

7. Anonymous, "Time for a Change," Microsoft case stories on-line, <http://www.microsoft.com/office>.

8. Anthony B. Perkins, "John Doerr: The Thinker," the *Red Herring* magazine, March 1995, 3, <http://www.redherring.com/mag/issue19/thinker.html>.

9. Perkins, "John Doerr: The Thinker."

10. According to Intuit; also see Web site at <http://www.intuit.com/corporate/just_for_editors/company_history.html>.

11. According to IDC and PaineWebber.

12. Daniel Levine, "Executive of the Year: After Bringing Bill Gates to His Knees, Scott Cook Plans to Revolutionize the Finance Industries," *San Franscisco Business Times,* 6 January 1995.

13. Dave Mote, "Intuit," ed. Tina Grant, *International Directory of Company Histories,* vol. 14 (Detroit/New York: St. James Press, 1996), 263.

14. Mote, "Intuit," 262.

15. Levine, "Executive of the Year."

16. Evan I. Schwartz, "Financial Planner to the Masses," *Business Week,* 20 May, 1991, 1, via online archive.

17. According to annual reports.

18. See <http://www.bmc.com> for general and technical news.

19. See also Peter Elstrom, et al., "It Must Be Something in the Water," *Business Week*, 25 August 1997, 1, via Web archive.

20. According to Netscape company information.

21. Alex S. Vieux, "The Once and Future Kings," the *Red Herring* magazine, November 1995, 9, via Web archive, <http://www.redherring.com/mag/issue25/once.html>.

22. See also Peter Elstrom et al., "It Must Be Something in the Water," *Business Week*, 25 August 1997, via Web archive.

23. For further details on the bowling alley market development approach, see Geoffrey A. Moore, *Inside the Tornado: Marketing Strategies from Silicon Valley's Cutting Edge* (New York: Harper–Business, 1995), 22-24, 35-40.

24. Anonymous, "Bill Gates Launches Ramco Marshal 3.0," company press release, 5 March 1997, 1, via <http://www.ramco.com/press/gates.htm>.

25. Manjeet Kripalani, "The Business Rajahs," *Business Week*, 14 April 1997, 1, via Web archive.

26. Christian Deysson and Matthias Wulff, "Unter die Fittiche" (Under one's wings), *Wirtschaftswoche,* 33, 10 August 1995, 48.

27. For example, Lothar Kuhn, "Ausflug in Davos (Excursion in Davos)," *Wirtschaftswoche* 13, 19 March 1998, 100.

28. Kate Farnady, "Netscape Charm School Trains Evangelists," *Wired News*, 11 February 1997.

29. Nick Wilgius, "Things to Come: Preaching the Technology Gospel," *The Bangkok Post*, 26 November 1997.

30. Gerd Meissner, *SAP—die heimliche Software-Macht* (*SAP—The Secret Software Power*) (Hamburg: Hoffmann und Campe, 1997), 131.

31. According to SEC filings.

32. According to SAP company information.

33. Anonymous, "Apple wirbt um Vertrauen (Apple Pleas for Trust)," *Werben & Verkaufen* 41, 10 October 1997, 26.

34. Anonymous, "Marketing Communications Head Christofer Recker About Attacks from the Competition and Image Building," *Werben & Verkaufen,* 26.

35. According to personal interview with Richard Roy, general manager Microsoft Germany, 7 July 1998; also see article Anonymous, "Millionen-deal für Werbebutton (Million Deal for Ad Button)," *Horizont* 17, 23 April 1998, 62.

36. Anonymous, "Software Marketing in Multimedia Look," *Horizont*, 28 August 1997, 24.

37. Survey by ORC International, 1998. From ORC report extracts received directly from ORC.

38. Jeff Brown of ORC International, telephone interview, 20 August 1998.

39. Cathy Booth, "Steve's Job: Restart Apple," *Time*, 18 August 1997, 4, via Web archive.

40. Described also on the company Web site <http://www5.baan.com>.

41. See also anonymous, "Doomonomics," in survey "A World Gone Soft," *The Economist*, 25 May 1996, 16.

42. According to Business Software Alliance (BSA), the largest organization to protect intellectual software property rights. Based on 1997 interview with Bob Kruger, vice president of enforcement at BSA, in "The Cost of Software Piracy," *Business Week Online*, 10 March 1997, 1, via Web archive.

43. Pete Engardio, "Microsoft's Long March," *Business Week*, 24 June 1996, 1, via Web archive.

44. Kruger, "The Cost of Software Piracy."

45. Anonymous, "Auch die IBM will nicht verzichten (Even IBM Doesn't Want to Go Without It)," *Computerwoche*, 25 June 1995, 16.

46. According to IDC, PaineWebber estimates, and company reports.

47. According to PaineWebber.

48. According to a Microsoft press release, via Web at <http://www.microsoft.com/MSCorp/Museum/timelines/microsoft/timeline.asp>.

49. See Doron P. Levin, *Irreconcilable Differences: Ross Perot versus General Motors* (Boston: Little, Brown, 1989), 24–27.

50. Meissner, *SAP—die heimliche Software-Macht (SAP—The Secret Software Power)*, 109.

51. Anonymous, "Microsoft kooperiert mit Software-Kunden (Microsoft Co-operates with Software Customers)," *Horizont* 47, 20 November 1997, 18.

52. Anonymous, "Europaeischer Marktanteil des Betriebssystems verdroppelt (European Operating System Market Share Doubled)," *Computerwoche* 42, 21 October 1994, 13.

53. Deysson and Wulff, "Unter die Fittiche (Under One's Wings).

54. According to Dataquest.

55. Dataquest "PC Operating Platforms," 1996, and McKinsey analysis.

56. Christian Deysson, "Fundament sprengen (Blast Away the Basic Platform)," *Wirtschaftswoche*, 10 August 1995, 55.

57. P. McNamara, "Notes-Exchange Race Getting Tighter," *Network-World* 15, 23 March 1998, 7.

58. For a further strategic perspective on the topic of early product announcements as a signaling technique, also see Oliver P. Heil, George S. Day, and David J. Reibstein, "Signaling to Competitors," section "Announcements," in *Wharton on Dynamic Competitive Strategy*, ed. George S. Day and David J. Reibstein, with Robert E. Gunther (New York: Wiley, 1997), 283–288.

59. Information about this event from Mike Wilson, *The Difference between God and Larry Ellison* (New York: Morrow, 1997), 169-170.

60. Wilson, *The Difference between God and Larry Ellison*.

61. Anonymous, "IBM Hits Out," *The Economist,* 11 January 1975, 66.

62. This was part of a larger antitrust verdict against IBM, and although the larger antitrust ruling was partially overruled later, the point about early product announcements remained.

63. Meissner, *SAP—die heimliche Software-Macht (SAP—The Secret Software Power)*, 115.

64. Andrew S. Grove, *Only the Paranoid Survive: How to Exploit the Crisis Points That Challenge Every Company and Career* (New York: Doubleday, 1996), 118.

65. Kathy Rebello, "The Glitch at WordPerfect," *Business Week,* 17 May 1993, 56–57.

66. Lee Patterson, "Tanking It Five Ways," *Forbes Magazine*, 2 June 1997, 3, via Web archive.

67. Michael H. Martin, "Conversation with the Lords of Wintel," *Fortune Magazine,* 8 July 1996, 8, via Web archive.

68. According to Microsoft and WordPerfect company timelines, via Web archives.

69. The article also appeared in other newspapers around the world in August 1995 (e.g., Bill Gates, "The Surging Power of the Internet," *The Guardian* [London], 17 August 1995, 7.)

70. According to SDC filings, 7 March 1999. See also Ira Sager and Catherine Yang, "Power-Play: AOL-Netscape-Sun," *Business Week*, 7 December 1998, 1, via Web archive.

71. Alex Grove, "Money Can't Buy You Love," the *Red Herring* magazine, February 1997, 39.

72. Kathy Rebello et al., "Is Microsoft Too Powerful?" *Business Week*, 1 March 1993, 6, via Web.

73. Industry analyst Martin Marshall of Zona Research in an April 1998 interview with ABCNews.com, the online branch of ABC.

74. Christian Deysson, "Fundament sprengen (Blast Away the Basic Platform).

7. PROFESSIONAL SOFTWARE SERVICES: EXPERTS AT MARKETING TRUST

1. David Maister, *Managing the Professional Services Firm* (New York: Free Press, 1997), 114.

2. The details in this case are sourced from "United to Simplify Denver's Troubled Baggage Project," *Computerworld*, 10 October 1994; "Baggage-Handling Snags Hold New Airport at the Gate," *IEEE Spectrum*, August 1994; and Stephen Flowers, *Software Failure: Management Failure. Amazing Stories and Cautionary Tales* (West Sussex, England: John Wiley & Sons, Ltd.), 91–93.

3. "Computer Problems Persist at New Airport in Kuala Lumpur," *The Asian Wall Street Journal*, 3 July 1998, 5.

4. The details in this case are from James Geoffrey, "IT Fiascoes . . . and How to Avoid Them," *Datamation*, November 1997; and Bruce Caldwell, "Andersen Sued Over 'Flawed' SAP *R/3* Job," *InformationWeek*, 3 July 1998.

5. *Revolution and Risk: IT into the Millenium. A Report into the Challenges Facing IT Managers in Business*, unpublished report, commissioned by Sequent Computer Systems, conducted by the RONIN Corporation, 1997.

6. Steve McConnell *Rapid Development. Taming Wild Software Schedules* (Redmond, Wash.: Microsoft Press, 1998), 81.

7. Information Technology Services Marketing Association (ITSMA), ed., *ITSMA Benchmarking Study on Services Marketing Practices*, 1997–1998 edition (Lexington, Mass.), 213.

8. Mindy Blodgett, "Group Efforts," *CIO Magazine*, 15 November 1997, 2 from <http://www.cio.com/archive/111597_group_content.html>.

9. Bob Violino, "Where CIOs Meet Online—High-Level IT Executives Take to Members-Only Web Sites to Discuss Technology and Business Issues," *TechWeb News*, 27 April 1998, 1.

10. Name was changed.

11. Kevin Carnahan, team partner, Andersen Consulting Europe, personal conversation, June 1999.

12. Information Technology Services Marketing Association (ITSMA), ed., *ITSMA Benchmarking Study on Services Marketing Practices*, 167.

13. David Maister, *True Professionalism: The Courage to Care about Your People, Your Clients, and Your Career* (New York: Free Press, 1997), 185.

14. Quoted from Andersen Consulting's Web page <http://www.ac.com>.

15. "Unternehmensberatung—Mit Hilfe einer weltweiten Imagekampagne will Andersen Consulting internationaler Marktführer werden" (Consulting—With a Worldwide Image Campaign Andersen Consulting Wants to Become the Global Market Leader), *werben und verkaufen — W&V*, 30 January 1998, 104–105.

16. "Andersen Consulting Unveils New Global Brand Strategy. First Identity Change in Firm's History Marks Effort to Further Distinguish Its Marketplace Image," *PR Newswire*, 12 June 1998, New York, 1.

8. GROW YOUR PARTNERS TO GROW YOURSELF

1. Baan Investment is now called Vanenburg Business Systems BV.

2. Stephen Baker, "Is Baan Stalling Out on the Infobahn?" *Business Week International Edition*, 25 May 1998, 1, via Web archive.

3. Baan Company, "Microsoft and the Baan Company Deliver on a Common Vision for the Integrated Enterprise with the 'Digital Nervous System,'" press release, 21 April 1998, via Web archive, <http://www5.baan.com/press/>.

4. Estimated 1997 revenues.

5. Thomas L. Friedman, "The Internet Wars," *The New York Times*, 11 April 1998.

6. Everen Securities, "Microsoft," 1997.

7. According to personal interview with Don Nelson, 29 June 1998, company brochure, and Web site <http://www.greatplains.com/partner/circle.htm>.

8. Baan Company, "Baan Joins Forces With More Than 27 Business Partners and Announces Channels Initiative," press release, 22 April 1997, 1, via Web archive, <http://www.baan.com>.

9. According to company information about Microsoft *Windows* Logo Program at <http://www.microsoft.com/windows>.

10. According to company information; see also <http://www.intershop.com/partners/list_partners.htm> and <http://www.intershop.com/partners/tech_partners.htm>.

11. Steve Hamm, "This Intuit Hunch May Pay Off," *Business Week*, 15 June 1998, 123.

12. According to company information on <http://www.intuit.com/corporate/just_for_editors/press_releases>.

13. Hamm, "This Intuit Hunch May Pay Off," 124.

14. According to Dataquest.

15. According to Intuit company information on <http://www.intuit.com/corporate/just_for_editors/press_releases>.

16. Cathy Booth, "Steve's Job: Restart Apple," *Time* 18 August 1997, 9.

17. Apple Computer, "Microsoft and Apple Affirm Commitment to Build Next Generation Software for Macintosh," press release, 6 August 1997, via Web archive, <http://product.info.apple.com/pr/>.

18. According to Yahoo! company information. See also <http://docs.yahoo.com/info/misc/history.html>, "in early 1995 Marc Andreessen, cofounder of Netscape Communications in Mountain View, CA, invited Filo and Yang to move their files over to larger computers housed at Netscape. As a result, the Stanford [University] computer network returned to normal, and both parties benefitted."

19. Yahoo!, "Yahoo! Unveils Platinum Visa Card," press release, 23 February 1998, 1, via Web archive at <http://www.yahoo.com/doc/pr/release150.html>.

20. Yves L. Doz and Gary Hamel, *Alliance Advantage: The Art of Creating Value through Partnering* (Boston: Harvard Business School Press, 1998), 1–2.

21. Anonymous, "Sony to Buy Part of Justsystem to Develop Software," *AsiaBizTech*, 4 June 1998, 1, via Web archive, <http://www.asiabiztech. com/Database/98_Jun/04/Mor.02.gwif.html>.

22. According to personal interview with Mr. Ramadorai on 15 May 1998. See also similar comments on <http://www.tcs.com/alliances/alliances. htm>.

23. Robert D. Hof, Kathy Rebello, and Peter Burrows, "Scott McNealy's Rising Sun," *Business Week*, 22 January 1996, 1, via Web archive.

24. From interview with Dr. David Cole, a renowned U.S. automobile industry expert from the University of Michigan Transportation Research Institute, on 16 June 1998.

25. Information from Web site <http://www.sap.com/partner/part_pro.htm>.

26. Graham Sharman, telephone conversation with author, July 1997.

27. Andersen Consulting, "SAP AG and Andersen Consulting for Global Alliance to Create New Business Solutions for the Utilities Industry," press release, 21 April 1998, 1, via Web archive, <http://www.ac.com/ topstories/currnews/ts_98-0421b.html>.

28. Patricia Nakache, "Secrets of the New Brand Builders," *Fortune Magazine*, 22 June 1998, 167.

29. According to Kennedy Information, "SAP Continuing to Drive ERP Market," *Global IT Consulting Report*, November 1997, 15.

30. Microsoft, "Microsoft Announces Certification for Leading Developer Technology and Skills," press release, 1 June 1998, 2, via Web archive.

31. John Hagel III, "Spider versus Spider," *McKinsey Quarterly*, January 1996, 4–18. See also *Net Gain* (Boston: Harvard Business School Press, 1997) and *Net Worth* (Boston: Harvard Business School Press, 1999).

32. See Jagi Shahani and Steve McClure, "1995 Worldwide Market for Object-Oriented Programming," *IDC Report*, June 1996, 4.

33. Dirk Anders, personal conversation with research team member, February 1998.

34. See also Adam M. Brandenburger and Barry J. Nalebuff, *Co-opetition* (New York: Currency Doubleday, 1996), and Joel Bleeke and David Ernst, *Collaborating to Compete* (New York: Wiley, 1993).

35. Kennedy Information, *SAP Battle Brewing Between AC and PW*, Global IT Consulting Report, November 1997, 15.

36. John Hagel III and Marc Singer, *Net Worth* (Boston: Harvard Business School Press, 1999), 140–141, 144–145, 157.

37. See also "Partnering" section at <http://www.pandesic.com>.

38. Described also on Baan's Web Site: <http://www.baan.com>.

39. Ralf Felter and Stefan Spang, "Primer: The Integrated Standard Software Package SAP," internal McKinsey analysis, 23.

40. Dietmar Hopp, "Globale Strategien der SAP AG (Global Strategies of SAP)," in *Strategische Erneuerungen fuer den globalen Wettbewerb (Strategic Renewal for the Global Competition)*, ed. Erich Zahn, (Stuttgart: Schaeffer-Poeschel, 1996), 129.

41. Irene Kunii et al., "The Games Sony Plays," *Business Week*, 15 June 1998, 129.

42. Kunii et al., "The Games Sony Plays."

43. According to Dataquest, "PC Operating Platforms," 1996.

44. According to Dataquest, "PC Operating Platforms," 1996.

45. Robert D. Hof, "Commentary: Java Can Be A Contender—If Sun Lets It," *Business Week*, 6 April 1998, 1, via Web archive.

46. Alex Grove, "Perk Elation Waning: Venture Capitalists Adopt More Realistic Expectations of Java," the *Red Herring* magazine, June 1998, 1, via Web archive at <http://www.redherring.com/mag/issue55/whispers.html>.

47. See also Seanna Browder, Steven V. Brull, and Andy Reinhardt, "Nintendo: At the Top of His Game," *Business Week*, 9 June 1997, 2, via Web archive.

48. See also Intellicorp, "Intellicorp Announces Acquisition of Equity Interest By SAP AG," press release, 9 August 1996, 1, at <http://www.intellicorp.com>.

49. IDS, "SAP AG Acquiring an Interest in IDS Prof. Scheer GmbH," press release, 20 June 1997, 1, via Web archive <http://www.ids-scheer.com/news/June20-97.htm>.

50. According to company information. See also <http://www.microsoft.com/mcsp/preview.htm>.

51. Kay Anderson, "TeamSAP—the Critical Role of Partners," *SAP World* (SAP employee newspaper), January 1998, 1.

52. Michael Duffy et al., "Microsoft's Trophies," *Time*, 1 June 1998, 58.

53. According to IDC.

54. According to company information.

9. THE LANDSCAPE OF THE FUTURE

1. According to SEC filings of the respective companies.

2. According to SEC filings of the respective companies, ranking according to revenues.

3. Era 5 according to our taxonomy explained in Chapter 2.

4. John Hagel and Arthur Armstrong, *Net Gain* (Boston: Harvard Business School Press, 1997).

5. Gartner Group.

6. IDC.

7. Thomas Koll (general manager of worldwide business strategies embedded systems, Microsoft), personal communication, August 1998.

8. Charles P. Wallace "Psion of the Times," *Time*, 23 November 1998; and Owen Thomas, "Microsoft, Qualcomm Launch Mobile Venture," the *Red Herring* magazine, 10 November 1998 (online).

9. Koll, personal communication.

10. Lowell Bryan et al., *Race for the World: Strategies to Build a Great Global Firm* (Boston: Harvard Business School Press, 1999).

11. Ranking according to revenues.

12. McKinsey's Global Institute, internal report.

13. Peter Solvik (CIO, Cisco), presentation at Cisco Executive Briefing Center, San Jose, February 1998.

14. 1998 figures from Richard L. Nolan and Kelley A. Porter, "Cisco Systems, Inc.," case study no. N9-398-127, 17 August 1998, Harvard Business School, 8.

15. Prof. Dr. Ernst Dehnert, personal communication with author, Munich, March 1998.

16. Stephen Bradley and Richard Nolan, *Sense & Respond* (Boston: Harvard Business School Press, 1998), 3–29.

17. Capers Jones, *Estimating Software Costs* (New York: McGraw Hill, 1998).

18. Paul Taylor, "India's Software Industry," *Financial Times*, special issue.

19. Ralph Müller, Bernd Klosterkemper, Detlev Hoch, and Detlev Ruland, *Making Off-Shore Software Development in Emerging Markets Pay Off,* forthcoming.

20. Müller et al., *Making Off-Shore Software Development in Emerging Markets Pay Off.*

21. Dewang Mehta, personal communication with author, May 1998.

22. Kerry Lamson, personal conversation with author, February 1998.

23. *1997 Database of the Computer Industry,* unpublished McKinsey internal database.

24. For more detail on this slicing or slivering phenomenon, see Lowell Bryan et al., "Winning the World through Slivers," in *Race for the World: Strategies to Build a Great Global Firm* (Boston: Harvard Business School Press, 1999).

25. Stephen Ladwig, personal conversation with author, at IBM's Executive Seminar on the San Francisco project, Brussels, 28 May 1998.

26. *Financial Times IT Special,* 20 October 1998.

27. Andrew Maluish, Perot Systems Europe Ltd., London. Quoted in "Outsourcing in Neuen Dimensionene," *Handelsblatt*, no. 138, 21 July 1992, 13.

28. According to company information at <http://www.adp.com/home/about/adpstory.html>.

29. Marc Andreessen, quoted in *Welt am Sonntag,* 4 October 1998.

30. Tim Jackson, "Free Rein on the Net," *Financial Times,* 16 February 1999; and Jason Pontin, "Free PCs!" the *Red Herring* magazine, April 1999.

31. Collin Frye, "Gauging the Industry," *Software Magazine,* June 1998, cover story.

32. Lloyd Gray, "Oracle Testing Online Service Delivery Waters," *PCWeek,* August 1998.

33. Timothy S. Mullaney and Peter Burrows, "Application Providers Are Changing the Way Programs Are Sold and Delivered," *Business Week*, June 1999, 134.

34. Broadview Associates, *1997 Technology M&A Report: First Half 1998*, New York.

35. Robert Strauss, personal communication with author, July 1998.

36. Stephen Baker, "Look Who's Bait Now, The Rise and Fall of a Software Legend (Baan)," *Business Week (European Edition)*, 28 December 1998, 21.

37. Frye, "Gauging the Industry."

38. *Business Week*, June 1998.

39. David C. Moschella, *Waves of Power* (Amacom, 1997), 69.

40. Bill Gates, *Business @ the Speed of Thought* (New York: Warner Books, 1999).

41. Bradley and Nolan, *Sense & Respond*.

42. Patrick Butler et al., "A Revolution in Interaction," *The McKinsey Quarterly* 1 (1997), 4–23.

43. Gates, *Business @ the Speed of Thought*, xiii.

44. Gates, *Business @ the Speed of Thought*, xviii.

10. STAYING ON THE BULL

1. Charles H. Fine, *Clockspeed* (Reading, Mass.: Perseus Books, 1998), 239.

2. Chapter 2 has already outlined the basic strategic differences and "commonalities" between professional services, enterprise solutions, and software mass-market product companies. The analysis of the differences is based on a correlation analysis between companies' overall performances and specific factors of success, across the different segments.

3. Melanie Warner, "Inside the Silicon Valley Machine," *Fortune*, 26 October 1998, 112.

APPENDIX II. SOFTWARE HISTORY: AN OVERVIEW

1. Martin Campbell-Kelly, "Development and Structure of the International Software Industry, 1950–1990," *Business and Economic History* 24, no. 2 (winter 1995): 82.

2. Campbell-Kelly, "Development and Structure of the International Software Industry, 1950–1990."

3. See Gilbert Burck, The Computer Age and Its Potential for Management (New York: Harper &Row, 1965); James L. McKenney et al. *Waves of Change: Business Evolution Through Information Technology* (Boston: Harvard Business School Press, 1995).

4. From SABRE Group's Web page <http://www.sabre.com/corpinfo/history.htm>.

5. Campbell-Kelly, "Development and Structure of the International Software Industry, 1950–1990," 80.

6. Elmer C. Kubie, "Recollections of the First Software Company," *IEEE Annals of the History of Computing* 16, no. 2 (1994): 65–71.

7. Elmer C. Kubie, "Recollections of the First Software Company," 69.

8. Campbell-Kelly, "Development and Structure of the International Software Industry, 1950–1990," 84.

9. Franklin M. Fisher, James W. McKie, and Richard B. Mancke, *IBM and the U.S. Data Processing Industry: An Economic History* (New York: Praeger, 1983), 323.

10. Jacques Lesourne and Richard Armand, "A Brief History of the First Decade of SEMA," *IEEE Annals of the History of Computing*, 13, no. 4 (1991): 341.

11. Jacques Lesourne and Richard Armand, "A Brief History of the First Decade of SEMA," 342.

12. See Luanne (James) Johnson, "A View from the 1960s: How the Software Industry Began," *IEEE Annals of the History of Computing* 20, no. 1 (1998).

13. Johnson, "A View from the 1960s: How the Software Industry Began," 38.

14. Revenue statistics vary widely depending on the source. See Alfred D. Chandler, Jr., "The Computer Industry, The First Half Century," in David B. Yoffie, ed., *Competing in the Age of Digital Convergence* (Boston: Harvard Business School Press, 1997), and Walter Bauer, "Software Markets in the 70s" in Fred Gruenberger, ed., *Expanding Use of Computers in the 70s: Markets, Needs, Technology*, (Englewood Cliffs, N.J.: Prentice Hall 1971).

15. Richard Thomas DeLamarter, *Big Blue: IBM's Use and Abuse of Power* (London: Pan, 1988).

16. Information is from JoAnne Yates, "Application Software for Insurance in the 1960s and Early 1970s," *Business and Economic History* 24, no. 1 (Fall 1995): 123–134.

17. Hesh Kestin, *Twenty-First-Century Management: The Revolutionary Strategies That Have Made Computer Associates a Multi-Billion Software Giant* (New York: Atlantic Monthly Press, 1992).

18. Campbell-Kelly, "Development and Structure of the International Software Industry, 1950–1990," 74.

INDEX

ABOUT THE AUTHORS

Detlev J. Hoch, a Director at McKinsey & Company, Inc., Düsseldorf, joined the company in 1980. He specializes in information technology applications that resolve top management issues and has made major contributions on an international scale toward identifying and utilizing improvement potential for software and services providers and users. Until recently, he led McKinsey's competence center IT/S and currently is a member of the global leadership teams of McKinsey's Electronics and TIMe sectors. Hoch initiated and directed the global research project "Secrets of Software Success." He earned an M.B.A. from Queen's University in Kingston, Canada, as well as a Diploma in Computer Science and Operations Research from Technical University Karlsruhe. He worked as a systems analyst at the Nuclear Research Center in Karlsruhe and at IBM, Frankfurt. Hoch was a scholar with the German Academic Exchange Service and is a member of Gesellschaft für Informatik, Verband Deutscher Wirtschaftsingenieure, the New York Academy of Sciences, the Planetary Society, and the editorial board of Wirtschaftsinformatik.

Cyriac R. Roeding, a Senior Associate in the Munich office of McKinsey & Company, Inc., has recently transferred to McKinsey's Silicon Valley office. He specializes in the software, Internet e-commerce, and media industries. He acted as the "communication engine" for the "Secrets of Software Success" project since January 1998. Roeding previously worked for Hewlett-Packard, the DaimlerChrysler Research Institute, Roland Berger & Partner, and as a journalist and reporter at several leading radio and TV stations in Europe. He studied at Sophia University in Tokyo and holds an M.B.A. from the University of Georgia in Entrepreneurship and Strategy and a Masters

Degree in Business Administration and Engineering from the University of Karlsruhe in Germany. He was a Foundation of the German People scholar.

Gert Purkert, a Senior Associate in the McKinsey & Company, Inc., Berlin office, focuses mainly on the software, IT services, and media industries. He worked in polymer physics at the Swiss Federal Institute of Technology, Lausanne, and was a freelancer for several leading German publishing houses. Purkert holds a Masters Degree in Physics from the University of Leipzig, Germany, in addition to studying at the Swiss Federal Institute of Technology and at Michigan State University, Lansing. He received several scholarships from the Foundation of the German People and the German Academic Exchange Service (DAAD). Currently, Purkert is working on his Ph.D. thesis at Technical University of Berlin.

Sandro K. Lindner began his career at McKinsey & Company, Inc., in Munich working on the "Secrets of Software Success." Prior to joining McKinsey, he gained business and IT experience at Deutsche Bank, NatWest Securities, and Siemens. He holds a Masters Degree in Business Administration and Engineering from Karlsruhe University in Germany, in addition to studying in Seville, Spain, and at Carleton University in Ottawa. Lindner is currently finishing his Ph.D. thesis on professional IT services management at Technical University of Berlin.

Ralph Müller is an Engagement Manager in the Business Technology Office of McKinsey & Company, Inc., focusing on IT solutions from a user and provider perspective. He holds a degree in Business Engineering from the University of Karlsruhe and a Ph.D. from the University of St. Gallen (Switzerland). Ralph was the initial project manager of the "Secrets of Software Success" research project from its beginning in October 1996 until September 1997.